THE SOUTHWOLD DIARY
OF JAMES MAGGS
1818–1876

A.C.B.

12.1.85

Volume II

James Maggs in old age.
(with his dog, Leo)

THE SOUTHWOLD DIARY
OF JAMES MAGGS
1818–1876

Edited by

Alan Farquhar Bottomley

Volume II   1848–1876

Published for the Suffolk Records Society
by The Boydell Press
VOLUME XXVI

© Alan Farquhar Bottomley

Published for the Suffolk Records Society
by The Boydell Press, an imprint of
Boydell & Brewer Ltd, PO Box 9, Woodbridge
Suffolk IP12 3DF

First published 1984

ISBN 0 85115 411 5

British Library Cataloguing in Publication Data

Maggs, James
  The Southwold diary of James Maggs 1818–1876.
  —(Suffolk Records Society; v.26)
  Vol. 2: 1848–1876
  1. Southwold (Suffolk)—Social life and customs
  I. Title   II. Bottomley, Alan Farquhar
  III. Series
  942.6′41   DA690.S78

  ISBN 0-85115-411-5

To
my mother
and in memory of
my father
Leonard Farquhar Bottomley

Omnium parentum
Optimi parentes
Vobis hunc librum
Filius iam dedit.

Printed in Great Britain
by Short Run Press Ltd
Exeter, Devon.

Contents

List of Illustrations

Note on Abbreviations

Some of Maggs' habitual abbreviations are idiosyncratic and, as such, have been kept. Most are self-evident, such as agt, for against, et for etc, and vd for *vide*. Several are not, and a complete list follows:

acct	= account	mo	= month
ag/agd	= aged	ob	= observe
agt	= against	Obd	= Obadiah
amt	= amount	offc	= office
b.d	= birthday	p	= past
bot	= bought	pd	= paid
brot	= brought	qrtr	= quarter
C.B.	= Common Book	sd	= said
C.H.	= Custom House	sh	= share
cr/crs	= creditor, creditors	solor	= solicitor
chwdn	= church warden	tempo	= temporary
daugr	= daughter	T.B	= Town Book
dec	= deceased	U.Ho	= Union House
dro	= drowned		(workhouse)
ec	= each	wd	= widow
et/et.et.	= etc	wk	= wreck
exor	= executor	wt	= with
fro	= from	yt	= that
furnr	= furniture	ye	= the
-g	= -ing		
interd	= interred	Blkshore	= Blackshore
k	= killed	Blythbro	= Blythburgh
masr	= master	Haleso	= Halesworth
memo	= memory	Misner	= Minsmere
mess	= messrs	SoWold	= Southwold

Introduction to Vol. 2

In the general introduction to the Diary, all but one of James Maggs's children were accounted for, either by marriage or death. The exception was Maria, the youngest, who remained at 20 Park Lane to keep house for her father after the death of her mother in 1865.[1]

On March 20 1868 the diarist made his will, leaving a double share in the residue of his property to Maria in 'acknowledgment for her kindness and attention to me since the death of my wife'.[2] Neither this will, nor any other, seems to have been proved. The reason for this may have been that shortly afterwards, on June 10, this, the last of his daughters, was married here, in St. Edmund's church, to Lieutenant Alfred Brown of the United States Navy.[3]

The old man was not left completely deserted. Minnie Aldrich, Maria's illegitimate daughter, now five, was left in the care of her grandfather.[4] By 1881, when Maggs had but nine years of his long life left to him, she was still at Park Lane and had taken over her mother's duties.[5]

Maria's grandfather had most probably been a sailor; her uncle, William Maggs, had been drowned off Happisburgh; one of her brothers, Edward, went to sea at the age of twelve (though he did not much like the experience); and sister Ellen had married Charles Durrant of the Customs and Coastguard Service. Durrant, who signed the register at her wedding as one of the two principal witnesses, may perhaps have introduced the bride to her husband, who was himself the son of a Custom House Officer.[6]

It is thus easy to demonstrate the way in which the sea lapped at the lives of many of the nineteenth century inhabitants of Southwold. And it had ever been so. In pre-Conquest times the island, for such it was then, had been the means by which the men of Reydon had found access to the herring fisheries and upon it they had doubtless beached their vessels, landed their catches and dried their nets.

The pounding of this sea is audible in the pages of the diary. It was a fickle and treacherous friend to the ports of East Anglia. Strong north to south currents eroded any projections along the soft coast while even more potently the ebb and flow of the tide attacked what lay between. Maggs records that in 1827 four acres were swept away at Easton Bavents and that in the same gale there were losses, though much less severe, at Southwold between Gun Hill and New York Cliff.[7] When the town lost the protection afforded by Easton

1. Maggs I, p.15.
2. ibid.
3. Southwold Parish Registers.
4. Census of 1871.
5. Census of 1881.
6. Southwold Parish Registers.
7. Maggs I, p. 67.

and Dunwich, the 'horns' of Sole Bay, it was bound to suffer, though relatively immune until then. Just over twenty years later the breakwater was repaired at the foot of Gun Hill but this did not prevent alarming inroads being made there in 1853 and damage being suffered from New York Cliff to the south to Long Island Cliff to the north.[8] The beach at the foot of these cliffs was lined with beach houses and fish houses but these the sea attacked in 1856 and finally swept away in 1862.[9] Two years later the Coast Guard watchhouse, exposed in 1853, finally fell when serious erosion swept away the path from New York Cliff to Gun Hill.[10] In the closing decades of the century, after Maggs had made the last entry in his journal, coastal defence was to become and remain a living issue in the town as methods of coast protection were fiercely debated until our own time.

The sea carried south what it had washed away, creating spits and choking harbours and estuaries. This was a more considerable problem for Southwold than the erosion itself for its prosperity was closely linked to the state of the haven. The Free British Fishery of 1750 had been doomed by the sand banks that had formed at the mouth of the Blyth and the problem had not gone away in Maggs's own day. In 1833 and again in 1839 steam dredgers had been hired to clear the river but in the latter year, and again in 1843 when it was possible to walk across to Walberswick, the harbour was blocked.[11] In 1852 an attempt to haul a schooner across the bar using a cable and capstan ended in failure and the loss of the vessel.[12] Maggs recorded that three years later men were digging a channel through a new obstruction.[13] Yet three years more and the channel was again blocked.[14]

The state of the harbour was not the only discouragement to shipping. The coast was lined with treacherous sandbanks, inconstant in their siting but lethal in their effect. When the wind was strong and from off the sea ships could expect to be driven upon them. In 1829, with a gale blowing from the east three vessels were lost, one off Walberswick and two off Dunwich.[15] Gales blowing from the E.N.E. in the winter of 1835–6 drove twenty-three ships on shore between Kessingland and Corton on one occasion and five colliers on to the Barnard Sands on another.[16] Shortly afterwards twenty-

8. Maggs II, p. 64.
9. Maggs II, pp. 86, 110.
10. Maggs II, p. 113.
11. Maggs I, 79 & 65. The mouth of the haven had been dug out six times in 1810 and 1811. (Maggs 'Hand book etc. . . .', p. xiii). Between 1805 and 1818 it was dug out thirteen times. (ibid., p. xii). In 1839 a number of ships belonging to Patrick Stead of Halesworth were trapped inside the harbour. (Report of Evidence given before the Harbour Commissioners at Southwold. 1839.)
12. Maggs II, p. 52. 'Even at the best of times it was a job to get a fully-laden ship in without first lightening her.' (Roy Clark, 'Black Sailed Traders', p. 116.)
13. Maggs II, p. 79.
14. Maggs II, p. 96.
15. Maggs I, p. 72.
16. Maggs I, pp. 92–3.

2

seven ships came on shore between Kessingland and Lowestoft and in 1843 one vessel was lost at the pier and two others on the Barnard.[17] After the fearful east coast gales in November 1855 the shore at Southwold was littered with grounded vessels, the brigs 'Nelson' at North Cliff and 'Hylton Castle' at Long Island Cliff. Just south of Gun Hill lay the brigs 'Ocean' and 'Emma' and the barque 'Cape Horn'.[18]

In between these dramatic losses there were numerous individual casualties, for the east coast in Maggs's day was as dangerous as the stormy south-west. Yet the coastal trade throve and the horizon would more often than not have been alive with sail and later with steam and steel. In addition the fisheries were active and in 1840 forty-seven mackerel boats appeared in the bay.[19] Three years later Maggs counted seven to eight hundred vessels of unspecified character between the two nesses.[20]

Southwold itself suffered regularly when its men and ships were lost at sea and many who were baptised at St. Edmund's failed to find burial in the churchyard outside. When the 'Lady Nelson' foundered off Margate in 1837 it took with it James Sterry and two of his sons as well as the two remaining members of the crew.[21] The following year Maggs is organising a collection for twelve widowed mothers and thirty-two fatherless children after fifteen men were lost when the yawl 'Peace' was lost on the Newcome Sand.[22] Particularly distressing were the casualties among youngsters: when six-year-old Daniel Magub was accidentally drowned in the Thames, probably from his father's boat, in 1834, or thirteen-year-old Job Spoore and his friend Samuel Jarvis met the same fate four years earlier, when their boat was upset.[23] Older boys, who were starting their careers at sea, fell victim to their own lack of experience, on more than one occasion by a fall from the rigging.[24] Sometimes a wife would be lost with her husband, as when the 'Villager' went down in the North Sea in 1823.[25] Life at sea was not only dangerous but hard, as young Edward Maggs was to find aboard the 'Irwell' in 1836.[26]

Maggs himself made a substantial part of his livelihood from disasters at sea and his diary is full of notes and details of auctions that he held on the shore from Covehithe to Minsmere when there was a wreck to dispose of, the remains of which were bought for re-use or re-sale by local men. Salvage also could mean a valuable windfall for the beachmen. These, as at Aldeburgh,

17. Maggs I, pp. 93, 121.
18. Maggs II, p. 82.
19. Maggs I, p. 108.
20. Maggs I, p. 119.
21. Maggs I, p. 96.
22. Maggs I, p. 100.
23. Maggs I, pp. 84, 74.
24. Maggs I, pp. 85, 92, 93, 98. Maggs II, pp. 7, 13, 56, 57, 119
25. Maggs I, p. 58.
26. Maggs I, p. 82.

were formed into companies: at Killcock, Long Island and New York Cliffs. Whether they were 'bold, artful, surly and savage' as they have been described, they were certainly bitterly competitive as they launched their yawls in search of pilotage or salvage. Each had their look-out that was constantly manned when the opportunity for either was proffered. It is said that on April 3, 1814 the famous yawl 'Jubilee', racing another to a salvage job, cut her rival clean in two, probably on purpose. Maggs himself reports that in 1855 the 'Swiftsure' cut the 'Reliance' in two and sank it.[27] Three years later the oars of the 'Cricketer' and the 'Teazer' became locked together as they raced out to a Russian steamer. As a result 'Teazer', with its crew of thirteen was capsized and it was decided that in future pilotage should go by rotation.[28]

Whatever may have been the ruthlessness of the beach-men, the people of Southwold were not 'wreckers'. It is true that it might fleetingly have seemed so when the new gas light that they put up on Gun Hill led to two vessels in succession running aground between there and the harbour, mistaking the unexpected illumination for the light at Lowestoft![29] 1840 saw the establishment of a lifeboat at Southwold but before that the men of the yawls were noted for their courage and success in saving life at sea.[30] Later they formed the backbone of the crew of the 'Conservative' lifeboat and its successors, the exploits of which verged upon the legendary and were faithfully recorded by Maggs.

It was partly to exhibit the prowess of the men of the yawls that the annual Regattas were started at Southwold in 1835.[31] Always held in August, the Regatta brought something of the spirit of carnival to the lives of the poorer inhabitants: there were brass bands and fireworks upon Gun Hill; competitors from Lowestoft and elsewhere along the coast increased the excitement of the races.

Smuggling appears to have been on the wane. Maggs has only trifling incidents to record. The heaviest duties had been removed, and though the landlord of the 'Bear' at Reydon was tempted to restock with contraband in 1852, this was a late and apparently isolated episode.[32] A century before and there had been fighting between the Preventive Men and smugglers along deserted stretches of the coast, but now there was only the small addition to an otherwise legal cargo.[33]

Dabbling in contraband may have eased the economic problem of the

27. Maggs I, p. 132. Maggs II, p. 84.
28. Maggs II, p. 97.
29. Maggs II, pp. 17, 19.
30. Maggs I, p. 110. (See also Cooper, E. R., 'Seventy years' work of the Southwold lifeboats', 1912.)
31. Maggs I, p. 91.
32. Maggs II, p. 59.
33. In 1732 there was a fight between customs men from Southwold and a gang of forty smugglers. (Copinger, W. A., 'County of Suffolk', sub. Southwold.)

individual townsman, but nothing short of a vast and unreasonable expenditure could safeguard the future of the port. A succession of surveyor's reports by some of the most distinguished experts available gave little hope.[34] Whether the fault lay with the embanking of marshland by self-interested landowners or the constantly forming shingle bar across the mouth of the Blyth the landed interest that dominated the Harbour and River Commissions was unlikely to reflood the marshes to provide an adequate scour, nor could they decide upon the expensive lengthening of the piers that might have alleviated the situation. Maggs, if it was indeed he that wrote the carefully phrased introduction to his 'Hand book to the port and shipping of Southwold', carefully avoided any mention of the enclosures or the criticism of the landed interest that has been made by a modern writer.[35]

As the port was certainly doomed so was the local fishing industry that operated from both harbour and beach. The rise of Lowestoft with its superior facilities and communications was to kill the industry at Southwold,[36] so it was to survive for long after the demise of the diarist himself. The future of the town lay with its holiday visitors. We have already seen how Maggs himself took advantage of the new fashion for watering places that gave fresh life to old ports at the beginning of his own century.[37]

34. 1814 Smith, 1819 Rennie, 1828 Cubitt, 1839 Lieutenant F. W. Ellis, R.N. (Harbourmaster, etc., at Southwold), 1841 James Walker, 1844 E. K. Calver (a native of Southwold and a distinguished Admiralty expert), 1856 William Teasdel.
35. Roy Clark, 'Black Sailed Traders' (1961), Chapter VI.
36. Victoria County History. Suffolk. Vol. II. 'Industry—fishing'.
37. Maggs I, p. 8.

Testimonial Accompanying silver inkstand presented to the Reverend
John Henry Young by 125 persons, on the occasion of his
marriage, November 5 1847. (Died Aug 2/61)

1848 Jany 12th The Revd Mr Young & Mrs Y returns to Southwold to
Lodgings. See 27th inst.

Cutting Presentation to the Reverend John Henry Young. (Jany 27 1848.)

Jany 12th Removed from the House of Mr Benj.Palmer, his Furniture &
Effects to the "Southwold Arms", by order of Mr Fulcher, for rent. 15th I
sold them by Auction.

Jany 12th Eliza (See April 28 1847) leaves Lowestoft and comes home. Mr
Jesse Grossmith the waiter also left—and came to my house—left 17th
returned on the 20th—left 24th—returned 27th left 28th. July 7th 1850 Eliza
came home—from Southampton. vd. Aug 7.

Jany 20th Mr Wm Turner, Wangford, Agent to Mr Galsworthy, Ipswich,
Solor: serves Me and Mr John Parker with a Writ. See Aug 16 1847.

Rudland v. Mills

Feb 25th Self & Parker, served by Mr Wm Turner a Declaration, dated 22d
inst.

1848 Jany 25th Married at Yarmouth—Elizth relict of Mr Jas Boyce, to
Foster Bokenham, both of this place.

Jany 24th Sale of Trawl Boat, Fishg gear et: the property of Lewis Curdy—
Jany 25th Fire at Covehithe.

Cutting Barn belonging to Mr Edmund Cottingham at Covehithe, a tenant of
Sir Thomas Gooch, catches fire. A north-east gale blowing, it was
reduced to ashes in two hours. The exertions of labourers from
Covehithe and Southwold and the Southwold fire engine saved the
threatened farm. Because of the good relations between Gooch and
Cottingham and their labourers it was not likely to have been caused
by incendiarism but accidentally from the pipe of a tramp sheltering
in a turnip shed.

Jany 26th. Put to Sale Cottages of Mr Fredk: Gowing—No bidding :—

Jany 29th At St Matthew's, Friday Street, London, by the Revd Wm
Durham M.A. Nicholas Robilliard Esq. of Southwold to Catharine, daughter
of the late James Simmons Esqr . . . . . . of Seaford, Essex.[1]

Feby A Revolution in France, Louis Philippe and Queen Amelia arrives in
England 3 March

From an Almanack Mar. 1848 "A certain monarch "the Napoleon of Peace"
may require all his prudence and power to
restrain the revolutionary spirit of his people.
Barricades are not yet obsolete."

1848 Feby 3 Sale of the Furniture & Effects of Mrs Mary Poynts for Mr Wm
Sutton and also of the Furniture & Effects of Mrs Maria Palmer for Mr
Jellicoe—at the Crown Hotel.

---

1. Maggs must have meant Sussex, not Essex.

Feby 4th Sale of Trawl Boat, Fishing Nets et of Mr Frs Wayth.

Feb 7th Unanimously elected by a shew of hands by a Majority of the Members present of the "Albion" Club, held at the "Lion Inn" Lydia Martin—*Myself* a Member thereof.

Feby 9th Died at Huntingfield in his 90th yr. The Revd Henry Uhtoff 65 years, rector of the consolidated parishes of Huntingfield and Cookley, and during the same period rector of Aldham, in this county.

1871 Feb His daughter Died at Putney, ag 80

Feby 15th Mr Wm Rogers, Custom Ho. Officer leaves this Town to reside at Burnham, nr. Maldon, Essex.

Feb 16th. Odd Fellows, Society of. A meeting was called at the "Red Lion" Inn, Lydia Martin by a Mr Daines and Mr Allen from Norwich—

two of the directors of the Manchester Union of Odd Fellows for the purpose of establishing a Society of Brothers in this Town—when it was agreed to meet again on Wednesday the 15th March following when a Society was formed and established—about 12 or 14 were initiated. The Lodge being held at the "Red Lion" Inn and denominated the "*Sole Bay*". Mr John Sutherland, Surgeon.

Cutting Founding of the Sole Bay Lodge. (April 11 1848)

1848 Feby 20th Sunday *William* Son of Mr David Green, Masr of the "Heart of Oak" of this place, accidentally fell overboard from a Vessel lying next the "Heart of Oak" at "Union" Wharf, London, and was drowned. dec. was not found 'till the followg day, and then under the bottom of his own Vessel—He was brought here by his Father 28 inst and interred on the 4th March followg. He was in his 21st Year and had been Married only 6 weeks, to Jane, daughter of Mr John King of this Town, Sailmaker.

Feby 22d At the Rectory, Carlton Colville the Revd Edward Jermyn A.M. 41 Years Rector of that Parish, Aged 76.[2]

1848 Feby 22d The Brig "Vesta" Coal laden, belonging to Colchester, Yeoman Masr. was taken to Yarmouth, leaky—by the Pilot Boat "Swiftsure" belonging to this place—Paid 60 £'s shared 50s/ec

March 4th The Rev H.W.R. Birch's Curate came, commenced his Curacy followg day. Revd Rd. Henry Bicknell. Nov 27th/50 Mr Bicknell ordained at Norwich. Left Southwold Dec. 6th 1852.

March 2d Sale of Furniture et. of Mr Hy Burwood.

March 16th Meeting held at the House of Mr Chas Sawyer's for the purpose of instituting a Masonic Lodge—principals Mr Sawyer and Mr Thos Rounce.

Cuttings Southwold Lifeboat rescues the crew of nine from the brig "Cleofrid of Newcastle, driven on to Sizewell Bank during a gale. March 21. Letter from the master, James Simm, acknowledging the services

---

2. Edward Jermyn was the brother of James, the High Steward of Southwold, Maggs' one time employer.

rendered by the Lifeboat and the town. (Mar 21st 1848) (2 Nov 1848)

March 22 I sold Ropes, Sails, Mast, Yard et et Salved from her, and brought to this Beach by Auction.

March 27th John Henry Heigham, Hunston Hall, Esq & family leaves this Town. see Sept 2 1847.

1848 March 27th. Mr Samuel Cornaby of this place in the act of Cutting a piece of Wood at the Saw Mill (see Nov 26 1847) at Wangford, accidentally cut his left fore-finger as to cause an immediate amputation which was performed by Mr Cottingham, Surgeon, Wangford.

1848 April 2d Sunday—A Child of Mr Thos. John King's—Blackshore, interred in the Baptist Chapel—the Wife of—*Alexander* of Reydon accidentally walking into the grave unfortunately *broke her Leg*.

Monday April 3 Sale of Mr Wm Turner's Furniture et et.

Wednesday April 5th Sale of Mrs Rix's Furniture et   Wrentham.

April 12th *Charles* Son of Mr George Mayhew, leaves home to a Situation as Druggist et—Feversham, Kent.

April 24th Sale of Cloths et by J.T.Salomon to the 29th inst at the House of Mrs Lydia Martin's, Red Lion Inn

Cutting The "Poor's" or "Town Land" in Reydon to be let for eight years from October 11 1848. Two pieces of excellent arable land, one 24 acres, the other 3. Tenders to Thomas Holmes Diver, Reydon.

This Land was occupied by the late Mr John Hadingham. Now hired by Mr Ed. Gray 24 Acres L 28 Mr Pashley 3 Acres L 5 Mr H gave 17£ for the former and 1£ for the latter v. May 16/51

1848 April 25th Miss Knights leave this Town   27th I sold their Furniture by Auction.

Notice Southwold Pasturage 1848   April 25th 1848   Rates given.

April 26 Charles Cullingford bound *by me* an Apprentice to Mr Rt Allen of this town, Stone Mason, for 3 years from the 27th March ult.

April 28th Edwd Smith ag' 17 Son of Mr John Smith and Servant to Mrs Bokenham, Old Swan Inn, absconded with a Sovereign which he was instrusted with to get changed. return'd May followg

Apr 30th   Boon of Walberswick accidentally drowned in a Sluice in that Parish

May 1st "Pilot" Coach commenced running from the "Crown" to Norwich —Proprietor Mr Harber of Thurton "George"—Coachman "Benj Friar"— Sept 23d Discontinued—1849 May 14 re-commenced—Discontinued Oct 13th 1849. re-commenced May 27 1850. Discontind 5th Oct 1850. June 2d 1851 Commenc'd   discontin'd Aug 4 1851.

May 8th "Blue" a Buss, branch to the London Coach "Blue" commences running from the "Old Swan" to Wangford twice a day, Proprietors Rivett & Rowell. horsed by Mrs Bokenham, "Old Swan" Inn SoWold   Discontinued 22d November inst. May 31st 1849 Commenced again. Discontinued July 22nd 1850 vid July 15 1850 Blue Coach

1848 May 1st The Revd H.W.R.Birch—& family leaves to reside at Hereford returns v Nov 25 the Revd Hen Symons D.C.L. Vicar of St Martin with All Saints. Hereford comes to reside here, & officiates for Mr Birch, commenc'd his Services Sunday 14th inst. July 10th the Doctor gets thrown out of his Gig turning the Corner from the Market place into Mill Lane and broke his Collar bone see Oct 29

Augt 20 Preached a Sermon for the benefit of the National Schools Collected £13

May Sunday 14th Died at Mrs Sheriffe's Lodgings—South End, Wm Fredk Sherlock, agd 7 Months—Son of Mr Ed Gooch M.P. Interred at Benacre.

May 17th Commenced New Roofing the South Side of this Church—

Sunday 21 & 28th No Service at this Church. 28th Prayers read at the National School by the Revd Wm French—June 28th The new roof & leading South Aisle completed—upon the Wall plate near the South Door is D. Fulcher M.C.W. R.R.Boniwell. C.W. P.Palmer, G.E.Child Fecit 1848

May 19th (See June 7 1847) Died at Bulcamp House, Mary Ann, Wife of Mr. Wm Pashley—41 Interr'd in the Chapel yard there.

May 20th Myself, Mr Hy Smith & Mr Rob Carter took up the supposed Grave Stone of the burial place of the late Captn Jo Steele and cleaned it. May

1848 Monday 22d Sale of Wm Turner's Furniture et at Wangford June 1st Mr Turner leaves Wangford to reside at [   ]

Printed leaflet Rules and Regulations of Southwold Cricket Club. May 24 1848 (Discontinued 1850)

May 25th Sale of Mr Wm Green's (See Feb 20th) Furniture et. et.

May 28th Thunder Storm and heavy Rain

May 30th Married by the Revd Dr Simmons D.D. at this Church Mr Benj Haward Carter to Mrs Mary Simpson, lt of Walberswick.

May 31st Dr Wake returned, left 1st April last in ill health.

Cutting The bells rung and flags displayed upon the return of the universally respected Dr. Wake.(vd Jany 10/49)

June 1st Sale of Growg Crops of Grass upon the Marsh Walls, Saltings et £4.12.6.

June 5th. Mr Fisher Jnr. elected Relievg Officer in the place of his Father— deceased.

1848 June 16th Opening of Masonic Lodge in this Town—at the House of Messr Wright & Sawyer. See Aug 4 1848 (afterwd at the Town Hall)

June 17th Daughter Eliza embarked on board the Steamer "Earl of Liverpool" for London—thence to Southampton—J.S.Eldridges Esquire—came home July 7/50 returned on the 24th inst. Sarah went with her. Eliza leaves Dec/50 and comes home Jany 20 1851.

June 20th German Brass Band 20 in number here—Second Fair day.

June 23d Charles Rudland 39 Chemist and Druggist of Aldborough where he resided, committed Suicide by cutting his Throat—Interred at 11 o'Clock at Night without the Funereal rites.

July 2nd at Halesworth. Died Sarah Norman Cracknell agd 23—daughter of Mr Thos Cracknell of the above place, Brewer.

July 12th Mr Henry Knevett Bransby comes from Dunwich to reside here in the House of Mr Edmund Child's Market Place and opened School on the 24th inst. v' April 22nd 1850

Prospectus Sole Bay Academy—Market Place—Southwold. Mr H.K.Bransby is moving his establishment from Dunwich to Southwold at Midsummer next. Fees, for boarders, above 10, 22 guineas p.a. under 10, 20 guineas. Weekly boarders, above 10, 18 guineas, under 10, 16 guineas. Day boarders, exclusive of tuition 2 guineas a quarter. Day pupils, above 10, a guinea a quarter, under 10, 15s. Parlour boarders, 30 guineas p.a.

Extras, Greek,Latin,French, each a guinea a quarter. Drawing half a guinea, Navigation a guinea, Land Surveying 5s 6d. Music and Dancing by approved masters. Each young Gentleman to bring a pair of Sheets and Six Towels. School to start on July 24 1848.[3]

1848 July 6th Sale of Freehold property of Mr Obd Boyce. Solicitor Mr Hallet 7 Staple Inn Auctioneer myself J.M.

1848 July 17th Died at Walberswick agd 80 Simon Gorrard—many years servant to Mr Whiting   March 16 1854 in America Ann Wife of Wm Whiting

1848 July 17 Sale at Dunwich of Growing Crops of Corn et of Mr Henry Knevett Bransby.

Cutting Died 18th ult. in the United States of America aged 72 years Mr William Whiting formerly of Thorington (and many years Merchant at Walberswick.)

July 27 To Henham & Sotherton—Valued the personal Effects of Mr Rd. Ludlow of Henham—dec. 3 Augt under the direction of his Son Rd. Ludlow 13 Victoria Place Norwich I sold the Effects by Auction at the "Cross Bow" Sotherton—Searle,Landlord Mr Ludlow died 17 July inst. ag 49.

July 28.J Jermyn Esqr—Reydon Cottage came to Southwold—nearly 4 Yrs since he was here before.

Rudland v. Mills and others

Augt 1st 1848

Ipswich Assizes

Cutting Action brought by Miles Willis Rudland, a surgeon, formerly of Southwold, but now of Wangford, against Edward Mills, gentleman of Norwich, John Parker, Inspector of Police and James Maggs, auctioneer and appraiser, for an excessive distraint for unpaid rent. Nominal damages of one farthing awarded by jury.

Subpoena For the above case, directed to William Smith and Richard Roe.

---

3. The Sole Bay Academy occupied the present Lloyd's Bank building or possibly the adjacent property.

1848 Aug 4th Consecration of Mason's About ½p.11 A.M. *A Thunder Storm* commenced with a heavy rain—Mr Mayhew of Wangford—Farmer—had 14 Lambs killed by the Lightning—2 Persons at Lowestoft much injured by the lightning—see June 16/48

Aug 7th Daughter Mary Ann to her Uncle's—Stocton—

Aug 10th Thunder Storm accompanied with a heavy rain—happily no damage done.

Aug 14th—Blaxall of Halesworth—elected Porter, Bulcamp House in the room of Geo Tuthill, resigned.

Aug 14 Mr B.Moulton, Woodbridge, Auctioneer came to see me respecting Tink's premises.

Aug 18th *Hannah* relict of John Barrell (who died March 6th 1845 agd 80) I conveyed to Bulcamp House, in a derang'd state of mind. Also *Mary Ann* daughter of Mr Bela Crisp a lunatic 24 inst—See Sep 18 1844

I took the latter to Melton Asylum.—

Cutting "THE REGATTA—We have much pleasure in recording the reviving prosperity of our small but much frequented watering place. The recent institution of a Masonic Lodge in this town has wonderfully improved the aspect of things, changing still monotony into animated life". At a meeting of masons held at the home of Thomas Wallace Esq. a regatta was suggested, which took place on Wednesday August 23. The shops were closed, business suspended, the bells rang throughout the day, Taylor's brass band from Woodbridge played, the battery on Gun Hill fired its salutes, the principal buildings and the shipping in the bay and the harbour were decked with flags, as was the High Street. The regatta started at half past one o'clock, at six a dinner was held at The Crown, at nine there were fireworks on Gun Hill and the ascent of a fire balloon.

Cutting Announcement of the Regatta. Races between yawls, punts, gigs and a duck hunt.

Cutting Regatta to take place on August 23 at "one of the most delightful watering places upon the coast" An excellent day's sport is promised by the Stewards. May their efforts be crowned with success and "their reward be the gracious smiles of a numerous assemblage of the fairer portion of creation at the ball, to be held at the Assembly-rooms in the evening."

1848 Aug 20th Sunday Afternoon Service, Church, Robert Haylock of this town—was ordered out of this Church for *swearing* and *brawling* in it.

1848 Aug 21st *An unexpected Gale of Wind*—the previous day (Sunday) was calm & quiet—not a ripple on the shore—about ½ p 8 A.M. this morning a fresh breeze came up fro the S at ½ p 11 it blew a heavy gale—Signals of distress and for assistance were hoisted—the life boat went off but could not board only 1 Ship—on board of which Mr Ed Taylor, Trinity Pilot was put on board 8 P.M. Wind W—nearly a calm.

On Sunday Aug 20th—the Brigs "Mary" Brown and the "John Lees"   Roberson of Newcastle brought up in this bay with flags flying half mast upon ascertaining the cause it was found the latter had lost to the great grief of his friends & crew a young man named Robert Tann 18 a native of Wangford in this county—deceased was the previous evening coming down the river Thames when in Gravesend reach, for some occasion stepped into the Ship's boat, which from the current of Tide and the surging of the boats painter she immediately upset—every effort was used to rescue the poor fellow from a watery grave but without success. John, Son of Michael Ashmenall of this place was shipped in deceased's room. The following day was a heavy gale of Wind—the life boat went off to 2 or 3 Vessels   See Aug 21 1848

Sunday Eveng Aug 27 Mr Jo Chittleburgh of the "Mary Ann" of this place, in the act of stepping off the staithe on board his vessel lying at Middlesboro' dock accidentally fell into the River and was Drowned.

Aug 27 The Revd Nathaniel Hopper Arthey A.M. preached in this Church. *also Sep 3d*.left Oct 18th/48 Sep 9 1855 His Son—Nat first read the Lessons in this church.

Aug 31st The "Helen" Easter, belonging to Yarmouth brought up off this place hoistd a signal for a Boat from the shore—upon boarding the Vessel it was ascertained a young Man named John Baldry belonging to this Town was very ill—sent for a Surgeon—Mr J.A.Stamford went off to the Vessel but Baldry was dead before the Surgeon got on board—An attempt was made to bring the body on shore for interment—but fearing deceased died of some contagious disorder—Mr D. Fulcher, Mayor went and met the Corpse, directing it not to be brought ashore—it was however taken to Yarmouth awaited an Inquest and interred—great displeasure arose in the minds of the Yarmothians respecting the proceedings of the Mayor of Southwold.

Sep 6th Dined with Mr C. White & Wife Mr & Mrs P.Palmer at Mr Denny's, Wrentham.

1848 Sep 7th Take an acct of the Furniture Stock in Trade of Mr Rd Newson. Tailor. Insolvent.

25 I sold them by Auction

27 Newson passes thro' County Court. No opposition *I was present*

Oct 18 Newson pass'd again no opposition

Sep 11th Sale of Droits et. F.W.Ellis agent

Sep 5th Mr John Arthur Clubb Kilwick to *Rosamund* daugr of the late John

12

Church. Masr. Mariner. Same day—Mr Jos Blowers to [   ] daugr. of Mr Jas Fisk

Sep 6 Her Majesty Queen Victoria passes here for Scotland—return'd by Land

Sep 13 Mr Richard Waggoner—C Ho.Off. is removed to [   ] after a period of 17 Yrs residence here.

Sep 24th Robert Bryant agd [   ] yrs Grandson of Mrs Lydia Martin "Lion" Pub Ho.—drowned—dec. on his passage from the North—fell from the Rigging of the Geo IV   Park of Maldon.

1848 Sepr 7th   The "Ruby" Thomas Jarvis Masr. launch'd, built at Black Shore—by Mr.T.J.King—who left this Town to reside at Yarmouth—Ship-building discontinued. 30th, the "Ruby" first went to Sea.

Sep 24th Robert Bryant agd (Grandson of Mrs Lydia Martin, Lion Inn) was drowned in his passage fro the North dec. was in the Geo IV   of Maldon. Park Master and in the act of going aloft—fell from the rigging to rise no more.

Cutting COOK'S CIRCUS   Cook's celebrated equestrian company in the town for afternoon and evening performances. (Sep 26th 1848)
Sep 14th 1850   Oct 9/55

Notice Sermon to be preached by the Bishop of Norwich in Southwold Church on Sunday, September 24, 1848, at 3 o'clock, in aid of the Southwold Dispensary

Notice Sermon to be preached by the Reverend J.H.Young B.A. on Sunday October 1 1848, at 3 o'clock in Walberswick Church in aid of the Southwold Medical Institution

Cutting Report that £32 17s was collected after the Bishop's sermon. The "principal chapels" in the town were closed on the occasion.

Oct 2d. Sale of Live and Dead Stock et. of the late Mr. John Hadingham who died Sep 19th. 1847. agd 79.

Oct 14th Mr T.H.Diver's Sale—Mr D. leaves the farm Oct 11 and succeeded by Mr. [   ] Chilvers—Mr. D goes into the farm formerly occupied by his Father. Apr 1 1854

1848 Oct 4th   D.Fulcher.Mayor—Peter Palmer—Alderman—& Jonthn Gooding, Town Clerk, goes to London.

Oct 5th Sale of Mr Edwd Howes Effects, Wangford.

Oct 6th Sale of Mr David Laws' effects at Westleton.

Oct 9th Sale of Mr Benj Rt Manning's Effect Reydon Easton   Mr & Mrs M come to reside here.

Leaflet Maggs to auction at the Swan Hotel, on October 10, bankrupt stock consisting of electro-plated and papier machee goods, guns, revolving pistols etc etc   (Long list)

Cutting Death on the 28th at Southwold of Mr George Wyatt, aged 65, after nine years lingering illness. Up to then there have been 29 deaths in Southwold, averaging but 2 more than 1 % of the computed population. 10 of these averaged 80 years, 6 sixty four, 6 thirty one and the remaining 7 were minors or children.

1848. Oct 11th. Mr Jos Dix, leaves "Ship" Inn Dunwich, after [ ] Years occupancy—Mr D Succeeded by Mr. [   ] Fisher, late of [   ]

Oct 11th Met Mr Attoe, and his Solicitor from Litcham, at Wangford—to compromise matters of rent et between Mr. Attoe and Mr. Wm Turner—late tenant of the sd Mr Attoe—Mr T. did not attend—On Friday I met Mr. A. & Mr. T. (Solor leavg us) and by allowg Mr. T. 20£'s damages from the loss he made it appear he sustained at his Sale on the 22d May ult—we came to terms.

The fact is this—Mr Turner hires certain houses of Mr Attoe in Wangford for a term of 3 yrs;—last April a half year's rent of £15 was due—for which Mr A applied for at the Sale and upon non-payment, Attoe serves me with a Notice to be paid from the proceeds of Sale—this Turner objected to—Attoe then puts in a Distress—which Turner upset—upon the grounds that it was *not* upon the premises where the rent was due, but actually upon a seperate and distinct hire, and of another person, a Mrs Barber. After some long delay I proceeded to selling—Turner observing several persons leaving both before and at the sale made a demand for damages, which from the error of the distress—and evidences to persons leavg the Sale—Turner made a demand of 20£'s—which was allowed him—*tho' not much to his (Turner's) credit.*

1848 Oct 20th. Sale of Mr Raven's Effects et at Wangford.

Oct 26th Sale of Furniture & Effects of Mary—the wife of Mr Jo Chittleburgh See Aug 27/48

Oct 29th Sunday Dr Symons preaches a Sermon in this Church for the benefit of the Sunday-Schools—collected £9 — s   4½ this was his last Sermon   The Dr leaves 7th November followg   See May 1 1848

Cutting Annual General Meeting of the Southwold Life Boat Society on Thursday November 2 1848. Sir Charles Blois in the chair. The subscribers gathered in the Town Hall were read the letter from the Master of the Cleofrid, wrecked on March 21.

Novr 6th Monday—Rufus son of Mr R.R.Boniwell receives an accident from the explosion of a Squib in the face.

Novr 9th Rd. Son of Mr T Diver—leaves this Country.

1848 Novr. 9th Election of Mayor.

Cutting On November 1 nine candidates presented themselves for election to the four vacant seats on the council. "The manner in which the Inhabitants of this place conduct their municipal elections is worthy of the imitation of towns of greater pretensions; no question is asked, is he Whig, or is he a Tory, but what are his abilities to serve; no bribery is here thought of." The present mayor, Mr Fulcher, has held the office for the past four years and though he is universally respected, an opinion is gaining ground that Members of Parliament, though fond of long tenures for themselves, would not have enacted annual elections if the office was intended to be hereditary.

14

Cutting Letter to the Editor of the Ipswich Journal from "your constant reader" "A BURGESS". November 9 1848.

Defends the re-election of Fulcher for a fifth term of office.

Cutting Letter to the Editor of the Ipswich Journal from "ANOTHER BURGESS" November 15 1848.

At his feast prior to the election the mayor mustered only half the council and as there was another candidate who could claim the remainder it seemed likely that he would have to use his own casting vote to gain re-election. However, using intimidation, which his fellow tradesmen on the council already thought prudent to submit to, he managed to secure the withdrawal of the vote of one of his opponent's supporters and was thus unopposed. Fulcher is not so superior to the rest of the corporation that he can take a lease upon the mayoralty.

Notice   List of Members of the Corporation 1848–9

Catalogue Of the household furniture of Mr Richard R. Boniwell, which Maggs is to auction on November 16 1848. Boniwell is declining lodging house keeping. Included is grand piano by Stodart.

Cutting Announcing the auction of the household furniture of Richard Rufus Boniwell.

Cutting Aurora Borealis sighted in all parts of Great Britain. (1848 Novr 17th)

Cutting Charge proved against a sub-inspector of the county constabulary stationed at Bungay. No obvious Southwold connection. November 23.

1848 Nov 24th I settled with B's Auction and took the Agency of his Houses Mr Garnham Fisher, Mortgagee of Heveningham.

Nov 25 see May 1 Mr Birch returns. Bells rang. Mr B. for the first time Sunday 26th preached wt *Spectacles*

Decr 1 see Oct 29 1814 Mr. A. Leman leaves the Salt-works—an Execution being put upon the Premises Nov 28th ult by a Mr Wilkinson & Littleboy of Norwich, who carries on the Works 'till [   ]

June 16 Leman & family leaves the Town

1848 Sep 20th James Williams Esqr Surgeon—commenced practising here in the place of Dr Wake, havg disposed of his practice to him. Dec 7th Mr Williams came to reside here. (Dr Williams Died Jany 9th 1862 May 16/62 Mrs Williams left Southwold. Dr Blackett succeeds Dr Williams.)

1848 Novr 28th Stanfield Murders. Maggs inserts many cuttings and notes.

                     Conclusion of the Inquest.

                     Mr Press Coroner.

                     Tuesday 19th Decr. 1848

                     The jury after consulting upon the evidence received from Emily Sandford, Rush's Housekeeper, and Eliza Chestney, Mrs Jermy's wounded Servant, for only ten minutes—returned, and the foreman stated, that they were agreed on a verdict against James Bloomfield Rush, for the *wilful murder* of Isaac Jermy, and Isaac Jermy Jermy Apr 21/49 I saw Rush executed at Norwich.

Cutting Isaac Jermy, only son of Isaac Jermy, Esq. of Stanfield Hall, Recorder of Norwich, to Sophia Jane, fifth daughter of the late Clement Chevallier, rector of Badingham and Cransford, Suffolk, at Gorleston by the Reverend John Chevallier. M.D. (Jany 1846)

Monday 1848 Decr 4th

Cutting Southwold lifeboat goes out to the "Ury" of and from Sunderland, sailing to Dunkirk, which dismasted during a heavy gale from the south west, was driven on to the northern part of the Barnard Sand on Monday December 4 1848. Sighted from Kessingland at 8 a.m., a local yawl was unable to reach her because of the heavy sea. A messenger was despatched by horseback to Southwold. Two men rescued and taken to Lowestoft where they were lodged at the Suffolk Hotel. These were John Courtnell and Charles Holly. The master, Charles Hume, the mate, Thomas Nicholson and a boy were drowned.

21st inst The Crew of the Life Boat were remunerated by Lloyds for saving the 2 men on the 4th inst. viz John Fish £5 Master £2 Mate £2 Men each 9s Amounting in all to the sum of £19 10s

8th inst a Subscription was set on foot for the Crew of the Life-boat shar'd 7 shillings each.

See Mar 29/49 Fish presented with a Silver Medal.

6th inst. the body of Thos. Nicholson wash'd on Shore at Covehithe.

1848 Decr 14th John Fish (vd 4th inst) Thos Bugg, Wm Bedingfield and Wm Brown—Fishermen, in coming to the Shore in a Small fishing Punt (the property of Mr Jas Woodard "Pilot Boat" Public House) owing to a heavy Sea on the main, were upset—had not immediate assistance been at hand they must have perish'd, the boat being whelm'd over them. Providentially they were rescued, but greatly exhausted.

1848 Decr. 16th The "Norfolk" Jo Soans, with Malt for London, lost on the "Pye" Sand.   Crew Saved.

Decr. 19th A Pedestrian (who was here before, about 2½ yrs since) undertook to pick up a 100 Stones lying a yard from each other & depositing each in basket at the place of starting—to run a Wheelbarrow a Mile, and 2 miles afterwards, in 1 hour—he exceeded his hour 35 seconds!

Same day Mr Seaman of Chediston, and Mr Jas Martin, "Fleece" Inn Bungay met respecting £100 claimed by Mr S of the wd of Mr Jas Oldring— butcher, dec. for a debt. I met the parties seperately—nothing settled.

24th Sunday Evening—The "Blue" Stage Coach from the train Ipswich, brought several passengers from thence, by Wolsey Bridge to the "Bear" Inn Reydon, for Southwold.

26th The "Leda" of Whitby was observed upon our Beach at the S end of

Gun Hill—about 4 A.M. the Captain stated he mistook the lights upon the Gun (the Gas lamps) Hill for Lowestoft Lights—Being a flood tide and in ballast, she was got off by our Cliff men, at an expence of about 70£'s

Decr 27th Pilot Boat "Cricketer"—launch'd built by Mr Jas Critten.

Dec 28th Albert Garrod of Halesworth—while engag'd in Pigeon Shooting at [   ] his Gun bursting, so mutilated his left hand as to cause immediate amputation.

On Thursday 28th Decr. at the house of his Son-in-law the Rev Thos. Fison B.A. of Romsy Hants. in his 69th year—the Revd Andrew Ritchie for 42 years the respected pastor of the congregational church at Wrentham, Suffolk.

1849 Jany 4th. Marshall Twaddell "Sophia"—a letter was received announcing his safety—he had been missing upwards a fortnight—and all hopes given up of his return. Arrivd on the 9th

Jany 5th I sold by Auction at "Long Island" Cliff—the Gig "Welcome Home" to Mr Jo. Rogers for the New York Cliff.

Jany 8th Mr Garnham Fisher of Heveningham here respecting Mr R.R. Boniwells houses.

Cutting Inquest before the Coroner, J.E.Sparrowe Esq., on Saturday, at Henstead upon Mr William Wilby Carter, aged 34, farmer of that parish, who had hanged himself in his barn. His wife had left him about three years previously and the body was discovered by William Manning his neighbour. On Tuesday night, about 11, when in bed, the latter was called upon by Miss Carter, the dead man's sister. After a vain search at the house of another neighbour, she gave him a note which she had found in her brother's Bible. It read "Let my dear beloved son have my fiddle and squirrel cage; and now I must depart. Read the 16th chapter of St John and that will inform you full particulars" At the top of the note was interlined "Give my love to my wife". Carter was found suspended from a beam in the barn by a plough line, he was quite cold and stiff and had been dead some hours. A verdict of "Temporary aberration of intellect" was returned.

1849 Jany 10th Dr. Wake leaves, succeeded by Mr Jas Williams, Surgeon fro. London. Died Jany 9. 1862. 46

1851 Sep 20 Dr Wake returns to reside here

Notice Lecture to be given in the National School Room by W.A.Rackham, Esq. on Thursday evening, January 11, 1849, on the subject of Shakespeare. The first of a series of lectures under the auspices of the Southwold Union Book Club. Admission free. Chairman—F.W.Ellis Esq.[3a]

1849 Feby 1st Mr Thos Ayscough Thompson, clerk at the London and County Bank, Abingdon,

---

3a. Little is known about this short-lived Book Club. There had been a Southwold Book Society from 1811 to 1820, the records of which still survive.

whilst engag'd in a shooting party on the river at the above place his gun accidentally discharging and his *forefinger* of the left hand, which was imprudently placed over the muzzle *was blown off*.

Cutting Maggs to auction 30–35 tons of clover and trefoil stover and 25–30 tons of second crop stover at Reydon on January 15, 1849.

1849 Jany 15th Sale of "Stover" at Reydon for Messrs Plant & Rounce.

Feby 1st Married John Sones, widower, (his wife dying July 13th. 1848) to Hannah Hurren of and at Peasenhall.

Feby 1st John Bedingfield Hurr had his forefinger of the [ ] hand amputated by Mr Jas Williams—Surgeon.

1849 Feby 2d Died Mr Wm Wells—14th Dec 1848 Mrs Margt Cooper.

Cutting Few deaths in Southwold compared with the rest of the country. Its population is about 2700, yet there were only 35 deaths in the year ending December 14 last, just over 1% of the total population. Of these one was 93, six 83, four 76, six 65, one 36, three 34, two 26, one 19 and nine children. Since December 14 when Mrs Margaret Cooper died at 86, only Mr William Wells, on the 2nd inst, aged 78, has died.

Cutting Religious services held at the Independent Chapel at Wrentham to celebrate the two hundredth anniversary of the foundation of the church there. The Reverend William Hopkins of Southwold preached the opening sermon. (Feby 1st)

Cutting Mr H.K.Bransby of the "Sole Bay Academy" delivered a lecture on Thursday February 8 on the subject of "Elocution" under the auspices of the Southwold Union Book Club. Capt. C. Rayley R.N. was thanked for "his courteous conduct in the chair."

Cutting Notice of assignment for the benefit of his creditors by Richard Rufus Boniwell of Southwold, carpenter and builder, to John Bicker of Wangford, timber merchant, Joseph Farrow of Bungay, timber merchant and James Terry of Wangford, sadler and harness maker. February 14, 1849.
Notice of the auction of his household furniture etc by Girling & Son on March 1 1849.

Cutting Notice of a dividend to be paid to Boniwell's creditors at the Old Swan, Southwold, on November 3 1849.

1849 Feby 11th Mr Spalding leaves Southwold.

Feby 16th Sale Mr. Cassidy Wangford

Feby 17th Died at Henham Mr Thos Freeman—Steward to Lord Stradbroke agd 54 years.

Feb 22d.Put to Auction the letting of a Salt Marsh being a proportion of the Saltings and Common Pasture Land, lately enclosed near the entrance of the Buss Creek at its junction of the River Blyth—including all the Woods End Marsh Wall, and the Pit up to the rails on the common Pasture land, containing 13 Acres & 21 perches. Hired by Jonathan Button at 9L 9s per year. On lease for 11 Years. from 6 April 1849

Feb 23d Mr Saml Moss Jnr. leaves for Sea.

Feby 19th Wind W.S.W fresh. "The Robt & Jas": Jamieson of and for South Shields fro London—grounded upon the "Sand Pan Hole" near the Harbor at 4 A.M. but was got off with assistance at ½ p 6 A.M. and proceeded. Cost 5£'s

This is the second case—owing to taking our Gas Lights upon the Cliff for other lights. See 26 Dec 1848

Feby 28th Blowing hard with heavy rain—during the night heavy fall of Snow—on the Morng of March 1st sharp frost, rapid Thaw during the day
The [   ] of [   ] from [   ] to [   ]
        [   ] Master put in here laden with Cheese

March 1st   Saml Gayfer   )   Jas Boyce   )
) Assessors   ) Auditors
             Wm Abbott   )   Frederic W. Denny)

Cutting Lecture delivered at the Town Hall on March 15 1849 by Jonathan Gooding Esq., on the "Origin and Design of Freemasonry" The hall was "embellished with the symbols of masonry and several emblematical paintings, recently presented to the Lodge by Brother Rounce, adorned the walls. The Brethren of the Southwold"Lodge of Fidelity" arranged themselves on either side of the chair." (Mar 15/1849)

March 21 Sale at Wrentham of the Household Furniture & Effects of The Rev Andrew Ritchie dec: See Dec 28th, 1848.

March 7th Mr Wm Garrod, Ipswich call'd upon me—I had not seen him since we left School in 1814.

1849 Mar 12th Served a copy of Writ upon Mr D Fulcher for £111.17s.6d debt and £3 10s Costs from Obadiah Boyce—Mr Hallett 7 Staple Inn Solicitor 22d I recd a copy of writ for Mrs Charlotte Boyce. (viz Mr. Fulcher's Wife) which I left with Mr Gooding—Solor. and return'd the original which not being indors'd by Mr. G. for his appearance for the Defendant—was returned on the 28th and endorsed same day I sent it to Mr Hallett 7 Staple Inn Holborn Plaintiff—Obd. Boyce.

Debt £200.   Costs £3.10s.   Mr. Hallett—Solor

Obadiah Boyce is a Grandson of Mr. Richard Boyce (v Feb 28th 1844) by his Will it appear'd that 2 Lodging Houses upon East Cliff were left by him to Charlotte Boyce his daughter—now the Wife of Mr Danl Fulcher (*ob this Charlotte Boyce is Sister to Mr Fulcher's first Wife, Maria Boyce*) that Obd. Boyce's Solor Mr Hallett proved the Will to be *bad* and that the property belong'd to Ob Boyce—& that expences for recovering the Houses et appears to be the sum of £200 et et for which Sum the plaintiff Ob. Boyce sues Defendant Charo Boyce—the matter is settled and Mr Fulcher retain the Houses. See July 31st 1849.

1849 Mar. 12th Sale of Coleby's & Jellicoes Furniture

Commenced the Open Benches in this Church.vide Feb 11/50

March 28th Mr Wm Hotson of this Parish went under an Opperation for the Stone. Surgeons, Jas. Williams—Bales & others.

March 30th. Wm Cock's baker—fails and goes into the County Court, His Sale May 2/49

Lecture by F.W.Ellis, Esq.R.N. At the Town Hall. Thursday 29 March 1849.

Cutting Lecture delivered at the Town Hall on March 29 1849 by F.W.Ellis Esq R.N. on the "Life Boat and on other means used for the preservation of life from Shipwreck". The room was decorated with the flags of all nations and some beautiful models of naval architecture were displayed   At the lecture a medal was presented from the Royal National Shipwreck Institution to John Fish of the Southwold Life Boat for his bravery in rescuing two men from the "Ury" in the previous December. The Vicar was in the chair.

Cutting Death at Southwold on the 20th inst of Sarah, relict of the Reverend Thomas Sheriff, late of Uggeshall, aged 77. "By her decease the tradesmen lose a good employer and the poor a generous and consistent friend."

Cutting Protection Order for William Cocks, late of Curriers Arms Lane in Ipswich, then of Back Street, Southwold and now of High Street, Southwold, baker and confectioner, an insolvent debtor.

> 1849 Apr 6th.Market Place let to Mr Saml. Strange by tender for 3 Years at 8L.8s a year.

1849 April 4th Sale of Mr Geo Crisp's Effects Westleton—who leaves for Australia.

April 12th Sale of Building Materials for Jas Jermyn Esq. at Southwold.

April 9th I went to Uggeshall with Mr Dunham, valued the Household Furniture et of his Mother's Sold to Mr Rt. Dunnet, Cherry Tree Inn Stoven. 14th I sold the Effects by Auction.

> Apr 9th Mr Fulcher Parish Churchwarden and C. Rayley the Ministers in the room of Mr Boniwell See Ap 8/44

April 12th Thursday Mr Jas Critten—boat builder—his Son Jas.—brother George and a boy of Wm Pott Spence, on their way from Covehithe in an open Boat were accidentally upset—Jas Critten Snr and his brother George swam to the Shore—Jas Critten Jnr. being entangled in the Sail & rigging, after extricating himself therefrom—he then proceeded to the safety of the boy whom he extricated from a watery grave, but very much exhausted, so much so, that medical aid was applied and the next day the boy came home.

April 14th Mr Robt Pierson left here for America—with his Son-in-law and Daughter from Cambridge. Mr P. returned to SoWold Mar 7. 1856.

20

1849 Apr 15th. The Sloop "Friendship" (the property of Mr. Edwd. Goldsmith) Ed Gillings, Master—upon her passage from the North—sprang a leak 7 Miles South of the Dungeon Crew Saved by takg to their boat.

Apr 17th Mrs. Francois fails in the "Crown Hotel" Mr Hy Garrod late Landlord, put in to conduct its business 'till May 24th when Mr Cracknell puts his Clerk Mr. Fisher into it—who continued in 'till 21 June—when Mr. Giles Austin took it. Novr 7th Mrs Francois leaves Southwold (She had been at Lodgings at Mr Rt. Carter's)

18th Apr. To Wenhaston—took a view of my old School—which I had not seen for nearly 30 Years—the premises have been converted into Cottages for several years—

21st April I went to Norwich—saw James Bloomfield Rush executed.

19 April John Andrews Sale. Southwold.

27 . .   Andrews Sale of Drapery—at the "Bear" Inn Reydon.

Apr 19 Mr John Dillon. Bookseller opens a Shop in this town—left July

Cutting Mr H. Birch M.A. has resigned from his assistant mastership at Eton to become tutor to the Prince of Wales. Birch is the son of the Vicar of Southwold. (April 1849)

Cutting The London correspondent of the Oxford Herald reports rumours that the Prince Consort is interfering with the education of the Prince of Wales, objecting to his being taught the Church Catechism, and his tutor has resigned as a result.
(March 1850)

M.S. insertion The Town of Southwold in Suffolk which under its Charter Sergeant Mereweather has represented as a Model of Excellence is now under the Municipal reform Act to be regarded as a Model of Imperfection.

With a population little exceeding two thousand persons great difficulty was encountered in forming a Town Council of sufficient ability and independence to carry out the Act; but the principal Inhabitants lent themselves to the attempt, and to a certain extent succeeded; but however for some time ceased to take any interest in it, the Council is now composed altogether of Tradesmen—its Head being a Common Carpenter deficient in Education and in the knowledge of right from wrong.

As a Member of the Council the present Mayor who is in his third year of Office and also the late Mayor who held the Office for five consecutive years; were for six out of the eight years in the employment of the Council, doing most of their work and finding materials for it, receiving large Sums of Money from them, directly and indirectly—This violation of the Municipal Act was so common that other Members of the Council acted upon the same principle, and many Members took their Seats

21

in the Council, unqualified, either by Rate or Estate, without objection; perhaps lest one objection should lead to further inquiry. The Committees necessary to carry out the forms required by the Act have been generally appointed, but their utility has been invisible—many of them do nothing and some do wrong—thus, the Estate Committee employs its members in work, and the Finance Committee pays them—holding Money which ought to be in the hands of the Treasurer, to their hands, for that and perhaps other illegal purposes.

The Accounts kept by the Treasurer have always been badly kept, and are now necessarily so, through the interference of them with his duty—they are also carelessly audited and so stated in the printed Copy as to defy all common understanding—Still however they are remarkable for the illegal expenditure of money both for public and private purposes.

The Income of the Corporation amounts from nine hundred to a thousand pounds, a part only of which is paid into the hands of the Treasurer, who is improperly anticipated by other Receivers who give no account of their receits. In the expenditure of Income, the Improvement of the Town is so far from being considered, that the repair of its public buildings and the maintenance of its public works are altogether neglected. That the Town Council may have had difficulties in providing for expences incurr'd through improvident & illegal contracts which they have recognized; is perhaps beyond question—but the Income of the Corporation is undiminished and it appears to be a mistaken Economy which leaves public works to fall into decay for want of repair.

Amongst the Complaints of the Commonalty it is complained that various and very valuable rights and privileges which they enjoyed under the Charter, as administered by the powers that were; not one remnant remains to them, under the Municipal Reform Act, as administered by the powers that be, viz the Mayor & Town Council in which Improvement is beyond hope as it has been so degraded by the abuse of its powers that no person, who puts any value upon his Character, will suffer himself to be connected with it.[4]

Cutting Letter to the Editor of the Ipswich Journal from the Reverend H.W.R.Birch of Southwold Parsonage, dated April 30 1849. Birch defends the report made by Bardwell upon the state of Southwold Church which was published in the Journal in September 1847 and he invites donations for carrying out urgent repairs. Letters between Birch and the Archdeacon of Suffolk are reprinted *verbatim*.   Birch

4. This is in the handwriting of James Jermyn, the probable author.

to the Archdeacon (April 26 1849) The roof of the south aisle has been repaired at a cost of over £300. It was in a ruinous condition, far beyond that anticipated by the Southwold carpenters. During Birch's absence in Herefordshire a massive piece of timber fell from the side of the north aisle roof, it was fortunate that this did not happen during a service, when it would have killed anybody within reach. Quantities of decayed wood were falling from the roof on the north side of the altar. Within the last six weeks a piece of wood over the pulpit was dislodged after a cricketer from the town had been employed to THROW at the board, when it fell into the nave. The roof of the north aisle lets in the rain.

Archdeacon to Birch (April 27) Will visit the church within the next two months. The present state of St Edmund's is humiliating to all connected with the parish.

Birch to the Archdeacon (April 28). Mr Bardwell is second only, if at all, to Mr Cottingham, the talented restorer of Hereford Cathedral. He wrote to defend his reputation and to refute the report made by Mr Stannard. He himself, in spite of the implication made at the close of the Archdeacon's letter, had not been negligent in carrying out repairs. He had carried a motion in the vestry to repair one or two windows each year, but this proving expensive, the first costing £13, this policy had been abandoned. He had opposed the replacement of pews with benches when one of the most exposed churches in England was neither wind nor water proof. He suggests a meeting between the Archdeacon and Bardwell and has friends who will raise money to pay for the architect's visit from London or elsewhere.[5]

Cutting Verses entitled "Southwold Church", of no merit, but asserting that there is a conspiracy within the town to thwart bids from outside Southwold for repairing the church and to give the work to local men, in spite of it being publicly advertised. The last two verses read:

> Moreover, trickery to prevent
> And see things fairly thro'
> Their Warden shall have Five Per Cent
> Upon all costs when due.
>
> Thus is the town to jobs a prey
> Each patronizing trader,
> Will tax himself—the trade to pay,
> And keep out an Invader.

5. Lewis Nockalls Cottingham, 1787–1847, was born at Laxfield, the son of a farmer and served an apprenticeship at Ipswich (ex. inf. John Hutchinson). He would thus have been related to Lewis Orlebar Cottingham, farmer, of The Grove, Reydon, and John Cottingham, the retired farmer, of Southwold. Birch would have seen his restoration of Hereford Cathedral when he was there in 1848.

April 28th We were visited with a Thunder Storm at ½ p 2 A.M.

Mr Birch resigns his Tutorship Sep 23/51

April 29th I & Wife with Ellen went to Stocton—I left them at her Brother's—returned May 17th followg.

Same day I went to Kirby Cane saw Mrs Doe.

Poster SOUTHWOLD—REDUCED FARES—The public are respectfully informed that ELLIOTT'S FAST OMNIBUS Will start every morning from the Red Lion Inn, Southwold, through Wangford, Stoven, Brampton, Shaddingfield, and Weston, to his booking-office at Beccles; from thence every Monday, Wednesday, and Saturday through Loddon and Thurton to the White Horse Inn, Old Haymarket, Norwich, and leaves in the afternoon of the same days. Every Tuesday, Thursday, and Friday morning on the arrival of the Omnibus at Beccles from Southwold, Moore's Railway Bus will convey passengers, parcels &c from the King's Head Commercial Hotel, Beccles, to Haddiscoe, in time for train to Yarmouth, Lowestoft, Norwich, Wymondham, Attleborough, Fakenham, Dereham, Swaffham, Lynn, Newmarket, Ely, Cambridge, Wisbeach, Peterborough, London, Birmingham, and Manchester, and returns from the above station every evening (Sundays excepted).

OBSERVE! Elliott's Fast Omnibus Starts every Morning from Martin's Red Lion Hotel, Southwold, at REDUCED FARES

LOYNS, PRINTER AND BOOKSELLER, BECCLES

(Commenced May 9 1849. Discontinued May 31)

May 1st Mr Rd Dunnett—"Cherry Tree", Stoven leaves home for London, being in embarass'd circumstances—returns on the 7th inst.*

Cutting Howlett and Lenny are to auction at the Cherry Tree Inn, Stoven on May 31 the household furniture etc of Richard Dunnett, late of Uggeshall, blacksmith, and now of Stoven, innkeeper.

I attended the Sale May 31 1849 and took Valuation of Fixtures, Garden et with Messrs Howlett & Lenny.

* Left the House Oct 11/49 after residing in it year—and goes to London succeeded by Mr. Chas Harvey.

May 31st. At the Old Swan, Southwold Put to Sale *Fish House* the property of John Braham June 14th Sold it to Jonthn Button £33

May 2d Thunder & heavy rain.

May 17 *Ascension Day*. Prayers at Church—by Revd HWR.Birch—this is the *first time* Prayers have ever been known to have been read upon this day—at this church May 25 1854 by Mr Crowfoot.

1849 May 27th I took an excursion upon the Sea with George Critten, John Skelton, Charles Alexander, & Jo Fish—Seamen—went on board 2 Dutch Vessels and 1 Dane The "Den junge Hermann" Capt T. Bornholdt—I brought a Tobacco pipe from each.

Cutting Maggs to auction two dwelling houses in East Street formerly

24

belonging to the late William Wells at the Crown on June 7 as well as the deceased's household furniture.
(Lot II Purchsd by Jo Barber
.. I .. .. Wm Warne 30 June/49)

Cutting To the Editor of the Ipswich Journal "The Vernal Seasons of England"

Cutting Prosperity of "this much frequented and deservedly admired watering place" Southwold has been long recommended by doctors for "the restoration of invalids, and inducing long life". 88 people living in the parish whose ages total 6,802 years. Sixty three average 74, eighteen 83 years 4 months, seven 92 years 6 months.

1849 June 7th Sale of Household Furniture Dwelling Houses et of the late Mr W. Wells. Exor. Jas Bloomfield Halesworth.

June 15 Ernest—Son of the Revd Mr Birch—leaves here for the Indies.

June 16 Mr Abraham Leman leaves this Town. Mr. A. was proprietor of the Saltworks here Died at Norwich Dec. 23. 1851

June 21 Mr Giles Austin takes "Crown" Hotel late Mary Francois—see April 17 (leaves June 21/50) vd June 21 1850 Westrup.

June 22d My Nephews John Banks & Amos Barber present Mr T.W. Thompson with a very handsome Bible from the Inhabitants of Walberswick for his great attention to them in religious duties. see July 6/49

June 22 Abbott's Theatre leaves this Town—came on Trinity Monday—the Fair.

June 23 Catharine daughter of Mr J.L.Pashley (see June 7th 1847) found drowned upon the Beach—Nr the North Pier—Coroner's Inquest *Found drowned* It is supposed she drownd herself on the Morng of the 21st. *Her Mother died on the 13th inst.*

June 26/49 Cap. Rayley advances £40 to Wm Prettyman upon his Premises Park Lane

1849 July 21st "John Bull" Pilot Boat (built by Jas Critten) was launchd

July 6th Mr T.W.Thompson leaves this Town to reside at Halesworth. Mr T has resided here about 34 Years and for several years was agent in this town for the Norwich Crown Bank—to which Bank he is now its agent at Halesworth Mr W.A.Thompson succeeds his Father to this Bank vd Aug 6 1850

July 19 Samuel Mayhew 54 hung himself in a Shed the property of Mr Ed. Goldsmith—The shed is in a Marsh, adjoining the Marsh where Mr W. Pashley hung himself see June 7th. 1847.

July 25th Sale of House & Premises in the occupation of Mr Artis at Wrentham and of one at Reydon in the occupation of Saml. Cutler—Sale at the "Eagle" Inn, in Wrentham. Solicitors Mess. Fiske Francis & Fiske Beccles Exors Jas Taylor & Wm Jos Wigg to the late Margt. Cooper.

Cutting Maggs to auction a messuage etc and a freehold dwelling house at the Eagle Inn, Wrentham on July 25 1849. The first is at Wrentham, the second, occupied by Samuel Cutler, is in Reydon.

25

South Cliff, Southwold, Suffolk

Leaflet Issued by the Proprietors of the Norfolk News announcing that they
will carry full reports of the meetings of the Royal Agricultural
Society at Norwich.

1849

July 26 Repository Sale at the Old Swan—Southwold

Augt 5th The "Lady Stewart" Geo Elliott—of Newcastle—came into this
Bay havg one of her Crew on board (Jas:Clark) dead with Cholera—He was
consigned to the deep—

Cutting "This favourite place of resort is fast filling and the season, it is
anticipated, will prove a propitious one . . . . the coming
Regatta will far surpass in interest and magnitude any previous event
of the kind remembered in Southwold." (August 4 1849)

August 8th Regatta

Cutting "The bright sun cast his golden beams on the ever-varying surface of
the deep, which bore upon its mighty bosom many a beauteous craft,
which like wild birds floated on the main, while ever and anon the
sweet strains from "Taylor's band swept upon the ear." Cannon fired
from Gun Hill at noon, dinner for the gentlemen at the Crown at
five, at ten a beautiful "pyrotechnic display, by Coe, of Norwich" on
Gun Hill.

1849 July 25th Simon Spicer comes home leavg his Vessel the "Victoria" at
Yarmouth. Wm Walker takes her as Master.

1849 July 26th A repository Sale of Furniture at the Old Swan Hotel Southwold. see July 26 1849

1849 July 31 Mr Wm Buckingham, and Wife came over to Mr Prettyman's

Cuttings "Boyce v. Fulcher. Mr Palmer and Mr Power were counsel for the plaintiff; Mr Prendergast for the defendant.

> The plaintiff is a tobacconist, living in London; the defendant who is related to him by marriage, is a builder, carrying on business at Southwold, where the plaintiff possesses several houses. The defendant was appointed agent to collect rents, and at the time of the action was brought it was alleged he had received the sum of £111 17s 6d, for which he had not accounted. The defendant paid £9 15s 4d into Court, and pleaded, among others, the general issue for the remainder." Because of the relationship between the parties, both counsel agreed to the case being referred. (Aug 11 1849)

Cutting Southwold Church Bells. At the last Ipswich assizes an award in the case above was given in favour of Mr Fulcher, mayor and parish churchwarden. "This success on the part of Mr Fulcher was deemed worthy of celebration by the ringing of the church bells without application to the churchwardens or to the minister of the parish, on the 22nd inst." Fulcher himself had not sanctioned this demonstration and the vicar, asking the cause, ordered it to be stopped.

Cutting "Southwold Church Bells" At Fulcher's request the correspondence between him and Stephen Jackson, the Editor of the Ipswich Journal, is reprinted in full. Jackson refuses to give the name of the writer of the paragraph above, which Fulcher considered untrue and injurious to his reputation. Jackson refuses to agree with him or to comply with his request. Jonathan Gooding, the Southwold solicitor and Town Clerk, takes up the cudgels on Fulcher's behalf, strenuously but unconvincingly and without success. (August 25–September 8 1849)

Cuttings The national cholera epidemic (August 11, August 18 1849 and later)

Maggs   )
)   Exors
Marshl Twaddel)

1849 Augt 8th Mr Henry Oldring Died agd 50   He was Sexton from Aug 6/ 32 to his death. vide August 6 1832.

1844 Mar 4 Eleanor, Wife of Henry Oldring died. 43

Aug 17th I had Gravestone put down to the Memo of my Sons

. . 21th Mr. Birch takes it up, and leaves it in the Church yard.

. . 26   Removed by Mr Birch into the Vestry. Novr 8th Mr Birch removes it into the Steeple—17th following Mr Birch and myself came to amicable terms, and through the interposition of Mr Fulcher it was put down to whence Mr. Birch took it up.

Cutting CLERICAL EXACTIONS   To the Editor of the Norfolk News.

> "Sir—I shall feel obliged by your allowing me a small space in your

widely circulated journal for the insertion of a few facts respecting the Rev. H.W.R. Birch, the perpetual curate of this parish.

On Tuesday last his reverence (while on his way to church to commit to the silent tomb the body of an aged parishioner) called on me, and demanded the sum of 5s for having had a gravestone cleaned, two additional inscriptions cut on the back, and then the stone replaced. Having previously paid the sums of 10s 6d and 5s for the same stone, I resisted the demand when the reverend gentleman gave me a strict injunction "never to take any further notice of him for the future" assuring me at the same time that "he would never speak to me any more if he resided in the parish the next hundred years." With the aid of the grave digger he has thought proper to remove the stone. I am now induced to ask the clergy generally if such conduct is in accordance with the principles of the New Testament and the authorised usages of the Established Church ? and the Rev H.W.R. Birch in particular by what authority he makes *any* charge for erecting monuments to the departed in this churchyard ? he being well aware a considerable doubt exists as to his possessing any right in the said churchyard whatever.

I am, Sir, your obedient Servant,

Southwold, August 22nd 1849   JAMES MAGGS.

NOTICE.

WHEREAS some Person or Persons did on Sunday, the 26th day of August, 1849, between the hours of Twelve & One o'Clock, immediately after Divine Service at this Church, remove a Tomb-Stone, the Property of James Maggs, from the Churchyard

BELONGING TO THIS PARISH.

Whoever will give Information of the Offender or Offenders, shall, upon conviction, receive a Handsome Reward.

Southwold, August 27th, 1849.

CROWE, PRINTER, STATIONER, BOOKSELLER, & BINDER, LOWESTOFT.

28

Handbill   NOTICE
WHEREAS some Person or Persons did on Sunday, the 26th day
of August, 1849, between the hours of Twelve & One o'Clock
immediately after Divine Service at this Church, remove a Tomb-
Stone, the Property of James Maggs, from the Churchyard
                BELONGING TO THIS PARISH
Whoever will give Information of the Offender or Offenders, shall,
upon conviction, receive a Handsome Reward.
Southwold, August 27th, 1849
     Crowe, printer, stationer, bookseller & binder, Lowestoft.

1849 August 25th. Incendiary Fire—at Wenhaston—the property of Mr
Charles White, Relievg Officer—[   ] is charged of the diabolical
Act—and committed to Ipswich for trial, property burnt—

Aug 31 Edwd Gooch Esqr M.P. made a Freemason of at this Lodge.
September 5

Cutting Maggs to auction four substantial brick and tiled freehold
          messuages with 3 roods of ground in Wangford at the Angel Inn
          there.

Sep 6th Sale of Wines and Spirits the property of Mrs Norton—at Mr P.
Palmer's House, Park Lane.

Cuttings Death of Dr. Stanley, the Bishop of Norwich. (1849 Sep 6th)
1849 Sep 14th James Alfred Stamford—Surgeon—to Ipswich Gaol for
debt—discharged under the Insolvent Debtors Act. On the 18th Oct came to
Southwold the day following. Nov 16 Mr. Stamford leaves Southwold

Sepr 15th Peter Francois died—at Sea.

Sep 27 Fire at the Union House—the fire was happily got under before any
great damage was done.

1849 Oct 4th. Died in London, aged 36—Harriet, Wife of Mr Giles Austin—
Landlord of the "Crown" Hotel, Southwold. June 21 1849

Sep 25th. William, Son of Mr John Sawyer, of this place—embarks at
London for New Orleans—leavg. his Wife and 2 children—

Oct 8th Very heavy swell & run of the Sea. took a large portion of Easton
Cliff. Had the tide been high, the Sea must have swept a great part of our
Cliff away—if not the Town

Oct 12th Sale of Mr Simon Spicer's Furniture et

Oct 13th Mr Ward (Austin's brother-in-law) leaves here for London.

Oct 13th A Dutch Skute—The "Opzeeman's Hoop" of Katwyk—came on
shore about 100 yards N of the bound Post—no one on board. She upset the
night before off Yarmouth—her Crew consisted of 8—Six of whom were
drowned, as stated by the Captain and One Man and Boy who where picked up
upon the Wreck and landed at Lowestoft. The 16th I sold the Wreck by
Auction—for £10. 10s 0d to Mr John Sawyer & Myself—the 25th She was
sold in lots by me on the 25th.

Cutting　Notice of Assignment of the goods of Arthur Baldrey Gray of the Tuns Inn, Yoxford, innkeeper and farmer, to Samuel Gayfer of Walberswick, merchant and brewer and John Bicker of Wangford, timber merchant. October 17 1849,

1849 Octob: 19th. Jas Jermyn Esq. leaves Reydon Cottage, where he had resided—since [   ] 18 [   ] And toke Lodgings at Mr Saml. Wayth's, Meetg House lane SoWold.

Oct 18th Sale of Mr Wm Sutton's Furniture et by J.Maggs. vd May 8/51

1849 Sep 20th Self and Mr Marshall Twaddell to the Rev. Mr. Atthills to prove Mr Hy. Oldring's Will.

Sep 22d. Mr Peter Palmer and myself signed a Note in hand for £40 from the Saxmundham Money Society for Mr Jonthn Button. He giving us a Bill of Sale of his Fish House.

Sep 24. Batty's company of Horsemanship here.

Sep 27 The Factory at this Union House partly destroyed by Fire—suppos'd to be an act of Incendary.

Oct 3d. Mrs Burch of Ipswich—came to see me respecting Tink's Houses.

Oct 11th. Mr John Croft leaves Wangford, "Lion" public House. Succeeded by Mr Ludden.

Oct 13th A Dutch Skute "Opzeemans Hoop" wash'd on Shore at Easton—Abandoned—16 I sold her by Auction. purchased by Mr John Sawyer, and myself for £10. 10s When I saw the Captain, name "Klaus Van der plas Leenderd" who stated she founder'd off Yarmouth, and 6 out of 8 of the Crew perished—25th I sold the Wreck in lots. 26th—The Captain's Nephew was picked up in this river—30th Inquest *Verdict found drowned.*

Oct 29th Died Suddenly at [   ] Mr Goff of Wrentham, Miller, aged vide 16th Oct 1850.

Oct 27th Wm Podd—son-in-law to the late Mr Henry Oldring—was accidentally killed at Maidstone, Kent.

Insertion Signature of Klaas Van der plas Leenderd

Cutting Notice of assignment of the goods of James Jermyn, late of Reydon and now of Southwold, gentleman, to Lewis Orlibar Cottingham of Leiston, gentleman and Read Crisp of Southwold, miller and merchant. November 1 1849.

Novr. 5th Sale of Furniture of the late Mr Rookyard's dec. Frostenden

Nov. 7 Sold by Auction. British Tar "Sun" "Star" and "Mayflower"

Cutting The sloop "Royal George", fishing vessel, of London, appeared in the bay and signalled for assistance. Boarded by the crew of the "Cricketer", who brought her safely into Lowestoft. November 16.

Catalogue Title page only (illustrated with engraving of Reydon Cottage) Sale of furniture,plate,china,library,paintings,engravings,scientific collections, the property of James Jermyn Esq.
To be sold at Reydon Cottage by Messrs Rix & Burton, November 19–21. Under Sheriff's order.

Nov 20th Valued Mrs Elizth Palmer's Effects for County Court. Settled without a Sale on the 24th.

Novr. 26th Valued Furniture & Effects of Mr John Lloyd, Brewer, under an Execution from the County Court.

Decr. 3d. Sold his Effects, by Auction.

Notice   Members of the Corporation etc. 1849–50

1849 Dec 5th Our Life Boat went to the assistance of 2 of our Fishing Punts—Cragie & Hurr—after taking the men on board, towed the boats on shore immediately she landed the boats and Crew—another boat—belonging to Pearl of Walberswick, was observed in great danger—to which she directly proceeded—and succeeded in bringing the Boat and Crew (7 in Number) safe to land—And not a little to the gratification to all of us—as the Wind was blowing Strong from the S.E.—and so heavy a Sea, that it would have been impossible to have landed. This morning John Rogers—Fisherman, and his Son upset in their boat upon the Shoal—and had not assistance from the Shore by a boat been rendered them, they must have perished.

5th My Self receives an appointment of agency for the Life Association of Scotland.

> 1849 Novr 28th—"Ronne Boonholm—The "Greyhound" Schooner Thos Foreman, Master of Yarmouth became a total wreck and crew perished (amongst whom was Wm Forder of Southwold) on the weathermost rocks of Eartholm, on the night of the 17th inst—some of her spars and the wk of two Boats marked "Greyhound" of Yarmouth, Thomas Foreman, and a bag of Wheat have come on shore from her.

Cutting Diagram (bar chart) showing the fluctuation in the average price of wheat during the six weeks ending December 8 1849.

Cuttings The high tides at Lowestoft and Reydon etc. At the latter place it was 10 feet on Friday morning last and 9 feet 10 ins in the evening. A "wretched work of rotten stakes, mis-called a breakwater, extending from the S end of Gun Hill towards the harbour" displaced at Southwold. The only damage there and no loss if it is replaced. (Decemb 27 and 28th)

Dec 12th To Wangford to take an Acct of the Effects of the late John Fenn—dec—Sale on the 21st inst.

Dec 13th. The Commissioners of this Harbor, appointed Thos Bailey Smith, Charles Naunton, William Chapman, and G̶e̶o̶r̶g̶e̶ Edward Elmy—Coalmeters.

(Elmy) resign'd Feb 11/50 and Jo P Hurr appointed in his room.

Dec 20th Sale of Admiralty Droits—by me   agent Mr F.W.Ellis.

Dec 17th I went to Halesworth, valued Effects under £20 to Mr John Davey of Halesworth—Auctioneer—who goes as an Insolvent thro' the County Court.

Tide Decr XXVII & XXVIII

Dec 25th Mr John Pritchard, 1 Widegate St Bishopsgate to Mary Lowsey of this place.

Cutting Few deaths among the adults of Southwold. With a population of about 2700 only 22 have occurred in the last 11 months and none last January and the town has been spared the devastation of cholera. Two males have died at 84, four at 76, two at 65, two at 52—these being averages. One female died at 92, one at 83, four at 76, one at 61, two at 55, two at 34 and one at 28.

> In addition to the deaths of the 22 adults were 35 children principally of "scarletina" and 2 Suicides see June 21st and 19th July making in all 59 deaths so had the same number in 1834   Ambrose Goodwin loses 2 children in 6 days George Savill 2 in one day   Wm Lincoln 2 in 10 days and Robert Allen 3 in four days.

1850 January 1st I went to Halesworth—Sold by Auction in the Angel Yard—A Cob, Cart and Harness—the property of Lockwood, under an execution from the County Court.

Mr Frs Stannard went to Halesworth with me.

January 1st Married Mr Gustavus J. Carson, London Church Missionary to Martha, daughter of Mr Joseph Arthey of this place.

Jany 1st At Halesworth Sold by Auction at the "Angel" Inn, Poney, Cart & Harness the property of Jas Lockwood, under an execution from the County Court.

8th Geo Blake, charg'd of robbing Mary Ann Bryant at Mrs Martins "Red Lion" Inn—9th examd and committed to Beccles Gaol for trial, Pleaded guilty-sessions Monday 11th March—Sentenced to 3 months hard labor.

Cuttings 1st inst., at Southwold Mr Wm Haken of Windsor to Eliza, daughter of Mr George Warne of Southwold

> 1st inst., at Southwold by the Rev Henry W. Rous Birch, Mr Gustavus J Carson, London Church Missionary to Martha, daughter of Mr Joseph Arthey of the above place, chemist and druggist.

Visiting Cards Mr and Mrs Gustavus J. Carson

Menu Banquet given by the Lord Mayor of London at the Mansion House to the Corporations of Hastings and Rye. Thursday January 24 1850.

1850 January 22d Revd H.W.R.Birch and family leaves and go to Strath-fieldsaye—24th May returned home.[6]

Feby 2d The Rev H. Martin came to officiate for Mr Birch, Mr Martin preached for the last time in this church on Sunday 28 April.

January 23d Self & Marshall Twaddell—exors to the late Henry Oldring dec. attend the County Court at Halesworth—versus John Soans for £4 16s 5d due to H Oldring's estate, expences £1.8.10—to be pd in 2 months

---

6. Strathfieldsaye was the seat of the Duke of Wellington.

Jany 24th Mr T. Wallace serves Mr Marshall Twaddell with a Notice from Mr. Fulcher—demanding his qualification to sit as Councillor.

Jany 26th Strong wind—the "Anna Maria" of So Shields ran on board off here by a large Bark and immediately went down—Crew all perished except 1 Man named Hunter—*Wm*: the Son of Mr Jas Cady of Walberswick was one who perished.

Jany 31st Sale of Mr Jo Burcham's effects.

Feb 2d Revd H Martin comes left April 28/50 vd Jany 22/50 preaching in the absence of Mr Birch.

1850 Feby 6. Sale of Mrs Hammonds effects. South Cove.

Same day

Heavy gale from the W. & N.W. during the day—½ p 10 A.M. a Vessel was observed with a flag in her rigging—the yawl "John Bull" and the Life Boat went off to her assistance—the former succeeded in boarding her first who took into Lowestoft—she proved to be the "Marys" of Guernsey for London, general cargo—"John Bulls" crew were rewarded with £125

Feby 11th (vd Mar 1849) re-commencd erecting Open Benches in this Church completed July. 1850. D.Fulcher & P.Palmer builders.

Feb 18 Sale of Jas Cutler's Effects—at Wrentham—

Feb 18th Lydia, daughter of John Lowsey to London.

Feby 20th Ann Waters, Will, Exors Wm Aldis Higham and Stegall Higham.

1850 Feb 22d I took an A/ct of Henry Haken's effects for County Court March 18—I sold the Effects, Stock in Trade et. by Auction.

Feb 25th.Wife and Self to Yarmouth to Mr Shelly's & Mr Palmer's, respecting Mr Oldrings—dec business.

Feb 26th Died at Yoxford Mr. Richd. Smith—late Butler to Sir C. Blois.

Feb 28th Died at Fressingfield, Mr Jo Doddington—tailor.

March 1st Died at Middleton—John Braham, agd 25, late of Southwold.

March 4th Married Geo Carter to Mary Oldring—at Southwold.

Mar 15 Sale at Wangford, Mr Charles Eastaugh, Shoemaker.

1850 March 19th I valued, with Mr. Randall of Ipswich, the Effects of Mr. Charles A. Everrett to Mr Alfred Wentworth—who this day succeeded Mr C.A. Everrett to the "Southwold Arms" Public House vd March 29 1851.

Mar 20. To Halesworth to the County Court.

Mar 21 Flour at this Union House, Contract 26s per Sack.

I went to Mr Lenny's Wrentham.

April 1st Easter Monday Mr Peter Palmer (the Mayor) Parish Warden and Mr Jos Arthey Minister's Warden elected Churchwardens in the room of Captn Rayley and Mr Fulcher—Robt Carter appointed Parish Clerk by the Minister, Mr Birch. *this is the first time a Parish Clk was ever appointed by either Minister or Parish—as no entry appears of such in any one of the Parish Books* Henry Oldring appointed Sexton—Jas Wigg and Geo Naunton elected *Vergers* or *Sidesmen* and Chas Carter—Organist—to play it without any *Salary*—depending upon Subscriptions.

Cutting Maggs to auction the twine and rope ground of Henry Oldring, rope maker and twine spinner, at six o'clock in the evening of Thursday March 28 1850 at the Old Swan. At one o'clock in the afternoon he will auction Oldring's stock in trade and household furniture. (Listed)

1850 March 30th Sold Furniture and Effects of Mrs Edwards at Blythburgh

Apr 6. Mr Thos Crowe, succeeds R.G.Turner to Mill, Wangford.

Apr 18th To the late Mr Winchop's of Blybro' & Valued property for Administration to the Will of his Wife Ann.

Apr 18 Sale of Rt G Turner's effects, Wangford, Miller

April 22d I valued Furniture and Effects of Mr H.K. Bransby—for Mr Thos Balls of Lowestoft—Auctioneer under an execution of a bill of Sale to Mr R.S.Haward of this Town Butcher—for 90£ expences included.

Cutting Notice to Henry Knevett Bransby of Southwold, schoolmaster, an insolvent debtor, to appear before the County Court Judge at Halesworth on May 22.

1851 Jany 29th Mr Bransby *leaves* SoWold Feb 6th Sale of his Furniture & Effects 1851 Bransby here 17 Augt left 23 inst Died New Orleans August 1855

Cutting Notice to Charles Anthony Everrett of Southwold, innkeeper and butcher, insolvent debtor, to appear before the County Court Judge at Halesworth on April 24.

Sunday April 28th Mr Charles White of Wenhaston a Weslyan Preacher—officiates for the Revd W Hopkins a dissenting Minister in this parish at the Dissenting Meeting House !!

May 14th To Halesworth with Mr M. Twaddell

May 18 Sale of Jas Welton's Boat et. et. to Frdk Alexander Esq.Reydon.

May 19 To Stocton with Wife and Sarah. I also went to Mr Jas Doe's, Kirby Cane.

May 29th Fishing Boat "Native" built by Henry Ladd at Mr Palmer's Fish Offc yard, was launched.

May 30th—Coe, Servant of Mr Ezekiel Read, Wangford drowns himself in a Meadow dyke.

Open Benches) about the middle part
Completed) of this month July 1850
Jas Holly sailed fro London May 4/50 In search of Sir Jo Franklin arrived 10 Oct 1851 no Intelligence

1850 May 22d (being 341 years this day since the date of Mr William Godell's Will) Upon the taking up of the old Pews in this Church between the Pulpit and the seats where the Bailiffs wont to set from 1490 to 1835 since which time has been the seats of the Mayor and one Alderman, for the purpose of erecting open benches—two large stones without plates or Inscriptions—but each with a carved figure thereon—the one representing a man and the other a woman was discovered curiosity led us that were present (namely Mr Peter Palmer and Mr Joseph Arthey—Churchwardens—Mr Jonthn Gooding—solicitor Mr Dnl Fulcher—myself—Mr Robt Allen, Stone Mason & Son also

3 or 4 of the Workmen) to ascertain if any one had been interred under them and the state of their remains—after digging down about 2½ feet—under the Stone bearing the figure of a Man we discovered two skull bones—the one of a Man and the other of a Woman lying so near each other and in a position that leaves but little doubt but that they were deposited by some rude hand at a subsequent interment—Under the Slab or Stone bearing the figure of a Woman were no human remains to be seen.

Some were of opinion the Skulls were those of Wm Godell and his Wife Margarett but Gardner says page 205 "On the East of the Pulpit by the North Isle are two Stones without Plates and Inscriptions *supposed* to have been Covertures to William Godell and his Wife" Gardner makes no remark of the figure upon each of them—nor is his opinion or statement only *supposition* and they were as likely to be interred where these skulls were found—as in the spot supposed by Gardner for in his Will "I bequeath my body to holy Sepulture within the church of Saint Edmund King and Martyr at Southwold aforesaid before the seat I am bound to sit in being a Bailiff" I examined the skulls—they were in an extraordinary fine preservation—particularly so—if those of Godell and his Wife—Mr Godell was Bailiff here in 1490 and 1491— his Will proved 26 June 1509—In what year Mr Godell died is not known— but certainly before his Wife Margaret—as she was requested "to offer every Day at the Mass of Requiem in the Worship of the Holy Trinity three pence et " The Stone bearing the figure of a Man—and the one in the middle Isle or Nave—"*Here Lyeth the Body of Mary Burges the Wif of John Burges Gent whoe departed this Life Januarey the 23 1673*" by the aid of the Mason this 22d May 1850 exchanged situations with each other . . . Witness Jas Maggs the 22d May 1850.

Cutting Notice of the assignment of the property of Simon Spicer, mariner, of Southwold, to Daniel Fulcher of Southwold, builder and Samuel Gayfer, brewer and merchant of Southwold and Walberswick, June 20 1850.

Cutting Maggs to auction four messuages on South Green near Gun Hill at the Old Swan, on Thursday May 30   1850. (did not sell)

1850 Nov 22d Present with Mr Jas Girling (Mortgagee to Mrs Susan Smith) Jo Read, Solor, and Mr Baggot at settlement of Premises £160 at the Old Swan

1850 Aug 31 I sold them to Mr Wm Baggot—of this town, Farmer for 168£ including conveyance and a Mortgage deed for £100   This property belongd to Mrs Susan Smith and was mortgaged to Mr Jas Girling of Cove.

1850 June 20th Sale of Hy Simpson's Boat & Nets.

June 21st Mr Philip Westrup succeeds Mr Giles Austin to the Crown Hotel. v. Oct 27 1853.

June 24th Robilliard v. Rayley respecting a difference of the former leavg the house of the latter.

June 24th *John Bevan* of the "Aid" of Whitby, John Crossby, Master was brought on shore here *dead*, and interred here.

35

1850 June 29th Robt Key—placed in the *Stocks* from 12 at Noon to 6 A.M.
for being drunk and disorderly   v July 25/53[7]

July 6 Sold Mr John Leverett of Walberswick—the late Henry Oldring's,
real Estate for   56£

pd Mortgage L50
 . . Interest   2 18 6
 . . Cash   3 1 6   56£

July 8th Jane Morby comes to meet daughter Eliza, returned 20th followg

July 9th Mr Wm Laws, Stocton to Rachel Abrahams.

July 15 Coach "Old Blue" Rivett & Rous commenced running to this place
once a day 22d *Twice* a day leavg at One A.M. for London, and 5 A.M. for
Yarmouth . Discontind Nov 23/50

Cutting detached

Purchased by Mr Jo Sawyer for 80£ for Mr Samuel Gayfer

1850 July 11th took an A/ct of Effects et of Mr Job Jeves Insolvent Dr in the
County Court. Sale of Stock et Aug 19 & 20

                 1850 July 6th Mr Gooderham of Beccles opens a
                 General Shop here—leaves 4th January 1851.

Cutting Maggs to auction twelve sixty-four shares in the brig "Victoria" of
             Southwold, port of Yarmouth, 88 tons, W.M.Walker Master, built
             at Southwold in 1839. At the Old Swan at 6 p.m. on July 18 1850

Notice (handwritten)   Caution

           All *Parishioners* are *Entitled* to *Sittings* in
           the *Parish Church* to the Extent of the
           Accommodation the Church Affords, Sub-
           ject to such arrangements as the Church-
           wardens may make to promote *order* and
           decorum No *Money* payment for appor-
           tioned Sittings can be *legally* or *justifiably*
           made
           Singned H.R.Birch
           Incumbent of Southwold, Suffolk
           Aug 7th 1850.
           A Copy of this was exhibited at the Shop
           Window of Mr Wm Abbott for several
           days previous to Sunday the 11th when one
           was affixed to the Church door which was
           removed by Parker the Constable by order
           of Mr P. Palmer Churchwarden
           After Mr Birch had concluded the Prayers
           in the Eveng Service of the 11th inst—he
           read this Notice to his congregation!!

1850 July 21st Hosannah Page, attempts drowning herself in the Sea, rescued

---

7. The stocks were on Bartholomew Green, in front of the church.

by Saml Mayhew. She had been for some time (at intervals) insane—And on the 25th inst I took her to Melton Asylum. vd 25th

July 22d Jonathan Button's insolvent Dr in the County Court, Sale, July 22/50

July 23d Mr James Welsh's Sale—of Furniture et who leaves SoWold to reside in London—as a Missionary.

July 25th Mr Benj Baxter Senr had a finger amputated by Mess's Sutherland & Williams, Surgeons.

July 25 I took Hosannah Page to Melton Asylum vd 21st inst   July 28 1856 I went and took her home.

July 31st To Lowestoft for Voting list.

Aug 2d Regatta—3d Races temporary.

Aug 6th. Mr Wm Ascough Thompson leaves the Bank—succeeded by Mr T Wallace Solor   24th inst   1852 Apr 8th I sold part of his Furniture and on the 24th Apr *inst he leaves* to reside in Chelsea London.

Church Rates   present C.W. Peter Palmer   late one C.W. Danl Fulcher

1850 Augt 10th Fire at Mr Tyrell's of Blyford—nearly all the outbuildings destroyed—3 fat hogs burned to death supposed to be an act of incendary

1850 Aug 11th Yawl "Swiftsure" & crew takes a North country Collier—to London, leaky   reward £100.

1850 Aug 26th Miss Rogerson, Beccles came to mine. returned Sep 2d

1850 Sep 6th Rd Rufus Boniwell Jnr to London by "Vigilant" Jo Magub Senr June 2 1851 came home returned 14th inst.

1850 Oct 3 Self, Wife, Maria & Ellen Mr & Mrs Twaddell & daughter—Mr Peter Palmer & Wife to Dinner et at Mr Robt Denny's—Wrentham.

Cutting Letter to the Editor of the Suffolk Chronicle from "Junius", dated Southwold August 13 1856

Parliament is procrastinating over the abolition of Church rates. The inhabitants of Southwold have however decided to act by themselves. The churchwardens proposed a 6d rate to pay a bill for £92. This was rejected by 42 to 10 on a show of hands and by 132 to 38 on a poll. Now that an oppressive and unjust tax that is insulting to dissenters has been refused, the sum needed to maintain "the truly beautiful fabric" should be raised voluntarily. For years the contractor has been without his money, the friends of the church should now discharge a debt that is a moral if not a legal obligation.

Cutting Reports the votes on the church rate, which was to pay for repairs to the roof and to maintain church services. Some episcopalians, though threatened, voted against and the decisive defeat means that after the vestry meeting of Thursday August 7 the rate will be abandoned. (Southwold, August 14)

Cutting Letter to the Editor of the Suffolk Chronicle by COSMOPOLITE. Southwold. August 14. 1850[8]

8. A MS. draft (to the Ipswich Journal) is in the possession of Mr. Barrett Jenkins of Southwold. This is in the handwriting of Jonathan Gooding, the Town Clerk, proving that he was 'Cosmopolite'. Lines in the MS. that were not printed are shown in italics.

Sir,—Having recently visited that very pleasant watering place, Southwold, I cannot do otherwise than express my satisfaction at its progressive improvement, within the last few years, in its public walks, nor the less so for the great alteration in its magnificent Church, by the removal of the pews—"those unsightly excrescences of modern times" as an archaeologist, of whom the county has a right to be proud, has spoken of them in one of his works—and in the substitution of "open benches" in their stead. My pleasure was a good deal checked on learning that some opposition had been made to the improvement, but much more so on finding that that opposition was not only headed by the minister of the parish, but was carried on in a spirit not at all likely to enhance the character of one whose duty it is by example, as well as precept, to teach "Peace on earth and good will to all men" Still more was I shocked at his continuing the crusade by publicly reading a notice on the subject of them from the desk during divine service *and immediately after having officiated at the "Lord's Table" in the Sacrament attacked in a very excited state the Police Officer of the Borough for having removed copies of the notice from the Church doors, and who is said to have reproved the Minister for his intemperance with a mild and respectful manner.*

But leaving this *personal affair* "petty quarrel" between the minister and some of his parishioners to be settled by themselves or to die away by its own innocuousness, by "wasting its sweetness on the desert air," I regret its publicity at such a time, and from such a place, and as an individual will only say with the satirist "Odi profanum vulgus et arceo" and that too whether headed by a man habited in *toga clericalis* or by an *equally* self-important occasional church-going dissenting *shopkeeper*

But reverting again to the demolished"pews and open benches" I am at a loss to understand how so orthodox a person, as this minister is said to be, could for a moment be an advocate for the retention of the former, knowing as he does, they were, if not positively intro- duced, at least considerably promoted by the puritans, a set of men not likely to be greatly admired by him, whilst the "open seats or benches" were originally used at the building of the present edifice, some remains of which were late standing in the north aisle, such seats having been used at Exeter as early as 1287 and are alluded to by Durandus in his time. A learned man of the adjoining county (Norfolk) writing on the subject of pews says "It is earnestly to be wished that our churches were as free as those of the continent from these vile incumbrances. The warmth, which is afforded by them, might be more efficaciously and cheaply obtained by double doors or stoves. They are not only grievously injurious to architectural effect, and frequently conceal or deface the venerable monument and sepulchral tablet, but they also give rise to petty jealousies and

38

disputes, very discordant indeed with the feelings which ought to prevail in us, on entering the temple of that Being who "is no respecter of persons" I cordially agree with what is so well expressed, and will only add that the removal of the pews brought to view two fine slabs of Purbeck marble, which once bore brasses in effigie of the persons buried beneath, who they were has not been satisfactorily ascertained, and it remains for the local historian to elicit. The brasses I need scarcely add, are gone, probably removed by Francis Verden, one of Dowsing's "myrmidons".[9]

Talking of Dowsing and his crew, I am almost tempted to wish one of his clique would arise (*and I would forgive him if he were even an occasional Church-going Dissenter*) and exercise his iconoclastic tricks, in the removal of that vile wooden desk, which partially conceals from view one of those original polygonal pulpits raised upon a single stem, which are occasionally met with in the churches of East Anglia—and I say not only should he have forgiveness and I would exclaim with the historian Eliensis, "Sanctum sacrilegium, fidele furtum salutaris rapina" There is one other point with regard to the manner in which the service is performed at Southwold Church, which, methinks it would be well if the minister would give his attention to it, I mean the pompous, irreverent and sententious manner in which the Parish Clerk reads the responses, he, *poor, vain and foolish man*, thinks no doubt he performs in the most approved and orthodox manner, and it would be a matter for much fun and drollery, was not the subject of too grave a nature, And then as to his singing—for so I suppose he calls it, why it is true he has a strong voice, so has a bull, but it is so ill managed and ill timed that I consider it quite as much his misfortune as that of the congregation that he could be heard: *Just fancy Mr Editor a tall statured gawky looking fellow with a prodigious stiff white neckcloth round his throat—so stiff that if by any accident he dropped a leaf from his book—he could not, to save his soul alive, bend down within his elegant desk to pick it up.* However there is one thing I will say of him and his coadjutors, the men and boys in the gallery, what they wanted in skill they made up in loudness and variety, every one has frequently his own time and the result of all I heard was like of choosing parliament men, where every one endeavours to cry loudest.

"When screech-owls scream their note portends,
To frighted mortals, death of friends;
But when Corvino strains his throat,
E'en screech-owls sicken at the note."

Cutting Vestry meeting held on Thursday August 22 at which under the

---

9. Verden held property in Southwold on the north side of the High Street, opposite the 'King's Head'.

chairmanship of the incumbent a 2d rate was voted upon to pay for repairs carried out in 1848. After he had gone the chair was taken by F.W.Ellis Esq. when a rate of 4d was further agreed to. This would pay for work done on the south aisle in 1848. Similar contributions would be collected in 1851 and 1852 to discharge in full the debt due to the tradesmen. Birch wrote a letter of protest to the Vestry-Clerk and Ratepayers on the 24th, attacking the expense of the benches, while agreeing that the tradesmen should be paid. He has the support of the correspondent submitting the article when he asserts that the conditions under which the benches were to be introduced have not been fulfilled. The committee that was to supervise their erection has not functioned, they were not to be a charge upon the parishioners, being paid for by voluntary contributions. Yet the work having been "completed by two carpenters of the town, one a present churchwarden, the other a late churchwarden, who have been levying contributions from house to house, and one of them (as it is alleged and complained of) accompanying the application with threats of depriving persons of their sittings on the benches unless they contribute to the cost of erection."

Notice   Public meeting of the inhabitants to be held at the Town Hall to adopt measures for giving the Lord Mayor of London a warm and cordial reception when he visits Southwold on the 23rd. Peter Palmer, the mayor, calls this meeting for the 17th, the day after the notice was issued.

Notice   The Committee of Management for the Lord Mayor's visit invite the inhabitants to illuminate their houses on the evening of the visit. Issued September 18

Programme for the procession to welcome the Lord Mayor. (Amongst the Councillors "Myself (Jas.Maggs) and Mr Moses Storkey in the absence of Mr Councillor Twaddell and Wayth")

1850 Sep 23d Lord Mayor of London—T. Farncomb.—Visit to Southwold

Cutting Grand Masonic Demonstration – very long and detailed account of the Lord Mayor's visit.

Insertion   Printed address to the Lord Mayor and his reply. The principal reason for his coming was to meet fellow masons.

Cutting From the Freemasons' Quarterly Magazine of December 31. "The late Lord Mayor at Southwold"

Programme Town Hall, Southwold, Tuesday evening, September 24 1850. "Mr Moody's Vocal Entertainment entitled Notes for English Circulation" To Commence at Half-past Seven o'clock—Tickets 2s each.

Notice   By permission of the Mayor. Great Pedestrian feat of 125 miles to take place at Mrs Martin's, Red Lion Inn, Southwold.
J. Breck, (The Welch Pedestrian) has undertaken the extraordinary

task, never before attempted, of walking one mile and a quarter every hour, for 100 successive hours.
(Performed with ease)
R.Crisp, Printer and Bookseller, Market Place, Beccles
(late of this Town, Miller et, left Sepr 1850. Succeeded by Wm Boyden Jnr.)
1850 Oct 16th Died Mr. John Goff Son of vd October 29 1849—late of Wrentham. Miller. agd 20.
Oct 20th Sunday Morng The "Peterel" of Sunderland. Henry Baxter of this place—sail'd from this bay to California.
Oct 25th This morning, and until about 11 o'clock—Strong wind from the N.E.—about ½ p 11 the Wind abated when a large Shoal of Herrings were observed in the Bay—Boats & Nets were immediately in request—and I witness'd that in the course of 4 or 5 hours 100£'s worth of Herrings were landed—there would have been more—had the boats been larger as the Nets so soon as cast into the Sea, sank with the quantity of Fish. This was as an Old Woman observed a "lucky God send".
Oct 30th Betsy daughter of John Palmer, Mariner—in the service of Mr C Carter, in the act of lighting a fire and in order to hasten its progress—very imprudently applied some gunpowder to it from a flask containing at least half a pound—the powder ignited—from its explosition nearly every square of glass was shatter'd to pieces—and the unfortunate girl so injured that..
Visiting Card Edward Cottingham   Surgeon   Wangford
               (came Oct 11/50 Days of attendance at Southwold, Mondays,
               Wednesdays and Fridays from 4 to 6 in the afternoon)
1850. Oct 31st I sold Mrs Susan L'Estrange's Furniture et.
Cutting The retiring four councillors re-elected, receiving five votes each, "scarce half a dozen burgesses appeared to give the day of election a moment's consideration" (Nov 1st 1850)
"The Fifth of November 1850, will be long remembered by the inhabitants of Southwold. It is always usual here for the Mayor to give a quantity of furze off the Common towards making a bonfire on the beach . . . . . but some reckless parties, not contented with this privilege, about 7 o'clock p.m. set a part of the Common, called the Dock, on fire . . . . . soon . . . . between 7 and 8 acres were burnt"
1850 Nov 2d One of the Halesworth Wherries laden with Oats broke from her Mooring—went to Sea—2 of the Ladd's and one of the Rogers picked her up—not all damaged—towed her into the Harbor & rec'd 15£'s for their trouble—Great blame attached to the Wherryman.
Cutting Sermon preached by the Reverend H.W.R.Birch against "the aggressions of the Pope of Rome" A petition against these "has been lying at our Bank for signature." (1850 Nov 17) Annual General Meeting of the Subscribers to the Southwold Life Boat Society. (Nov 14) Masonic Dinner at the Red Lion (Nov 13th)
Cutting Southwold fire engine attends the fire at Walberswick of the cottage

of a widow named Baker. Before it could get there "the cottage, its furniture, and a fat hog in an adjoining stye, were totally consumed." (Nov 20/50)

Cutting "SOUTHWOLD CORPORATION On Saturday last, the 9th inst., Mr Peter Palmer was unanimously re-elected Mayor of this Borough and Messers Palmer and Arthey, Aldermen. Unlike municipal corportions in general, the utmost harmony prevailed, all uniting in the laudable endeavour of cutting down useless expenditure, and extricating the borough from its financial difficulties. Mr Read Crisp, the treasurer, having left the town, Thomas Wallace Esq., solicitor and bank agent was appointed to fill the office. In the evening the Mayor invited a large party to meet him at the Crown Hotel, when, after partaking of a substantial tea, and enjoying the "social glass" and "joyous song" crowned by a monster bowl of punch, and backed by the consciousness that "each man had done his duty" they parted with a full determination to continue their efforts for the benefit of their fellow townsmen." (Nov 1850)

Notice   Members of the Corporation for 1850–51.

1850 Novr. 22d At Islington Died Susannah (daughter of Mr T.H.Diver, Reydon) Wife of Mr. Geo: L. Bokenham.

Cutting Samuel Gayfer, merchant, on his way home from Halesworth to Walberswick, with two of his children, was thrown from his gig as he approached Wenhaston. His horse had taken fright at the light from a gipsy's tent pitched at the roadside. (Novr 23d)

Decr. 7th Post office Orders for Money granted to this Post Office. Post Mistress Emily Bye.

Dec 10th—Sarah Ann Banks of Walswk. of a daughter. 1851 Apr 14th Child died at Brundish. Interred at Walswk

Dec 11th To Reydon with Mr Gooding—Solor viewed the property of the late Mrs Hading late Pooley for Sale—Mrs Elizth Palmer Excutrix.

1851 January 1st Jas Jermyn Esq removed from the office of High Stewd see Notice

Notice To Mr Alderman Arthy from the Town Clerk summoning him to an Especial Meeting of the Council at the Town Hall on Wednesday January 1 to vote on:—

Councillor Woodley's motion that James Jermyn Esq be removed from the High Stewardship.

Alderman Fulcher's motion that Black Shore be made a free quay.

The election of two members of the Council to serve on the Harbour Commission

The payment of interest due to the churchwardens on January 1 1837 and the bills of Snell & Bicker.

Feb 6th Let to Mr. Geo: Mayes, Watchmaker, Miss Wales' House for 7 yrs at £9 a year; from Apr 6/51—

Jany. 17. Sale of the Effects of Mr Geo. Bullen, at Westleton.

Jany 20th Dnl King—Coal Mercht his Credit Stopt—
26th He goes to London—return'd Feb 9/51.
Feb 12. Puts his business into the hands of Abbott & Gayfer
Jany 25th Riot at Bulcamp House   7 of the Rioters sent to Beccles Gaol.
Cutting SOUTHWOLD CHURCH A descriptive view of the interior
    arrangements since the demolition of the pews and the Substitution
    of open benches. Satirical verses ending—   (Jany 25/51)
                    Increased accommodation
                    Was the plea for spoliation;
                    Deceptive has been the cost,
                    Full eighty sittings have been lost!
Cutting Statement of the Merchant Seamen's Fund, Southwold, January 17
    1851 signed by James Maggs, Receiver. February 12 1851
Cutting Maggs has succeeded Edward Syer as Receiver on the resignation of
    the latter. (Feb 8 1851)
Jany 30th Put to Sale—Fish H. the property of myself and Mr Peter
Palmer—Not Sold.
Cutting Original poetry written upon the sermon preached at Blythburgh to
    upwards of 1,800 people by the Reverend Thomas Spencer of St.
    James, Notting Hill. (Feb:9th 1851)
                    1851 Feby 15th John Parker, Police Constable,
                    appointed Inspector of Weights and Measures,
                    Nuisances et in the room of James Jermyn Esq. See
                    Jany 1/51.
                    1851 Feby 20th Mr Jonthan Gooding of this Town,
                    Solicitor, appointed by Fredk Barne, Esq. High
                    Sheriff—Under Sheriff—and the Revd Rd. Gooch
                    of Frostenden to be his chaplain.
Cutting Riot by seamen at Yarmouth, March 21 1851
1851 Feby 8th Died at Tunstall, Oscar Miles, eldest Son of Mr. W. Rudland
Surgeon   agd 20, vid June 20th 1854.
1851 Feb 14th Chas Naunton receives a letter from his Son Chas at
Brentwood—of his enlistment into the 3d Company of the foot Artillery No
261. On the 13th ult. Colonel E Hay Commandant. Warley Barracks. Essex.
Feby 18th Jas Bloom's apprenticeship with Mr. Joseph Arthey—expires.
Feb 28 I and Mr P. Palmer purchases Fish House, situate upon the Beach, of
Mr Jonathan Button—and conveyed this day.
Feby 22d Riot at Yarmouth.

                              Feby 18 1851
Cuttings Petitions presented in the Lords by the Earl of Stradbroke, relating
    to Papal interference, and to the poor condition of able bodied
    labourers and of destitute farmers. Lord Hardwicke presented
    petitions relating to agricultural distress.
Cutting Maggs to auction (1) Shipwreck on beach at Walberswick, near

Southwold harbour, of the "Jeanne D'Arc" of Boulogne, 135 tons. April 2 1851.

(2) Three freehold tenements and a pightle on North Green (occupied by Edward Gray, farmer ; Dan Garrod, carrier ; and Samuel Clarke) with the freehold tenement and cottage pightle at the back (occupied by William Bedingfield) in Reydon, tenement (formerly a barn) at the east of the cottage pightle (above) (occupied by James Tink) and arable land in Reydon (occupied by Edward Gray) At the Old Swan, April 10 1851.

Cutting Inquest held on the 12th upon Thomas Girling Balls, aged 57. On the 22d last, he was seen, very drunk, going towards a beer house in Wangford. On attempting to open the door he missed his hold and fell heavily on the road. William Newberry put Balls into his cart, picking up John Bugg, also very drunk, at his own request. Reaching the "Bear" at Reydon, they all went in, where Mrs Pretty, the wife of the landlord, refused to serve Balls. Shortly afterwards he was found by George Lanham, man servant to Captain Rayley, sitting in the middle of the road about a hundred yards further on. He was led home by James King and for the next few days resumed his occupation, though complaining of pains at the back of his head. Mr Sutherland was called on the 5th and Mr Williams on the 7th. The next day Balls died and a post-mortem by Williams revealed inflammation of the brain. His daughter, who had dressed the wound, and William Downing, who had seen him daily, denied the rumour that was circulating that he had been ill-treated. (Died Mar 8th—March 12 1851, Inquest)

1851 March 4th I valued for Jas Jillings preparatory to going into the County Court.

Mar 5th Repository Sale—at "Swan" Inn Wangford. Wm Newberry, landlord—

Cutting The Schooner "Jeanne d'Arc", Francois Wacgone, from Blyth, of and for Boulogne, went ashore on Corton Sands. The captain brings her off and beaches her on Walberswick beach single handed, the crew of five refusing to remain on board were landed at Southwold. (March 5th)

March 13th at Walberswick I sold her Hull, Stores et Jo Preston, Yarmo agent.

Cutting detached (1851 Apr 10th 1/8 Share of the "Three Friends" sold to Mr P.Palmer   Hy Smith   Master.)

Cutting "John Fish, a fisherman of Southwold, was taken by warrant to Woodbridge on the complaint of Mr George Nunn of Aldeburgh, and convicted in the sum of £20 or three months imprisonment, for acting as pilot on board a foreign schooner after Mr George Kersey, a Trinity pilot, had offered his services. It came out in evidence that Joshua Chard, a fisherman of Thorp, brought Mr Kersey and Fish on shore and then pretended to Kersey that he was about to take Fish to Thorp; but instead he took him on board the said schooner and afterwards came and gave evidence against Fish for the purpose of getting a few shillings as poundage." (1851 March 19th)

Apr John Fish goes to Ipswich Gaol for 3 Months for non payment of Fine

1851 Mar 20th At the "Crown" Hotel I put to Auction the Schooner 4 Friends Wm Magub—late Master—not Sold.

Same Day. Wombell's Managerie here—left follwg Day.

March 21 Sale at Fox Inn—Darsham—of the effects of Mr John Berry. Landlord

March 24th Easter Monday—Messrs P. Palmer & Joseph Arthey—Chwardens—Thos K. Prestwidge—Clock winder et—Geo: Mayes being about leavg the Town.

March 27th Sale of the Effects of the late Mr. Wm Everrard, dec, by order of Mr Thos Hall, Trimmingham, nr. North Walsham, Norfolk

> 1851 March 20th Seven P.M. The Crew of the Brig "Naiad" of Hartlepool, David Myers, landed here in their boat the said Brig having been runned down by the "Vesper" of N. Shields off Sizewell Bank—that the mate Jas: Greener was so injured from the Mast falling upon him that he died on the 25th inst at the house of Mr. Jas: Woodward—Sign of the "Pilot Boat".

> 1851 Apr 17th Sale of Effects of Wm Hurr—mariner—Under distress for Rent. Mrs J.F. Bokenham Landlady.

1851. March 29—Kingston of Ipswich to Betsy daugr. of Mr P. Palmer of this place.

1851 March 29. Rd.Rufus Boniwell, succeeds Mr Alfred Wentworth to Southwold Arms, Public House March 19 1850 This House shut up to [   ]—when Saml Baker took it—left it June 22/60 and James Jillings fro the "Bear Reydon" took it June 22/60

March 31. Census. Mr Danl. Fulcher, Mr P. Palmer and myself. Enumerators. 2102

April 4 Sale of the Effects of Mr. Chas Welton, Wangford.

April 9 Mrs Mary Bardwell's Sale—who leaves the Town.

Apr 10 Sale of Southwold and Reydon Estate—re Mrs Mary Hadingham & Joshua Pooley her former husband exor Mrs Elizth Palmer, *not Sold.*

Apr 19 Mr Job Jeves accidentally falls down his Celler—seriously hurt but recovered.

April 24 Sale of Furniture et et of Mr Philip Westrups—"Crown" Hotel—

Apr 26 Took Valuation of Personal Estate of the late Wm Winyard, Frostenden—dec. Eleanor his Wife & Rob Borret Barfoot Exors.

> 1851 Apr 21 Sale of the Effects of Mr John Moody Excise off who left on the 3d May. A Aiticheson

succeeds Moody. May 3 1851. See February 3 1853

1851 April 28 Sale of Furniture & Effects of Mr Geo Mayes, Watchmaker who leaves the Town this day Insolvent. He is one of the Council !!

May 1st Sale of Furniture & Effects of Mr Jas Pretty—Bear Inn, Reydon who this day leaves it—succeeded by Mr Jas Howse—whom I valued for on the 16th April last—vd March 17 1847. Howse left Mar 20 1854

May 1st Mess's Saml Gayfer & Wm Matthew Woodley—Brewers & Merchants dissolves Partnership.

May 8th Sale of Furniture and Effects of Mr Wm Sutton Junior, vd Oct 18/49

May 3d Coach "Old Blue" commenced running from here, twice a day to London, Yarmouth et.

Cutting Tenders for the let of the "Poors" or "Town" land of 24 acres in
Reydon for 8 years from October 11 1851 to be delivered to Mr
Robert Chilvers of Reydon, churchwarden, before May 16.

Hired by Mr [   ] at £30 a yr   vd Apr 24/48

Cutting Southwold Brewery Samuel Gayfer informs his friends and the
public that he has taken over the Southwold Brewery in conjunction
with his business at Walberswick and Yoxford. May 8 1851.

1851 May 21 Hired House of Mr Cracknell. myself to do repairs—to be allowed 1 yrs rent £9 and Shop window—Agreement from Oct 11th. 1851 for 7 years, June 30th came to the office

May 23 To Melton Asylum with Sarah Naunton, of this Parish, fro the Union House. Dischard March 24 1852.

May 22d Nancy Wyatt's Sale—Mrs W leaves SoWold

May 26 & followg days Committe for revising Poor Rate.

June 13th To Mrs Elizth Booty's, Sluice House, Leiston with Mr Saml Gayfer—and took Valuation of Effects of the late John Booty, who died Augt 29th 1850

June 14th Revd Wm French leaves SoWold to reside at Reydon, late the residence of Jas Jermyn Esq.

June 24th Sale at Wrentham "Eagle" of the Effects of Mary Ann Newson—Lunatic in Melton.

July 1st To Valuation of Thos B Smith's effects who goes into the County Court for a Sum of Money he was bound for, for Job Jeves.

1851 July 2d Sold at Westleton the Effects of Mr Henry Fisk, dec.

1851 July 12 The House that "*Jack Built*"

Cutting A NEW VERSION OF THE HOUSE THAT JACK BUILT
As described to the Bishop on a recent Inspection
These are the Benches that Peter built.
These are the People intended to sit and to kneel on the Benches that
Peter built.
This is a "Poppy-head" slashed and cut
With the Southwold Arms in a Garter put;
And names remarkable carved thereon,

To show how much their owners have done
　　　In adorning the Benches that Peter built.
This is the wonder of every elf,
The Bench that Peter has built for himself !
There's a Door—on the "Poppy-head" carved a name,
From age to age to blazon the fame
Of this very great man—and his Crest's there too—
Where he got it's no business of me or of you ;
'Tis enough 'tis there and shews how true
Is his talent for carving and benching too.
And then there's a Cushion of scarlet hue,
Stuffed and padded and wadded too,
　　　To make soft this Bench that Peter built.
This is the Man who endeavours to sell
(Listen you now what I have to tell,)
To the highest bidder, the Seats that of yore
Were free to all People inside the Church door !
He has done you the kindness, willy nilly, to take
Your nice Old Pew, without sanction, to make
In its place a cramp't Bench ; and then meekly to say
For the priv'lege of sitting you now have to pay,
　　　On these splendid Benches that Peter built.
This is the Man, with the Coat and Gold Lace,
Who stood at the Bench with an impudent face
And his hands stretch'd across from place to place,
To keep the Woman from passing that way
To a seat she had sat on for many a day ;
But she was a Woman who would'nt pay
　　　To sit on the Benches that Peter built.
This is the P'lice-man, drest in state
To stand in his calling at the Church Gate
And face to face with the "Coat and Gold Lace,
Watch all who come to the Church early or late :
And again should this unruly Woman appear
T'wards the seat she's been used to, once more draw near,
They have orders to seize her and bear her away,
Since she's stoutly declared that she never will pay
　　　To sit on the Benches that Peter built.
These are the Doves, carved on Peter's own seat,
They're the emblem of all that's most gentle and sweet ;
And Peter has given with masterly skill
The fluttering wing, and the bill placed to bill ;
'Tis the token of love 'twixt the one and the other,
As the hand of a man placed in that of a brother ;
But empty's the token, and vain is the skill,

47

That give but the promise of love and good-will,
Far better the substance ! and more by the token
Some promises, like pie-crust, are made to be broken.
But here ends the Inspection ; enough has been spoken
Of the open Free Benches that Peter built.
(Alluding to Peter Palmer. Mayor)[10]

1851 July 21 Francis Hallows, Coast Guard Officer, fell down in the "Old Swan" Bar in a fit of Apoplexy and immediately expired dec. had not been in 5 minutes—had just sipped from a pint of porter, and was in the Act of lighting his pipe. His Wife died in London Sep 3/54
July 28 A total eclipse of the Sun, was expected—but to the great disappointment but very little was perceived, and that for not more than 5 Minutes   vd 1851
Aug 4th The Yawl "Friendship" built at Yarmouth for the North Cliff, came here.

> Mr & Mrs Woodley and family leaves to reside 8
> Prospect place Woolwich on the 13th August 1851

Augt 14th The Schooner "Richard Hill" of Exeter—Clapp, Master came into this Bay, in consequence of havg a Man on board named Wm Giles, who was stabbed with a knife by Samuel alias Richard Street. Giles was landed here taken to the "Red Lion" who being attended by Mr Sutherland—quite recovered from the wound—*Street* was then brought on Shore and lodged in the Station House—16th examined and committed to Ipswich to take his trial at the next assizes. Mar 22d–3d Assizes at Bury—Street sentenced to *One days* imprisonment.

Cutting Bankruptcy petition of Thomas Bayley Smith of High Street, Southwold, Superannuated Police Officer and Coal Meter to be heard at Halesworth, July 23 1851.

Cutting Farewell dinner at the "Old Swan" to W.M.Woodley Esq., who is leaving Southwold, where he has lived for the past seven years. (Aug 11 1851.)

> Anno Quarto & Quinto Gulielmi IV Regis 1834 August 13th An Act to amend an Act of the 20th year of Geo II for the relief and Support of Sick, maimed and disabled Seamen, and the Widows & children of such as shall be killed, slain or drownd in the Merchant service et et. *was pass'd* and continued 'till August 8 1851 when the Fund was wound up.
> see Rules for Constitutions

Insertion Explanatory Statement with reference to the Winding-Up of the

---

10. The actual benches bear the insignia of St Edmund and of Southwold on the one reserved for the Corporation but nothing to indicate the self assertion of Peter Palmer.

Merchant Seamen's Fund. Board of Trade. November 1851.
(Please return it   J.Maggs   Receiver   .)

Augt 16 Wm Wright charged of picking the pocket of John Stammers of 10/– committed to Beccles Gaol to await his trial Oct 13 Sessions Stammers refused to swear to a sixpence with a "doke" in it, as he had done before the Magistrates, the Court discharged the prisoner.[11]

Augt 21 I went to Haleso to County Court with John Parker.P.C.

Aug 28 Regatta.

Mr Charles Lillingston agd 47 Chauntry, Ipswich died here, and Interred in this Churchyard.

Sep 1 (vd Apr 28 1841) John Parker p.c. leaves here to reside at Nacton, Union House, Governor Thursday 4th Chas Spurgeon, lt of Lowestoft, elected p.c 9 for 3 agt. Samuel Strange, superintended 'till the 24th inst when Charles Spurgeon took the office.

1851 Sep 4th At Southwold Church by the Revd W.H.Andrews, Rector of Carlton, Rowland Jermyn, Lieut in East India Service company's Naval Service, to Louisa Emily, youngest daugr of Jas Jermyn Esq lt of Reydon Cottage. Mrs Jermyn, died at Pemlico Oct 29/58

Sep 8th Sold the Hull and Materials of the "Sarah" of White Haven— Wrecked on the Scroby sand on the 3d inst—picked up off here by the North Cliff men and towed on Shore near Gun Hill a *derelict* Sold to Mr Wm Martin, Red Lion Inn for £22.

17th followg sold this wreck in lots

Sep 9th Dnl Stammers hires the Town Mill—for the expiration of the lease.

Sep 11th Sale of John Parker's effects at the Old Swan.

Sep 12th Came to Mrs Chaston's House (Thos Cracknell of Haleso Trustee) 7 yrs fro Oct 11/51

Sep 15th Sale of Mr Bullock's Furniture et at Wrentham.

Sep 17th Let Poor's Land at Uggeshall under the direction of Revd W.C. Edgell to Jas Aldred for 8 yrs at L8 17s 6d pr yr fro Oct 11/51
1851

Sep 18th To Haleso to Mr Pedgriff's Sale with Mr Ed Goldsmith—Mr G. died Nov 2/51 48 yrs.

Sep 22 Rowland Twaddell of the "Isabella" of SoWold, convicted before John Sutherland and Peter Palmer, the Boro' Magistrates in a penalty of £1 for sending on Shore about 7 pints of Whiskey. The boat is the property of Edwd Palmer—which was seized.

Sep 24 Chas Spurgeon sworn into the offc of P.C. for this Boro'

Sep 25 John Norman Esq after many years residence leaves to reside at [   ] *ob Mrs N died in* [   ] Asylum on the [   ] inst

Sep 25 Jas J Colley leaves to reside Stoke Ipswich

Sep 27 Sale of Furniture et of Mr Simon Kemp, Westleton.

Oct 2 Sold Hull & Stores of the Barge "New Prosperous" of this Port at

---

11. A 'doke' or dock would be an incision on the coin.

Blackshore—the Property of Mr Jo Snell of Wangford to Mr Henry Truman, White Hart Inn, Blythbro for £31 who took her to Blythbro and broke her up *ob* This is the largest Tonnaged Vessel 61 ever remembered to have gone further than"New Quay—Nov 7th I *sold her again* at Blythbro' after havg been broken up.

1851 Oct 4th *Gennitts* company of Horsemanship performed here & June 26/56

Oct 8th Sale of Mr Geo Keable's effects Brampton "Dog" Inn—who went to reside at the "Sun" Halesworth.

Oct 9th Sale of Furniture et of Mr Michell's Wangford.

Oct 10th Sale of Furniture et of Mr T.O.Diver, Wangford.

Oct 13 Concert at Town Hall. Mr Hay manager.

Oct 16 Intelligence of the Death of Mr Benj Eaves—Aug [ ] 1851 at Calcutta.

Oct 22d Daughter Eliza to Raveningham took a School under Sir Edmd Bacon.

Oct 28th John Dandy Strowger, takes Public House at Blackshore.

Notice   List of Members of the Corporation 1851–52

Handbill Announcing that John J. Goff, miller and merchant, has taken over the Southwold business of Read Crisp   November 11 1851

Trade card J.J.Goff Miller and Merchant Southwold   (Novr 11th 1851)

1851 Nov 11th Mr John J Goff takes the Black Mill of Wm Boyden—left to go to the Mills at Wrentham. Oct 11/56 vd Oct 9 1856 June 9 1853.

Nov 13 I sold the Schooner "Mary Ann" by Auction at Blkshore to Mr Geo Butcher

Nov 15 To Melton Asylum with Henrietta Long—a Lunatic. Died May 1st 1852

Nov 16 Heavy fall of Snow—as have been remember'd for the last 11 years. The Streets & Lanes obliged to be clear'd out . see Mar 24/40.

Nov 17 Wife of Wm Sutton Jnr to Union Ho.

   . . 18 Sutton apprehended at Ipswich by Chas Spurgeon P.C. for refusing to support his Wife.

   19 Conveyed to this P.Office.

   20 Committed to Beccles Gaol. 1 Month.

Nov 20 I had a Repository Sale at the "Crown".

Nov 22 High Tide—Two Boats washd off the Beach—One picked up at Dunwich & One off Lowestoft.

1851 Monday 25th Novr—The Bark "Latena"—Clark Master of Hull—from Quebec was seen on the "Barnard" when this Life Boat went off to her assistance and found the Crew had abanded her—She was got off by our Men, and towed into Lowestoft Harbor by 2 of their Steam Tugs which had about £60 and after paying all charges our Boatmen receivd 600£—shared from £6.10s to L5 10s & 5£ each. This is what is termed a *"Gallooner"*[12]

12. A galooner/gallooner was a vessel requiring assistance, the salvage being divided equally between the crew and the 'floaters', the boat also receiving a share for its upkeep.

Nov 26 Mr Isaac Buxton, Butler to Miss Sheriffe—goes to reside as Landlord—Yoxford, Griffin Inn succeed Mr. [   ]

Trade Card Isaac Buxton, Griffin Inn, Yoxford   November 26th 1851

Nov 28 Jermyn's appeal agt the Poor Rate—on behalf of his daughter Emily Expences—Clerk, Subpoena's et £3 9s 4d

Stephen Clissold   )   County
)
B Bence   )   Magistrates

Subpoena To James Maggs and John Doe to appear before Southwold Magistrates November 5 1851 to produce Poor Rate Books re the appeal of Emily Jermyn

1851 Nov 28th—Valuation of Mr John Law's Furniture et to The Revd Holmes. with Mr Lenny

Dec 2d. Wm Waters apprehended and conveyed to Harwich, where he was charged in Robbing and obtaining Money et from the "Mary Ann" of this place—which vessel he was instrusted with as Master—in the room of Mr Joseph Read thro' ill health—3d Committed to Chelmsford Gaol for Trial—*Acquitted* Jany 6/52.

Decr. 3d. Sale of Mr. Saml. Hotson's Effects. who leaves to reside in London.

Dec 10 The "John", John Burton, Masr. of Newcastle 261 Tons struck Thorp Rocks, Coal laden, and became a total Wreck Sold for £35.

18 I went to Aldbro'—and sold her Stores et on the 19th—and returned home on the 20th. F.W.Ellis—Agent.

> 1851 Dec: 10th Married Mr. Read Crisp to Mary Ann. second daugr. of the late Mr. Peter Palmer Master Mariner

1851 Dec. 18th at Benacre Hall. Sir Thomas Gooch, Bart, Agd 85.

This Month Gig "Teazer" the 2d launched, built by Mr. Jas Critten.

Large catch of Cod Fish during this last 2 Months—No Herrings nor Sprats worth mentioning this Season.

Cutting The "William Cook" of Yarmouth, on passage from Hartlepool to Ramsgate driven on shore at Southwold under a heavy wind from the S.S.W. The life-gun apparatus was fired and the life-boat launched. The former saved the mate, William Jarrett and Richard Lucas and Thomas Holborn with the boy, Robert Newing Miller. The latter picked up the master, Corbett Cook. Another boy, Richard Newing Miller, brother of the one who was saved, jumped from the bowsprit with the cork fender but this was washed from him by the heavy sea and he was drowned. January 11 1852.

Cutting Maggs to auction the hull, lower masts and standing rigging of the English oak-built schooner "William Cook" (93 tons) on the beach at Southwold on January 20.

1852 January 8th Wm Sheppard Edwards, apprenticed to Fredk. Mayhew, Cabinet Maker—for 5 years, from 6th inst. Indenture Cancelled Dec 6/52.

Cutting The schooner "Spring" of Hull, R.Chapman, master, sailing from Middlesbro to Southwold with a cargo of coals, consigned to Messers Stratbarn and Paul of Halesworth, arrived off here on the 29th last. Unable to enter the harbour for want of water, she took refuge in Lowestoft roads because of the unsettled weather. On the 7th she tried once more to enter Southwold harbour, there being a fresh wind from the W.S.W. The Southwold harbour pilot boarded her and took charge, but proceeding to the harbour near high water she stopped at the bar. A tow line was run out to the capstan on the south and a stout ward to the north pier. But every effort to get her over the bar failed. When the tide fell, about noon, the wind veered to the S.S.W. and increased to a gale. On the flow of the tide the sea broke over the vessel, breaking the tow line and the warp and washing away the bulwarks. At midnight the life-gun was fired from the shore and the crew were hauled to safety. (Jan 6 1852)

16th & 17th I sold the Coals salved from her.—

20 Sold the Hull and her Materials purchased by Wm Magub and others for £82.

Feb 5th & 6th. Sold her again after being broken up. Company saved about £5.

January 22d—I put the Schooner "Happy Return" of Yarmouth—Wm Sharman, Masr. to sale at Blackshore—*not sell.*

Jany 23d—Wreck et Sale at Thorp—

Jany 23d Thomas Son of Thos. Wright, Shoemaker, enlists for a Soldier. Comes home July 1855. leaves July 21 1855 to the Seat of War.

Cutting A sheep stealer in Norfolk apprehended partly through the exertions of Superintendent Spurgeon of Southwold. (Feby 1st)

March 5 City Sessions Norwich Geo Copeman (he had been residing here by the name of Cook) was transported for 7 years for stealing 21 Sheep the property of Mr Palmer of West Wretham, his accomplice Precious was discharged, no evidence was offered against him.

1852 Feby 2d Prepared Bill of Sale, fro Mr. Jonathan Button to Robert Warne.

Feby 3d. Sale of John Crowford's effects, under distress for rent, by Mr D Fulcher—exor to the late Susan L'Estrange, dec.

Feb 4. Sale at Wenhaston of the effects of Mary Reynolds, widow—Valued Jas. Cullam's effects to Mr Henry White.

Feby 6. Henry Mildred Burch, appointed chaplain to Her Majesty.

This month he was presented with the sum of £5000 by Her Majesty from an Estate in [   ]

Feb 1st He first preached in Reydon Church and on the 8th in this [   ]

1854 Jany 22 He preach'd funeral Sermon here & Reydon for his Father who died 10th Jany 1854. Interred at Reydon.

Feb. 8th Robert Major, accidentally, broke his leg on board the "Charles" Pallant Simpson Masr. 28th Messrs Williams & others, Surgeons, amputated the leg. and he died the followg day.

Feb 10th Geo Gilbert Brittain of Lowestoft charged with having unlawfully assaulted and beaten Emma Haken of and at Southwold—Mar 3d Beccles Quarter Sessions—The grand Jury ignored the bill.

Feb 16th Sale of Wreck et Sizewell Gap

Feb 18th Fall of Snow at intervals for 6 days—many persons employed in clearg the Streets See February 8 1853

Feb 19. Robert Smith, Grocer, Boot & Shoe Maker, had his first hearing in the County Court.

March 1st I sold his Stock in Trade et

Feby 26 I sold the Schooner "Spring" for £200 to Mr. John Pratt of Wivenhoe—recd a deposit £50 which I paid to Mr F.W.Ellis, Lloyd's Agent. Mar 11th Mr Pratt sent a cheque for the £150 which I paid to Mr Ellis—less my expences of Sale—£6.9s.11d.same day Mr Saml. Wayth takes her to Wivenhoe see Jany 6/52

June 6th Mr Jellicoe gives up Bill of Sale to Mr Pratt

Feb 26 Edward Spence to Beccles Gaol for 3 Month for an assault.

1852 March 2d Wm Wells, Mariner, Committed to Beccles Gaol for 1 Month—leavg his Wife & family chargeable.

March 4 To Saxmundham with Mr Peter Palmer—In re Jonathan Button Saw Mr Cavell & Barnes—pd Cavell for the Society £3 as per receipt and to pay the principal off—as follows   v Sep 22/49

March 12th Sold Furniture, Stock in Trade et of Wm Bloomfield of *Stoven*

March 13th Samuel Mayhew, Fisherman, drowned at the Harbor, by his boat upsetting—17th the Body was found in the North Pier—& interred

March 16th I sold the Furniture et of Mr Wm Stockdale, Barnaby Green, Wangford—who is going to reside with Mr Taylor of Huntingfield.

1852 March 18 To Halesworth with Mr F.W.Denny—to the County Court—case Denny v Eelles—Debt & Cost about £30—Mrs E—to pay £1 a Month.

March 20th William Folkard of this Parish, Enlists for a Soldier.

March 20 John, son of Daniel King, committed to Yarmouth Gaol—for trial—falsely obtaining 18½ Tons of Coals from Mr Jo. Allen of Gt Yarmouth.

Cutting John King agreed to take 20 tons of coals from Allen for which he would give a cheque upon Gurney's Bank. At this point in the trial the Recorder stopped the case as being one for civil adjudication. If people were so careless as to part with their property without sufficient security for payment, they must not claim the protection of the law. King said it had always been his intention to pay and he would do so as soon as he could. (June 24 1852)

March22d,23d Bury Assizes. John Alfred Scott, Turner, late of Wrentham (See Dec 18/43) for burgariously breakg into the dwellg house of Jas Fish of Blythborough, and stealing therefrom six loaves of bread and other articles. Transported for 15 yrs.

March 24th Daughter Sarah comes home fro. J.S.Eldridge's Esq. South-ampton—returnd April 14 followg—when first went see July 24/50

April 1st Sale of Mr C.S. Marsh's Effects. (Mr M. was brewer for Gayfer & Woodley) and left Southwold on the 4th inst   succeeded by Mr Sevesque

Mar 31 Mr. Rt Jo Gooding   Vestry Clerk

1852. Apr. 8 Sold Furniture et of Thos Wallace, Esq.

1852 Apr 7. Wm Beamish's Sale, of Cove. Mr B. is emigrated.

Apr 8th Sale of Wm Wells' Furniture under distress for rent.

Apr 12 Pleasance Amy Ann to Union Ho.

. . 24 I took her to Melton Asylum.

Apr 16 Fitz Roy Kelly here and addressed the Voters et.

Apr 14. Dinner at Wrentham "Eagle" to Mr Hingeston

Cutting VERTUE—SUTHERLAND On Tuesday last at Finchley, Middle-sex, Francis Vertue Esq, surgeon, Southwold to Henrietta Maria youngest daughter of John Sutherland, Esq, of the latter place surgeon. (Apr 20/52)

Mr Vertue commd practice here in the room of Mr Jo Sutherland, surgeon

Mar 20. Mr V b'day born 1822 Vertue takes 8th division Parish Doctor

Sept 15/56. May 10th 1853 Mrs Vertue of a SON.

23 Fire—3 Cottages Burnt down in the occupation of Wm English and others—at Little Dingle—Dunwich

28 Wife & daugr. Ellen to Stocton—returned 13th May.

28th Sale of Jas Baker's Effects Frostenden

May 6 Sold Jas Upcraft's Effects—under distress for rent.

May 8. To Norwich with Mr. Peter Palmer—

May 13th Sold Mr Matthew Lambert's dec. Effects at Wenhaston—Chas White and the Revd Noott exors.

1852 May 14 Sold Mr Jas Smith's effects—Reydon

May 18th Lieut. Fredk Wetherell Smith, leaves this Town, for Chatham, in ill health. Died June 11/52   June 3d I sold his Furniture et et

May 20th 1852 Mr Jonthn Rt Gooding succeeds Mr. T. Wallace to this Bank

May 20 The "Eniglian" Cutter of Colchester, taken by the Coast Guard—with from 5 to 6 cwt of Tobacco.   Crew Levett and Crisp—committed to Beccles Gaol on the 25th inst. discharg'd Novr followg

(Wednesday Nov 17/52)

May 27 Christopher Andrews committed to Beccles Gaol, for stealing various carpenters Tools the property of Jonathan Robson—June 28—sentenced to 14 days hard labor, and then to be soundly flogged and discharged—

June 2d Mr Saml Gayfer removed fro Walberswick, to Reydon Cottage. Howes to Ips Gaol discharg'd May 16/53.

June 2 Mr. Frdk Burch of Shotley here.

June 3 Sold Crops of Grass upon the Greens & Walls.

June 3 Postponed sale of Brig "Victoria"—

June 7 At Frostenden.I sold Furniture et of Emily King.

1852 June 10 Frs Wilson Ellis, elected Treasurer in the room of Thos Wallace to find Sureties in the Sum of £500.

June 10th Sold Furniture & Effects of John Tink, of Wenhaston.

June 17 Ejected Wm Andrews from a House the property of Mrs Mary Burch. Chas Spurgeon, Constable.

June 29th Mr Job Jeves, leaves SoWold.

July 9th part of his Goods et were sold, at Halesworth under a distress for rent (which he had fraudulently removed) and the residue left upon the premises. I sold here on the 12th inst. Jeves at Sale & leaves.

July 1st I sold Mr John Palmer's effects at Reydon—Mr P. going to America.

June 28 "Pilot" Coach Ed Goldsmith commenced running fro Southwold, to Lowestoft, discontind 16 Oct 1852.

July 8th Mr John Dillers Bookseller hires the House (lt Jeves) of Miss Wales—fro 14th July at 1£ for month. left to go to Beccles. Nov 15/52.

Insertion Summons for Maggs to appear as a witness in the case between George Butcher, plaintiff, and Samuel Waythe, defendant , at the Angel Inn, Halesworth, on June 17 1852. Dated June 1 (Plaintiff brot the action agt Defend for £20 for the purchase of a Schooner "Mary Ann" on the 26 Feby last—by private contract—the Judge decided against Plaintiff there being no stamped agreement cost Plaintiff £9 19—)

1852 Feby 26th I sold at Blackshore, Southwold by Auction—the Schooner "Spring" of Hull—afterwards I left the Auction Room for some 10 or 15 minutes upon my return, I suggested to Mr George Butcher that I thought there was a very good chance in putting the "Mary Ann" (the vessel in question) to the hammer to which he replied *"I have sold her"*

1852 July 13th Sale Boats & Nets of the late Samuel Mayhew—vd March 13th ult.

July 22 Jonathn Gooding Esq. to Scotland returned, Aug 7th. followg.

July 26 The Body of a Man, supposed to be a Dutchman—picked up off here and brot on Shore for Interment—No doubt he had been drowned a long time being much decomposed—

Augt 6th A Terrific Thunder Storm

Cutting Storm at Southwold, with heavy fall of rain and hail, such as had not been experienced since August 5 1847, when Southwold, Reydon and Easton Bavents suffered greatly from the destruction of growing crops, windows to the value of £400–500. Lightning set fire to John Grimsey's house at Easton Bavents, the property of E.S. Gooch, lying about a mile north of Southwold.

Augt 7. Daughter Eliza came home from Raveningham and Lucy Doe— returned 25th inst

Sep 29 Eliza came home returned Oct 6/52.

1852 Augt 17. I took Nathaniel Pack to Melton Asylum, see September 27 1836

1852 Aug 17 Mr T. Wallace, here last—left 24th inst.

Aug 25 To Mr Miller's Westhall with Mr. Jonthn Rt. Gooding—valu'd a

House et for a Mortgage to the "Odd Fellows".
Aug 26 Shrimpton Mrs & daugr. Emily to London—returned
Aug 26 Rogerson—Misses here—
Aug 27 Siggar's Rd. Distrain'd his Effects for rent £6. 10. for Geo Clavering
Redman 34 Cornhill London Mr R. here on 18th inst. Sold Sep 2 1852
Aug 24 Tobias Gillings of Theberton, Shoemaker—drowns himself at
Dunwich—in the Sea.
Aug 28 Died at Wangford—agd 40 Mr Charles Wales, Grocer et.
1852 Sep 7th—New Life Boat "Harriett" came—Sent to the Life Boat
Society Feby 15/57.
Sep 10th To Mr. Thos. Doddington's of Cove—took A/ct of his Furniture et
for Auction on the 28th inst.
Sep 12th James Dennis—14 sent on shore from the "Resolution" of Seine.
[   ] Masr. with a fractured Arm, from a fall on board his Vessel—
taken to Mrs Martin's Red Lion—17th the Arm Amputated by Messrs
Williams, Bales, Vertue et.
Sep. 15. Sale of Effects of Mr Dnl. Brunning—Wenhaston
Sep 23d To Halesworth to Revising Barrister—
Sep 24.Sold Furniture et of Eliza Court. by order of Mr Wm Winyard
Oct 1st At Wrentham Sale of Mrs Wilson's Effects—and Let Wrentham
"Town Meadow " or Land for 8 yrs to Mr Johnson for Mr [   ] at £4 10s
pr annum, from the 11th inst   vd Apr 18/45.
1852 Oct 2d Sale of Effects of Mr. Mitchell, Wangford.
Oct 11th Jo Chinery's Sale.
Oct 12. Mr John Byerley—Directory Agent at Southwold—his address is
Sun Inn—Foregate, Clements Inn
Oct 6 Sale of Effects of Mr Thos. Turner, Holton.
Oct 8 Sale of Effect of Mr. Hy. Doddington—Henstead.
Oct 13—Valuing at "Cherry Tree"Stoven—for Mr Chas Harvey—outgoing
tenant—Mr Barnes of Saxmundham for Mr Youngs the incoming tenant.
Oct 14 Sold Furze upon the Common to Edwd Brown—for 1 yr £9 10s put
Town Mill to letting—not hired.
Oct 16 Mr Chas Harvey, Stoven Cherry, took a/ct for Sale. Sold on the 22d.
Poster Naming of Southwold Life Boat and Laying the Corner Stone of the
        New Building. , Procession of Masons etc.   October 8 1852
Cutting Report of the naming of the "Harriet", the new lifeboat, after Lady
        Gooch and Miss Sheriffe. Sir E.S. Gooch M.P. lays first stone of
        lifeboat house. Banquet at the Crown after service at the church.
Cutting Assignment of the goods of Henry Youngs, draper and grocer of
        Somerleyton for the benefit of his creditors. October 14 1852
Insertion Printed sermon "The tempest tossed Paul" preached by the
        Reverend Walter Melville Wright, Chaplain to the Royal Artillery,
        in Southwold church, October 8, when the lifeboat was named.
Insertion Ancient Free & Accepted Masons—Provincial Grand Lodge (for
        Suffolk) Ipswich Assembly Room Thursday October 14 1852. (Mr

56

Jonthn Gooding's Address upon being presented with a Silver Inkstand)

Insertion Visiting Card—Mr Richard E Garnham (came 21

(Oct 52

(returned 25

1852 Oct 21 To Lowestoft for Mr Rd.E.Garnham. 25th to Lowestoft with Mr G.

Oct 25th A man was washed on shore age between 50 & 60 about 5ft 6in high. a pair cased silver watch with brassguard—Maker's name James Ryland—Ormskirk No 823   Nov 4 in answer to a description given of him in the papers he proves to have been Henry Rhode—Master of a "Billy-boy" the "Enterprise" of Thorne—Yorkshire—dec was accidentally knocked overboard between Southwold and Lowestoft a few days previous.

Oct 30 Chas Pulford—Brooke, Norfolk over in re house late in the occupation of Mr Jo Chinery—appointed me his agent.

Nov 10th *Alexander Craig* Master of the "Hawk" (Geo Leslie—Owner) of Aberdeen brought on Shore to the "Red Lion" Mrs Martin's Jas Forbes 19 havg fallen from the topsail yard, and broken one Arm Leg and fractured his head, attended by F.H.Vertue Surgeon   Forbes sent home on the 19th Dec 1852 cured.

Lowestoft News

1852 Novr. 7th On Sunday, the brig "Victoria" James Hills of South Shields, from Tanganrag for Falmouth, with linseed, was brought into Lowestoft by Southwold men, by the Yawl "John Bull"—She set sail on her homeward Voyage on the 28th July last. While crossing the Bay of Biscay she experienced on the 27th ult a heavy gale & tremendous sea, during which she was thrown on her beam ends, which displaced her cargo, and listed her to starboard several streaks, in this unenviable state Falmouth was made on the 31st ult—when orders were received for Hull—Having started for that port she reached the Downs on Saturday last, and proceeded with a strong wind between the Galloper and Knock Lights. During the evening there were so many lights exhibited by various vessels, as obliged by the late act, that the Knock light from the confusion was not distinguishable, the consequence of which was that the vessel struck on the sand. She afterwards beat over and was brot up with two Anchors and chains the sea making a clean sweep of all the moveables on deck. At daylight they were compelled to slip from their Anchors which with the Chains they lost. On arriving off Southwold they obtained assistance, the crew being completely exhausted from pumping and working the ship—these men advised taking Lowestoft Harbor, where she was safely moved and extra hands employed at the pump—the cargo was discharged and forwarded to Hull—Southwold men paid £400—after deducting expences received £9 each, on the 12th Nov 1852

Notice   List of Members of the Corporation 1852–3

Cutting SOUTHWOLD It was announced in the last impression of the Journal that Alfred Lillingston Esq and John Leman Ewen Esq, two gentlemen of high character and bearing had been elected Town Councillors of this borough, a step which reflected much credit upon the judgement and discretion of the burgesses and which has been followed by another on the part of the council equally praiseworthy in the election of Mr Lillingston to the office of mayor and chief magistrate and of Robert Wake Esq M.D. to that of high-steward. There is occasionally a bright spot exhibited even in the dark history of municipal corporations; a tide in their affairs which like that of men if taken at the flood leads on to good report if not to fortune and these are of them. It is therefore a subject of congratulation to the town that a few gentlemen of intelligence, wealth and station and tradesmen of character and honesty of purpose are to be found willing under existing circumstances to take office upon themselves with the sole view of endeavouring to put an end to the disgraceful system of jobbing which has been so long carried on by certain members of the council and who became such members not for the purpose of conducting the affairs of the town for the benefit of the inhabitants but solely to advance their own interests by doing the work and being employed upon the estates of the corporation and other public works in the borough and this too not only in defiance of a resolution passed by the council at the period the ex-mayor first took upon himself the dignity of that office—with what grace it befits us not now to enquire—and by which resolution members of the council were to be restrained from being directly or indirectly concerned in any contract work, or even supplying goods for the use of the body corporate; as in like contravention of an express clause in the Municipal Act which not only prohibits such malpractices, but actually disqualifies the offender from office and renders him liable to forfeit £50 with full costs of suit to any person who will sue for the same. It is almost surprising that tradesmen can be found so utterly regardless of the consequences to which they are subject as to be avowedly guilty of such acts but their effrontery is only to be equalled by their recklessness. It would seem indeed to be something of a law of nature that if individuals in their private capacities be the first, yet, the same parties, when connected with public bodies are always the last to be aware of their own danger, and these worthies may be assured the danger is nearer their doors than they may be willing to know, for the time is at hand when they will be called upon to answer at the bar of public opinion, if not indeed, of public justice.

"We must not make a scarecrow of the law,
  Setting it up to fear the birds of prey
  And let it keep one shape till custom make it
  Their perch and not their terror."
(Ex Mayor Mr Peter Palmer)

Nov 9th Robt Wake M.D. appoint'd to the Office of *High Steward* in the room of James Jermyn Esq who died July 29 1852 and on Dec 24th Jas Maggs was appointed Bailiff for the Court Leet by Robt Wake 1st Court held Jany 14th 1853.

Cutting Inquest at Benacre on Samuel Moss, gardener, aged 79, found drowned by George Thrower, gamekeeper to J.H.L. Anstruther Esq, in a dyke near Latimere dam and half a mile from Spanton lane. He had parted from his brother at the foot of a hill near the lane at three o'clock in the afternoon of Saturday, October 23, as he proceeded down the lane to his place of work for Mr Knight. He was missing for a fortnight. (Nov 15 1852)

Cutting "SMUGGLING On Wednesday James Howes of the Bear Inn, Reydon, near Southwold was convicted on the evidence of William Crisp before Chas. Steward Esq, and the Rev. Jas Farr Reeve of being connected in a case of smuggling. John Latch Esq collector and Mr Jno Robertson appeared on behalf of Her Majesty's Customs and W.R. Seago Esq defended the prisoner—George Deal of the Coastguard deposed to boarding and seizing the smack "Eniglian" of Rowhedge off Southwold on the 20th of last May. Wm Crisp and Walter Levette were made prisoners and sentenced to a fine of £100 or imprisonment. Information having been given implicating Howes, Crisp after his release from prison was summoned as a witness for the prosecution His evidence went to show that James Howes, William Edmunds, William England and—Bullen had agreed to give him £25 for the run and that Howes also accompanied him to the continent had given him £10 to purchase the tobacco and cigars he had on board when he was taken prisoner. Other corresponding facts were also elicited which resulted in the Bench inflicting the usual fine of £100 or imprisonment until paid. It being stated to the Bench that Crisp was not the informer, he was called in, when Capt. Steward told him that the impression had been removed from their minds." (Nov 17 1852)

1852 Nov 18th Rt Carter versus Dn Fulcher lt chwdn in County Court at Halesworth for Bricklayer's Work done to Southwold Church—to the Amt of about £13. Judge's order for Mr F to pay *Bill* and *Costs* amounting to £22 & upwards.

Nov 19 Died at Beccles Jas Francois.24.

Nov 23 I witness with Dr Wake Mr Sutherland's signing his Will.

Witness'd Mrs S's will Feb 8/59 wt J.R.Gooding

Nov 24th Jas Lee to Phoebe Church.

Nov 27 Geo Critten & Wm Easey—accident from the fall of a Mast from the "Mary Ann" Blackshore.

Cuttings "THE CORPORATION OF SOUTHWOLD To the Editor of the Ipswich Journal   Sir—The paragraph which appeared in your paper this day denouncing the system of jobbing as practised by some of the members of the Town Council has produced its effect and will tend no doubt to make the Council cautious and the Burgesses watchful over the income of the Corporation and that it is expended legitimately, for the benefit of the inhabitants generally. It would be curious to have the bills analyzed in order to see what amount of money in the last four or five years has found its way into the pockets of two or three members of the Council for work done by them in repairing the buildings, making of gates and bridges, erecting of breakwaters, and in providing materials But all of this must necessarily follow under the new order of things.

There is however one point in the paragraph I will say a word upon—the re-appointment of a gentlemen to the office of High Steward—an office which the Council got rid of, in consequence of the great expence occasioned, far, indeed beyond any advantages to be derived from its continuance. Before therefore this office is re-established it behoves the Council to ascertain what are the advantages to be derived to the town from it ? what duties its officer has to perform ? and the annual cost for its maintenance ? These are serious questions for the Council to consider and it is to be hoped "the new order of things" will not rashly involve the Corporation in a useless expenditure. Renew it by all means if it can be made useful for any purpose at a small expence, but not otherwise,

I am Sir, your obliged servant, W"

"Sir—I had hoped the mania for abusive scribbling and bearing false witness against one's neighbour through the medium of the public press, had ceased in this town; but on perusing a paragraph headed Southwold in your Journal of the 12th inst, I find the snake is scotched, only, not killed—the venom and the will to use it still remain.

I wish I could believe that the paragraph alluded to had been written by one not an inhabitant of Southwold, but as the braying of the ass revealed his locality, though covered with the noble lion's skin; so of my learned friend's lucubrations, "his speech bewrayeth him" With the eulogy passed on the present Mayor and J.L. Ewen Esq I most cordially agree—"they are gentlemen of high character and bearing" Here my commendations must cease.

By all those who KNOW the management of the Corporation property during the past three years, the assertions of the writer are held in the most utter contempt; but for the information of those who do not know, and in reply to the slanders attempted to be propagated as truth, I will state the financial affairs of the Corporation in November 1849 when the ex-Mayor* was elected to the office of Chief Magistrate of this Borough I (like your Correspondent) will not allude "to the grace with which he accepted the office" or to the discomfiture of those fallen from their greatness never to rise again.

There was a large debt due to the Treasurer of the Borough who refused to advance another shilling until a second mortgage of the town property was effected—more than £700 due to contractors and tradesmen for work done and goods supplied—the members of the Corporation informed by their Town Clerk that "there was no means of avoiding the second mortgage" and that "the expence of obtaining such mortgage would be frightful" Mark the change in Nov. 1852. The debt to the treasurer has been paid, more than £650 of the arrears of of 1849 discharged and the balance in the hands of the treasurer, with arrears of rents due to the Corporation amply sufficient to discharge all its liabilities except the standing debt of £3,004, thus effecting a saving of more than £200 per annum. The economy practised is I perceive in the eyes of your correspondent "that disgraceful system of jobbing so long carried on" and if those "certain members who became such members not for the purpose of conducting the affairs of the town for the benefit of the inhabitants but to enhance their own interests "have worked such wonders as to do what others confessed they could not viz extricate the Corporation from its financial difficulties, the longer we have such men in office the better.

The sneers of the thwarted, the taunts of the envious, the slanders of the disappointed have not been able to effect the purposes desired by them. And the ex-Mayor on retiring from office, while thanking his FRIENDS for the assistance rendered him, so as to attain the happy results enumerated, may challenge the town to deny that he has done his duty.

In conclusion I would advise my learned friend (the writer of the paragraph commented on) to cease maligning his neighbours and bringing false accusations; but if he really must set to work in effecting a reformation let him begin at home and learn the first lesson—truth.

I am, Sir, your obedient servant
VINDEX (T.H.J.)"[13]

*Peter Palmer

Cutting Stranding of the brig "Ann and Mary" Collins of Sunderland, from Seaham to London with coal, upon Sizewell Bank on Sunday last about 6.30 a.m. in a gale of wind from the S.S.W. Turned on its beam ends and sank in 5 fathoms. The mate rescued by Joshua Chard of Thorp in the Thorp Lifeboat. Later the master was rescued and brought into Southwold, where he was revived by the local surgeons, Williams and Vertue. The "Friendship" yawl of Southwold rescues a further three of the crew from their drifting longboat. (Dec. 19/52)

---

13. 'Vindex' is Thomas Henry Jellicoe, the son-in-law of Peter Palmer, whom he defended.

Poster Request by the Mayor, Alfred Lillingston, that shops will be closed on Thursday, November 18, for the funeral of the Duke of Wellington.

Poster Concert by the Shapcott family of Exeter at the Town Hall. December 4th & 6th 1852.

1852 Dec 2d. Mr Marshal. Twaddell upset fro Cart—running in contact of a Waggon—in going to Blkshore—slightly injured in the head—but shortly recover'd.

Dec 10 Mr Thos Wales—dined at Mine—He had been out to [   ] et for [   ] Years—returned to Walberswick 21 Octobr. last.

Dec 18th Jonthn Button to Ipswich Gaol—upon a charge of Smuggling. 1854 June 17th He was discharged.

Dec 19 Sunday Morng. The brig "Ann & Mary" Thos Collins, Masr. of and from Sunderland bound to London, struck on Sizewell Bank and sunk the wind blowg. heavily from the S.W. by S. the crew with the exception of the Mate took to the boats—when a schooner in endeavouring to save these in the small Boat unfortunately struck her and she capsized and was only able to save two of the poor fellows—Joshua Chard alias George Osborne alias Joshua Chard of and at Thorpe seeing this distress manned his boat—and was the means of saving the Mate by taking him off the rigging—and afterwards the Master upon an Oar in a very exhausted state—and brought them on shore here. Our sailors seeing the position of the 3 Survivors in the long Boat drifting fast down to the Barnard Sand, gallantly ran off the "Friendship" yawl and providentially brought them safe to the shore. Seven out of the eight being saved. They were forwarded home on the Tuesday follwg by the aid of the Shipwreck'd Mariners Fund—although only the Master being a Member to it.

1852 Dec 24th Dr Wake, High Stewd appoints *me* his Bailiff of the Court Leet First Court held by Dr Wake 14 Jany 1853.

Dec 29 Put to Sale Mr Attoe's Houses & Meadow. not sell. see advertisement

Cutting Freehold and copyhold estate in Wangford to be auctioned by Maggs on Wednesday December 29 at 4 p.m. at the "Angel". Dwelling house shop, garden etc in tenure of John Rolfe, tailor and five cottages wheelwright's shop etc occupied by—Garrod and William Eastaugh. Also paddock of meadowland in occupation of William Newberry. The dwelling houses and shop front the street.

1852 Decr 29th Wm. Scarlett servant to Mr John Leverett of Walberswick *killed* dec was returning home with his team when near Walswk church some Colts were crossing the Road.frightened his Horses knocked him down and caused instant Death. Interred at Westleton.

Cutting Mayoral dinner at the Old Swan. December 29th. The Mayor & Council have sent for George Edwards Esq. the distinguished Civil Engineer, to inspect the sea defences, so that Gun Hill and the town itself may be saved.

Cutting Notice to debtors and creditors of the late John Sutherland. December 30. MARY ANN SUTHERLAND, Executrix

A.D.1853 Jany 1st Geo. Sones to Beccles Gaol for assaulting Mrs Howse "Bear" Inn Reydon. 2 Months.

Jany 4 Valuation et of Effects of the lt John Sutherland Esq for Administration

Jany 6 Sale of Furniture et of Mrs Maria Danford—relict of Mr Geo Danford—who died suddenly Oct 21/52

Jany 6th. The body of a Man unknown naked except a Small portion of a Flannel shirt marked X.W. washed on Shore, and interred here.

Jany 8th Daughter Eliza & Mr Jas: Tooke fro. Raveningham Hall here— returned on the 9th. again Mar 26 returnd Apr 2d.

Jany 12. Sale of Admiralty Droits.

Jany 13 Put to Sale a Stack of Hay, for Mrs Elizth. Goldsmith.

Jany 18 Wm Wright to Beccles Gaol for 6 Months, for breach of Peace agt his Parents.

Jany 22d Witness'd Indenture from Wm Sutton Jnr to Wm Sutton Senr re the purchase of a House by the latter of the former.

1853 Jany 22d Chas. Carter and Henry Sayer gives instructions to Mr Jo Read Solor and Mr Fisher of Halesworth, to pass through the County Court, for the Sum of £22 they were bound for—to the Saxmundham Money Club for Wm Sutton Jnr. I valued their effects

Jany 26 Married Mr Fredk. Palmer to Lydia Aldrich, daugr of Mr John Aldrich, Trinity Pilot.

Jany 27 The Schooner "[   ]" of "[   ]" Master put into this Harbor. The harbor pilot et after getting her in demanded Salvage—payment being refused—she was arrested. Feb 1 Bail was given and she sail'd on the 3d inst for the West Indies—to be employed in the Sugar Trade. Two of her Crew being unwilling to go in her, endeavour'd to make their escape—the one running away and the other by jumping overboard between the Piers. They were however both taken and placed on board and sailed with her. The case as to right of Salvage remains to be settled.

1853 Feby 3d Mr Thomas Rundle—Excise Officer, succeeds Mr A Aitchison.
    * 1859 Apr 1st Removed to Halesworth vd April 21 1851   April 1 1859

Feb 3 News arrived of the Death of James W age 18 Second Son of Mr John Lowsey—at Demarara Decr. 2d. 1852.

Feby 5 Sold Wm Welton's Effects, under distress for rent. Wm Sutton Landlord.

Feby 4 The "Alnwick" of Blyth, Jarvis Master, went on Shore upon Walberswick Beach. 8th got off by Mr Benjamin Herrington & Crew, and taken into the Harbor.recd £51

Feb 8th To Melton Asylum—and brought home, Mary Ann Crisp vd August 18 1848.

Sep 18/48 & Aug 18/48—and Amy Pleasance vd April 12 1852. both Cured

1853 Feby 8th Snow & Frosts—continued so 'till the [   ] heavy fall at intervals. Several persons, horses & Carts employed in carting it out of the Streets.   See Feb 18th 1852.

63

Feb 10th Married at Southwold Church Mr Phillips, Architect—to the relict of Lieut Walters, both of London. vd Feb 23/46.

1853 Feby 10th Apprenticed William Baldry Wigg to Robert Allen, Stone Mason, for 6 Years from 1st Jany

Feb 17 Put 50/64 parts or Shares of the Schooner "Louisa Elizth" to Sale at the Old Swan—reserve bid 250£ Bid £140, not Sold.

Feby 23d Gun Hill et High Tide Wind N.E. The Sea at intervals more particularly since Decr last—has made alarming inroads opposite the Gun Hill and as far to the N as the Long Island Cliff scarcely leaving sufficient width for the standing of the Bathing Machines opposite the Houses of Miss Sheriffe— The ground & flag pole in front of the New York Cliff house are all gone except of about 4½ ft the Watch House—belonging to the Coast Guard is so undermined that it is expected hourly to fall   It fell down May 9 1864, I saw it. The path which leads to the Gun Hill opposite the House belonging to Mr Delf is gone exposing the gas pipes so much so as the Gas Company was obliged immediately to remove them, but not until a great escapement of Gas. The distance fro the front of Mr Delf's house to the edge of the Cliff was in about the year 1816 62 feet—from that period this makes the 3d path taken off the lawn the distance from the front of the House to the edge of the Cliff is now only 40 feet: The Gun Hill is very much injured also the ground in front is so much destroyed and loosened that if something is not done immediately to check the sea—great fear is that it will all go.

Groins and faggot piling (the old breakwater being of no use) having been within this last 2 Months (costing from £250 to 300£) erected but proves ineffectual—as the sea has carried the groins in particular completely away. The opinion of Mr Reynolds Engineer and others has been given—that an efficient breakwater or Jetty is requird and that the estimated cost of either would exceed £1200   vd Dec 31 1840

During the Summer about £[   ] has been expended in putting down Stockes and filling with baulks Deals forming a Break Water opposite Gun Hill and Mr Delf's House under the direction of Mr Thos Rounce

Feb 8th to Mar 2d Heavy falls of Snow at intervals—Streets et clear'd out 3 different times—Feb 27 Sunday very heavy fall 10 to 12 inches on the level.

No Election of Auditors and Assessors

1853 Mar 1st Day appointed for the election of Auditors & Assessors *No election took place* not a Burgess interesting himself in the matter.

March 1st Sale of Mr Jas Fox's Furniture et of Wrentham.

March 16 Joseph Blowers to Beccles Gaol—One Month for non-payment of a bastard Child—The Mother of the child—daughter of Mr Jas: Leegood of this Parish but belonging to Ditchingham, Norfolk.

Mar 26 The "Pegasus" Jo Magub robbed of the clothes of Philip Tink by Richard Hoar—27 Committed to Beccles for trial.

April 1st Thunder Storm wt Rain.

April 4th Sale of Esther Mills Effects at Wrentham

Apr 6 Captn Chas Rayley R.N. purchases House and Premises of Jeremy Day

Esq late the property of Rd R Boniwell Long Isld Cliff for £[   ] John
Crabtree Solor   J. Maggs Agent

Cutting John King charged with having on April 5 last obtained at Southwold
from John Danby Strowger, agent for George Butcher of Wenhaston,
10 cwt of coals by false pretences. Mr Palmer, prosecuting, stated that
the prisoner, who was undefended, had borrowed a pony and cart
from Mrs Goldsmith of Southwold with which he went to Strowger's
coalyard and obtained the coals in her name. King was sentenced to 1
month's hard labour.

April 12th John King, committed to Beccles Gaol—for obtaining Coals under
a false pretence   June 27 Beccles Qr Sessions v. March 20/52

April 16 Saturday A.M. Mr John Laws 73 lt Master Mariner left his home—
last seen at "New Key"—he had been taking some beer at the Public House in
company with   —   Cleaveland of Walberswick after which they parted—
Cleaveland took his boat but Mr Laws took to the Wall under the idea of
walking home. Not hearing or seeing any thing of his return that night
search was made on the followg morning & for many days after. On the 18th his
Hat was found at the extreme end of the Buss Creek next the Sea by Jas
Howlett   See February 22 1844   April 18 1845

It is much feared he drowned himself—being never heard of or seen since the
16th inst, Until 18th May inst when his Body was observ'd floatg in the River
towards "New Quay"   Interred on the 20th   Verdict found dro by what means
unknown

1853 Monday 25 April Gale fro the [   ] On the Morning of the 26 "The
Three Friends", Henry Smith, Master, of this place, was totally wreck'd on
the Gunfleet sand—the Crew and the Master's daughter—all *saved* after
drifting over the sand in a small boat belonging to the Vessel were picked up by
a Vessel bound to London.

On the same Morning at 5 o'clock the crew of the "Eliza" of North Shields
G.G. Meldrum master were landed here, the Vessel having struck upon the
"Home" sand, and broken and unshipped her rudder, was abandond by her
crew—at 9 P.M. of the 24th there were 10 in Number—and were exposed in
an open boat to a tempestuous sea & gale for 8 hours.

A boat marked outside stern "Mary Young" N Shields, and inside "John
Knox" was picked up in this Bay and taken into the Harbor—no one in her.

Apr 29 Rec'd instructions fro the County Court to sell E Goldsmith's Wain
May 5 Sold it for £10 to Mr Edm Child.

Cutting Meteorological Observations. By Orlando   Whistlecraft of Thwaite.
April 30 1853.

Writ of Mandamus

April 22d date of Writ of Mandamus for non-
electing Auditors and Assessors the 1st March
Alfred Lillingston Esq Mayor   For Cost see
Abstract 1853
May 17 1853

Elected Frd Wade Denny ⎫
          Jas Boyce ⎬ Auditors
Thos Hy Jellicoe ⎫
          Wm Bagott ⎬ Assessors
             Jon Gooding   Town Clerk

Cutting Rewards distributed to Master and Crew of the "Glenmoriston" for rescuing the master of the "William and Mary" in Lowestoft Roads 24 June 1853

1853 May 5. Sale of Phoebe Botham's Furnr under distress for rent.

May 10th at Walberswick—by the Revd Thos. Harrison—Mr John Fisk—Officer of the Inland Revenue, Thornbury—Gloucestershire to Eleanor Markham—only daugr of Mr. Obadiah Palmer of the former place

Cutting On Thursday May 12 the schooner "William and Mary" of Southwold, Henry Wright, master, ran into the sloop "Lily" and sank in Lowestoft roads. The master was rescued by Francis Stannard of the"Glenmoriston" of Southwold. Lewis Cady, mate, saved, John Bullen and William Todd, drowned.

Cutting On June 2 the silver medal of the Society for the Preservation of Life from Shipwreck presented to Francis Stannard (Lowestoft June 2)

May 19 Sold Effects of Mrs Elizth Palmer for Mr S Gayfer.

1853 May 21st Mr F. Wade Denny—goes into the Shop lt Mr Wm Abbott dec.

May 23d.The Revd William Wellington Yonge—Curate came here—1854 June 4th preach'd farewell Sermon & left the Town. June 11 ordained a Priest

May 24 Wife to Southampton for my daugr. Sarah—returned 10th June.

May 28 John Barber, Louisa Elizth committed to Beccles Gaol—admitted Bail

June 27 Qtr Sessions.

Cutting John Barber charged with stealing at Southwold one ton of coals, the property of Messers Strathern and Paul of Halesworth. Barber, Master and part owner of the "Louisa Elizabeth", living in Southwold, engaged to take a cargo of malt from there to Grimsby. Then to proceed to Hartlepool and take on a load of Backhouse's Wallsend coals. He paid for 40 chaldrons (Newcastle measure). Arriving at Southwold, 21 tons were taken out before proceeding to Blackshore Quay. There the coal meter measured 86 tons 15 cwt. A carter named Wentworth carted 16 bags from the ship to Barber's house and 2 bags to his son's house, there being about half a ton or more in the bags. Mr Strathern did not know the weight of a Newcastle chaldron but had been told it was about 2½ tons. It was also usual for the master to have the sweepings of the hold. For Barber, Mr Palmer said that no loss had been proved, if it existed it was not more than half a ton and to this the master was entitled by custom at Southwold. Barber was given an excellent character and was acquitted.

May 28th Wenhaston Sale of Mr John Spoore's effects.

Cutting Destructive fires at Westleton originating in a spark from a chimney falling into a pig stye. Under a strong north easterly wind it spread to four houses belonging to Mr Tacon, a barn owned by Mr R Girling and a house the property of Mr Brown, that contained three dwellings. The thatched church was at one time in danger as also was the house of S.A. Woods Esq. When a cottage belonging to Lord Huntingfield was destroyed there were fears for the village itself. (May 25/53)

Cutting Richard Hoar accused of stealing a pair of boots at Lowestoft from William Swabey on March 13. Hoar went to Southwold and sold the boots to a man called Bird. He was also accused of stealing wearing apparel from Philip Tink at Southwold but no evidence was offered on this count. Hoar was convicted and sentenced to 6 months hard labour.(June xxvii 1853)

1853 May 30th Champness Family here—Instrumental Concert et at 1st Visit.

2d Visit Aug 20 & 21 1855.

June 7. To Blythbro in re of Jas Fisk's Sale Sold 15th—On the 20th Mr F. goes to Boyton Alms Houses.

June 9 Black Mill put to Sale. Sold to Mr Wm Wallace Bardwell—Mortgagee for £750 !!

June 24—3 P.M. We were visited with a heavy Thunder Storm accompanied with rain and hail—A Cottage near the "Bear Inn" Reydon was struck with the lightning—and two of the Inmates daugrs of Mr Jo Smith were Struck also severely burning the one and slightly the other—Mr S was in the house but escaped unhurt—All 3 were very much shocked but speedily recovrd.Mr John Soans "Two Friends" was going to Sea—when the lightning descended upon the rigging and greatly schorched one of his hands.

June 29th Sale of Harriett Wright's Effects wd. Wangford

Cutting Maggs to auction the household furniture etc of Mrs Chaston, who is changing her residence, on Thursday July 7 1853.

July 12th I went to Lowestoft Regatta.

. . 23d To Lowestoft with Marshl. Twaddell to his Vessel "Sophia" lying there.

July 13th Sarah Hambling

Cutting Sarah Hambling, 20, charged with stealing a woollen shawl belonging to Robert Page of Southwold, hostler at the "Crown", where Hambling had been engaged as a servant. She left in March and policeman Spurgeon stated that she had been arrested in Beccles with the shawl which she said Page had given to her. Mr Palmer, for the prisoner, quoted her excellent character and she was acquitted. She claimed that Page was fond of her and had given the shawl to her when she had been hanging out the linen on a cold day.

Cutting Robert Key transported for ten years for cruelly maiming a ewe belonging to Thomas Whitmore of Reydon, who had employed the 35 year old Key. (Ipswich Assizes July 25th 1853)

Cutting Shipping Dues Commission meets at Southwold Town Hall on July 14 1853. Jonathan Gooding, Clerk to the Commissioners of Southwold Harbour presented each commissioner with a copy of Maggs's "Hand Book of the Port and Shipping of Southwold" The port was not in debt but had £400 in hand. It emerged that no Parliamentary Act defined the inner limits of the haven, which was disputed between the Commissioners for the Harbour and for the Blyth Navigation.

1853 July 23d I went to Lowestoft—met Mr Marshl. Twaddell "Sophia" returned 24th.

Aug 8th "Hermandez & Stone", American Circus here.

Sep 3d & 4th A large arrival of Foreign Ships off here. 12 Trinity Pilots and 27 "Brummegers" were shipped for London. In 1814 We had a similar arrival of Foreigners. [14]

Sepr 6th Regatta

Cutting Regatta followed by dinner at the Swan. Fireworks on the Common, accompanied by Watering's band, which was in attendance then and during the sailing and the dining.

Sep 11th Mr John Larner & Mr [   ] Pipe Shopmen of Mr F.W.Denny's met with an accident at Theberton from an upset of their Cart.

Sep 19th "New York" Cliff House taken down by order of the Council. It stood upon the Cliff opposite the property of William Aldrich & Thos Reeve near South Green.

1853 Sep 21st Wm F. Boyden—leaves to reside in or Near London as P.Off.

Sep 21st I was elected Auditor to the Gas Company.

Sep 26 Wm Christopher—Mate of the "Sophia" Marsl. Twaddell knocked over board in a gale—upon his passage from the North, and *drowned.*

Sep 28th John Smith. Wrentham, Sale.

Sep 29th Geo. Skinner, Sotterley Sale.

Oct 1st The "Andrew" "Half & Half" Fishg. Boat launch'd—built by Mr Henry Ladd in the Fish Offc yard. This is the first boat of this description built here—vide 31st March/54

Oct 10 Mr Roe—Reydon, *Sale*

Oct 13—Crisp—Hulver—Sale I was there also on the 6th takg an acct of same.

Cutting Meeting of the Southwold Harbour Commissioners held at the Old Swan on September 20 1853. Quotations are made from a report submitted in 1844 by E.K.Calver R.N., Admiralty Surveyor and a native of Southwold, attacking a proposal to improve the port by extending the piers. The "chronic disease" from which the harbour suffered cannot be cured or even ameliorated without better understanding between the Commissioners respectively for Harbour

14. A 'Brummeger' was an unlicensed pilot. (Ex inf. David Higgins.)

and for River. "The neglected state of the channel of the river navigation between Reydon quay and Bulcamp lock is the great evil of the port" because it fosters and promotes a bad bar. Quotation was also made from Calver's recently published "The Conservation and Improvement of Tidal Rivers".

Cutting William Spelman and Sons are to auction the schooner "Isabella", Rowland Twaddell, master, built in Northumberland and now lying south of the Gas Works at Yarmouth, on September 21st. The ship (of Southwold) and 3,500 tons had been thoroughly repaired since her construction in 1846.

Cutting "SOUTHWOLD—MUNICIPAL ELECTION—Tuesday bringing the important duty of electing four new town councillors in the room of those four who vacate their appointments, there was no slight sensation, evident from the hour of opening the poll until its close. Southwold, in common with other borough towns has had woeful experience of the mischief arising from the folly of the electors, who have allowed such persons to have seats in the Council, as without any regard for the real interests of the Town consult only the means of benefit to themselves; and smarting under this experience, a general anxiety was evident that fit and proper persons should be chosen to fill these important offices. Seven candidates appeared viz James Williams Esq., Lieutenant Simmons R.N. Messers G.E Child, J. King, D.Foreman, P. Westrup and S. Wayth. No small amusement was excited by a paper posted in the Market-place to this effect "Friends of your old Mayor, Peter Palmer, who will come forward— Foreman, Wayth and Westrup ! " But notwithstanding this gentle hint from "Peter Palmer, the old Mayor" in his own handwriting ! upon an active canvass commencing the state of the poll at eleven o'clock showed—For Williams 62, Simmons 59, King 63, Child 63, Foreman 3, Westrup 3, Wayth 3 and at 4 o'clock, the close of the poll, the numbers stood Williams 116, Simmons 112, Child 111, King 108, Foreman 23, Wayth 21, Westrup 19. We congratulate Southwold upon the result of the day's work and feel convinced that the four elected Councilmen are fit and proper persons to represent the interests of the town." (Nov 1st 1853)

Notice   List of Members of the Corporation 1853–4
1853 Oct 8th—W. Simmons, Wenhaston. Sale.
Oct 10th—Mr Cooper's, Wrentham—Sale
Oct 10th   To Mr Jas. Crickmer's—Holton Farmer, with execution from his Landlord John Robinson Esq—Dunwich for rent & Arrears to the Amot of £798 13s 6d   13th I again enter'd for 150£ more   makg £948. 13s. 6d
* Oct 15th To Ringsfield & Ditchingham 16th To Harleston Dragon Inn.
17 To Halesworth wt Mr. Gooding to Mr Baas in re Crickmer
19 To Halesworth—met Mr Earl—thence to Holton to Crickmers—
20 To Mr Robinson's Dunwich, in re Crickmer.

22 To Holton—met Earl—in re same

28 To Holton & Halesworth with Mr. Gooding—in re same.

29 To Dunwich with Mr Gooding to Mr Robinson's in re same.

Nov 2 to Halesworth with Mr Gooding in re same

Nov 5 To Holton with Mr Gooding—for Samples of Corn et et.

Nov 8th

1853 Nov 8th To Holton & Halesworth Market to sell Corn—of Jas: Crickmer

Nov 10th To Holton in re Threshing.

Nov 12th To Holton in re Jas Crickmer.

Nov 15th To Holton & Haleso Market.

Nov 18th To Holton Jas Crickmer's Sale to Haleso in the evening—met Mr Howlett and Appleton—re Valuation of Crickmer's Covenants £426 11 6— at the "King's Arms"

Nov 19th To Holton & Haleso—re Corn.

Nov 22nd To Holton & Haleso Market

Nov 26th To Holton & Haleso with Mr. J. R. Gooding—met Mr Robinson, Baas. and Earl—settled J Crickmer's Sale et paid Earl Sheriff's Officer £164. 16. 6

Nov 28th Remitted to Mr Robinson from the Estate of Jas Crickmer £504.14s.9d

Cutting Maggs to auction farming stock etc of James Crickmer at Holton on November 18, under distress for rent.

Cutting Maggs advertises letting of a farmhouse, two barns and 247 acres of arable and pasture at Holton. November 19 1853. (Let in February 1854 to Mr Godbold)

Cutting Maggs to auction the wreck of the schooner "Lucie" of St. Malo, 82 tons, built within the last six months, on the beach at Covehithe on November 23 & 24 1853.

Cutting The Southwold Lifeboat (Ben Herrington and William Waters, coxswains) rescues the crew of nine from the brig "Sheraton Grange", William Turnbull, bound from Sunderland to London with coal. The vessel is now a grounded wreck opposite the town as the result of a gale of wind from the S.S.W. Miss Sheriffe "with her accustomed liberality" sent £5 to the lifeboatmen. (Nov 29 1853)

1853 Oct 18th Married at Raveningham Mr Jas.Tooke to my daughter Eliza. She then proceeded to a Sale at the "Green Dragon" Inn Harleston—where she was robbed of her Purse of £33

19th Mr Tooke took the above Inn at Harleston. Left Oct 11 1855

1856 Jany To live at Newton Nr. Long Stratton Norfolk in a School

Oct 24th & 25th Valued for Mr Westrup at the Crown Inn against Mr Robinson for Mrs Sh Hall incoming Tenant

27th Mr Westrup leaves Crown succeeded by Mrs Sarah Hall—fro June 21/50

1854 May Mr Westrup leaves the Town

1855 Oct 18 Mrs Hall distrained for rent 80£ Sale Nov 15 & 16 1856
May 25 Sale of Mrs Halls effects   June 3d Mrs Hall leaves "Crown" which
continues unoccupied until May 27th 1857 Taken by Mrs Lucy Mercer
Opening dinner Novr 19th followg.
Oct 29th Sold a French Schooner "Lucie" of St Malo—wkd on the Beach at
Covehithe the previous day—Crew perished—
Wk purchased by Messr Thurston & Benstead for £50—duty 50s
Nov 3d Let by Auction 3 Marshes—viz 1 to Mr Catling & 2 to Mr E
Cottingham and Blkshore Wharf to J.J.Goff 1 yr £2
Novr. 13th. Mr Peter Palmer, Ch warden requested by A Lillingston Esq.
Mayor to vacate his seat at Church (the seat that he sat in when Mayor &
Magistrate) to the present Magistrates—which he acceded to but persisted
in sitting in a seat on the opposite side also intended for the Magistrates—to
the displeasure of the Mayor (These seats are those where the *Bailiffs* and
Chamberlains sat previous to the passing of the Municipal Corporation Act
1835.) On the 25 inst it was agreed in Council, or rather voted that Mr Palmer
gives up to the Magistrates the seat without any further trouble—but on
Sunday the 27th Mr Palmer attended Church and took the seat where Mr
Fulcher J.P. had for several years been sitting—and where, as a Magistrate it
was agreed for him to sit—I should say on the Morning of Sunday the 20th &
27th the Police Officer, Spurgeon & his assistant—C. Naunton were order'd
to the Church to inform Mr Palmer the Mayor's objection to his taking any
One of these 4 *Seats*—when Mr Palmer goes to the back of Mr Fulcher's seat
climbs over and takes *possession*—and continues to do so until Sunday 5th
Feby 1854—when he Mr P vacates it, and retires to his Own Seat—in the
Middle Isle.
               See Revd Stephen Clissold's award Jany 31 1854
Cutting Howlett and Lenny to auction property on East Cliff-green that
          belonged to the late John Cottingham, gentleman, at the Old Swan
          on December 14 1853. A residence with adjoining double cottage
          occupied by James Waters and John Hur.
1853 Nov 16. To Melton Asylum with Harriett wife of Jas. Lowsey.
Novr. 28th Alfred Lillingston Esq Mayor gives the Burgesses a Dinner at the
Crown.
Dec 3d Sold the *Hull* of the "Sheraton Grange" to J.J.Goff & company for
132£
Dec 10th Self, Wife and Ellen—to my daugr Eliza's—Harleston "Dragon"
Dec 12th Sold Coals of "Sheraton Grange"
  .. 13   .. Stores & Materials of same
  .. 16   .. at Sizewell of part of Do and also some Admiralty droits.
Cutting Maggs to auction the fast-sailing brig "Victoria" 88 tons, built in
          1839 and lying at Blackshore, at the Old Swan on December 15 1853.
Victoria sold to Mr S.M.Fell of Yarmo by Private contract £555   Decr 27th
1853   1854 Jany Victoria sails for Yarmouth
Cutting Maggs to auction the wreck of the brig "Sheraton Grange" of

Sunderland, 261 tons. December 29 at Southwold and December 30 at Walberswick.

1854 Jany 1st Set in with Snow & Frosts—continued 4 days.

Jany 3th & 4th Heavy Gale E.done considerable damage to many houses in the Town—a great number of Vessels with their Crews—but happily none of this place.

Jany 6th. Charlotte King to Union House. and sent to Melton Asylum. Died at Asylum Dec 26/54 & interr'd there.

1855 July—Daniel her Husband died in LONDON.

Jany 9th At Brighton Aged 69 Mr T.W. Thompson many years resident here.

1854 Jany 10th The Revd H.W.R. Birch died   Interred at Reydon

Feby 23 & His family leaves Southwold March 8 & 9   Sale of his Furniture et. et.

Jany 14 Button Geo. petitions for a Pilots Warrant.

Feby 3. Pleasance Mrs A—to the Union House.

Feby. 9. Siggars Mr. Rd. leaves to reside in London.

Feb 16th Rd Siggars Sale—

. .   . . A.A.Pleasance wd Sale vd Feby 3d inst.

Letter   (Copy)   Wrentham Rectory. Jany 31/54

J. Gooding Esq.

Town Clerk

Whereas differences and disputes have arisen and are still depending between the Magistrates of the Borough of Southwold of the one part and Mr Peter Palmer, Alderman of the same Borough of the other part touching the right to sit in certain Stalls in the Chancel of Southwold Church namely the four Stalls in the Chancel adjoining the Screen, and facing the Organ Gallery.

And Whereas the said parties, in order to obtain an amicable adjustment of such differences and disputes have agreed to refer the same together with all proceedings originating in or connected with the same to my Arbitration and to abide the event and determination of my Award as binding and conclusive and each and every of the said parties. And whereas with the sanction and at the request of the Lord Bishop of the Diocese I have taken upon myself the charge and business of the said Award and whereas all Books, papers and Writings touching or relating to the matters in difference between the said parties have been delivered to me and having been attended by both the said parties and heard the allegations and proofs and investigated the Acts and transactions by and between the said parties concerning the several matters referred to me and have maturely considered the same I award and determine in manner following—

That the Magistrates of the Borough of Southwold and their official Successors Inhabitants of the Parish of Southwold have acquired a right to the occupation of four Stalls in the Chancel adjoining the Screen and facing the Organ Gallery in Southwold Church—and I do award order and direct that the said Magistrates be peaceably seated therein.

And I do further declare and Order that this my award shall in no respect whatsoever either directly or indirectly be used or taken as justifying or sanctioning either of the said parties in difference in reclaiming or taking possession of any other of the Stalls, Seats or Pews situate in the Chancel of the said Church and at present occupied by Parishioners. And I declare also my opinion to be in agreement with Dr Haggard's on this subject—namely— that the Corporation have no such power.

And further the more effectually to insure Submission to this my Award it is likewise ordered by and with the consent of the said parties in difference that neither of them shall prosecute or bring any Action or Suit in any court of Law Equity Civil or Ecclesiastical against each other concerning the said seats or concerning any of the Acts or Transactions of either of the said parties in relation thereto.   Stephen Clissold

> 1854 Jany 13th Mr Jo Burcham ejected fro his premises in High St—purchased by his son-in-law Rt Allen. Mr. B. was in custody at the Town Hall for breach of the peace fro the 13th to 16th released upon promising to be peaceable. Mar 16 Mr B. sent to Beccles 27 To Bury Assizes and was charged of Stealing two boards and three wood jacks belonging to a luggage cart, the property of Robert Allen of Southwold.

Cutting "A SCANDALOUS PROSECUTION John Burcham 76 of very venerable appearance was charged with stealing two boards and three wood jacks belonging to a luggage cart, the property of Robert Allen of Southwold. The Prisoner when asked the usual question replied in an excited manner "They were my own and are so to this day" Mr Bulwer appeared for the prosecution. The prisoner was described as a wheelwright and the property was alleged to have been stolen from his son-in-law who was called to give evidence and who gave his testimony with an animus calculated to disgust almost every person in court. The Judge : It is a case of family dispute. It is very wrong to bring up an old man like that and charge him with felony here. Let him be immediately discharged. It is a very scandalous case. The prosecutor here slunk out of the witness box. Mr Bulwer: The case was sent here my lord by the magistrates of Beccles* against the advice of their clerk. The Judge: But who made the charge of felony ? Mr Bulwer: The prosecutor, no doubt.   The Judge: The costs of the prosecution will not be allowed." *(read Southwold)

> 1854 Apr 13th John Burcham to Beccles Gaol for a Breach of the Peace agt his Son-in-law, Mr Allen. Committed for want of Sureties 6 mths Died at home Oct 30/54 76

Cutting Presentation made to the crew of the Southwold lifeboat in the Town

Hall by F.W.Ellis Esq. for their rescue of the crew of the "Sheraton Grange" (Feby 22 1854)

Cutting Maggs to auction a messuage in the Market Place, with Cooper's Shops Sailmaker's Loft etc lately occupied and owned by John King. At the Old Swan, February 16.

1854 Feby 13th Wm Girling pass'd for a Trinity Pilot—Obtained his Warrant a few days afterwds 1st Ship "Victoria" of Lobhitze to London. Feb 16–17–18 Strong Wind N.E. & Snow.

Feb 25 A Cottage at Reydon—belonging to Lord Stradbroke—in the occupation of Hy. Bedingfield and—Wale laborers *burnt* down—supposed to have originated from some sparks fro the Oven fallg upon the Thatched roof—Only a Pig and few articles of Furnitr partially burnt—Our Engine was there—

Feb 27th At Dunwich Mr Jos Dix—formerly of the "Ship" Inn—Died.

March 7th Sale of Boats & Nets of Mr Jo Waters & Isaac Jarvis—also of Mr W's Fishhouse.

March 12th Geo. Green—of Brighton to U. Ho.

March 16th Sale of Mr John Hall's effects.

1854 March 20th Henry Sayer—succeeds Jas: Gillings to "White Horse" Beer House. Jas Gillings succeeds Jas Hows to "Bear Inn, Reydon See May 1 1851

Mar 22d Sold sundry Effects of Mr B.S.Candler

March 25 Died Mr Dnl. Riches Junr of Frostenden 47. Apr 13 Mr Jos Riches 67 d Uncle to dec

1855 Feb 5 D. Riches Snr Dies Ap 19 Mary Ann Wife of Jo Read Halesworth 43 daugr of Mr Dnl Riches. Frostenden

Mar 28th Comet first seen here.

Mar 30th Hilleary Eliz. Sale of Effects.

March 31st "Alfred" Half & Half—Fishg Boat launch'd built by Hy Ladd— vd Oct 1/53

Apr 1st Sale of Furniture et of Mr. T.H. Diver—who left Reydon to reside at Kessingland. October 4 1848

April 15th Light shower of Rain—being the second during Lent—viz from the 5th March—Winds prevailing chiefly fro. the East—20th very dry Wind S. signs of Rain.

Letter Nacton House Aug 31. 1854

My dear Sir, I have just time to inform you, that in examining the Register of Deaths in the Wilford District I find Barnes Hill died on the 14 of April 1854 at Ramsholt Dock Inn—Yrs faithfully J. Parker

Mr Jas Maggs

Three years tomorrow (1st September) since I was Installed at Nacton Respects to all. J.P.

Cutting Haystack at Hinton Hall farm destroyed by fire after a ten year old boy had been playing with matches. (March xxiii 1854)

Cutting The weather. Letter from Orlando Whistlecraft of Thwaite April 11.

Cutting The comet 1854

Cutting Case brought in the Admiralty Court on May 27 1854. The 19 hands, the crew of the yawl "Reliance" claim salvage for bringing the "Leo", (laden with railway iron and bound from Newport, S. Wales for Bremen) into Lowestoft on December 17 1853 when she was in difficulties off Southwold. A pilot had been taken on board but it was not his services that saved the vessel. There were 2½ ft of water in the hold and it was the pumping done by 14 of the men from the "Reliance", after the crew of the "Leo" were exhausted that was decisive. They are awarded £150 instead of the £100 that had been offered by the owners of a property worth £2,832.

Handbill For W. Haken, butcher, of Market Place, Southwold, who has taken over the business of S.R. Haward. April 6 1854.

(Mr Haward goes to Lowestoft to reside. Mr Haken leaves June 28/54 Insolvent)

Cutting The Reverend John Rustat Crowfoot B.D. curate of St Mary's Cambridge, nominated by the Earl of Stradbroke to Southwold.

Mr. C. left SoWo July 23/60 went to Wangford. Rev. Barkworth succeeded him September 29 1860

Mr Birch d. 10th Jany. 1854. See Wake's History of Southwold Rev Wm French to the vicarage of Reydon. For their Union 1777 & Severance 1854 Wake p. 89

1854 May 21st Rev Jo Rustat Crowfoot B.D. Read himself into this Church.

April 24 A large quantity of Deals came on Shore between Lowestoft and Thorp Ness fro the "Albertina" [   ] Masr from Gothenburgh bound to Bordeaux wkd upon the Hasbro' sand—six perished and 7 saved by the Boat and picked up & taken into Harwich

June 21st I sold Deals at Walswick and Southwold
23 Dunwich 24 Sizewell and Misner sale fro 1000
to 1100£

April Wednesday 26th *Fast Day* Humiliation and prayer on acct of the War.

May 4th Sale of Paint for Mr Till.

First saw Mr Toogood Lowestoft.his accident

May 15 Many of the Inns raised Porter to 7d the Pot. Malt duty being raised fro the 8th inst—from 2s 9d to 4s the [   ]

Porter droppd to 6d the latter part of the Month.

May 23 Frs Palmer Fisherman upset out of his Boat—saved by clinging to an Oar 'till a boat went to his assistance.

May 25 Wm Chapman signs his Will Witnesses Mr F.H. Vertue and Mr Chas Spurgeon.

1854 June 16th To Melton Asylum for Harriett Lowsey—

June 19th Geo Bond from Hoxne—Tea Dealer came to reside here.

June 27th The "Dispatch" Wm Magub—lost Crew Saved.

June 29th "Hope" Henry Sayer, sold to Lowestoft.

July 15 To Lowestoft with Mr Sutton—re the purchase of Mr Thompson's

House "St John" New Church consecrated.

Insertion List of psalms and anthems at consecration of St. John's Lowestoft.

July 26 Sold Furniture et of Rowland Jermyn & others

Same day Fire of Stack et et the property of Mr Hugh Lawrence—at Walberswick.

July 27th Met Mr Frd Barnes of Epping at the Old Swan, Southwold for the purpose of putting property to sale, see Adv. I did not put it up. As Mr Robert John Debney of Southwold protested, claiming it as Heir at Law, John Wright marrying his Mother—then Sarah Stannard widow. Thus the matter rests.

London Gazette There to be no further burials in the church or within three yards of the church and of the independent chapel. Except for family vaults and graves, only one body to be buried in each grave. June 8 1854

Notice List of services in the church and information relating to the national, infant and Sunday schools, clothing club, lending library, dispensary etc. June 25 1854.

Cutting Maggs to auction the marine residence on South Green late the residence of T.W. Thompson and at present occupied by H.J. Debney. (1854 Aug 5 Sold to F.W. Ellis by private contract £305)
1854 Augt 5th Purchased by F.W.Ellis R.N. by Private Contract of Mr. Powell for £305

Cutting Cottages at Walberswick to be auctioned by Maggs at the Old Swan, Southwold, on July 27 1854. Occupied by William Easy, William Sewell and Thomas Bailey. Nearly all Walberswick belongs to Sir C.Blois.

July 29 The body of Mr Sadd of Lowestoft, Painter, picked up off here— buried 31st inst. dec was drowned on the 15th at Lowestoft in bathing.

July 31 Revd Rd. Gooch, leaves Frostenden—to the Continent—his Sale Aug 3/54.

Aug 20th Wm Warne—Trinity Pilot—29th first Vessel "St Michael fro Archangle Cap. Plauzango 13ft from Lowestoft.

Aug 19 Mr J.J.Goff struck with a piece of brass fro a chisel, and perish'd an Eye.
1854 Aug 24th Died at Yoxford Mr Calver Builder to Sir C. Blois fro accident

1854 Aug 23d Regatta.

Sep 6th Sale of Fishing Gear et et of Mr Frdk Denny.

Sep 7 Chas Fisk, elected deputy Harbor Master in the room of Francis Brown who died March 1/54 agd 54.

Sep 8th Sale of Mr Edwd Burwood's Furniture et. Wangford
14th Sale of Geo Bond's effects et.

Sep 18th To Yoxford to Revd Badley's Sale.

Sep 23d "Henrietta" built by Hy Ladd—launched—("Half & half Fishing boat")

Sep 25th Took an Account of Repository Sale, Walberswk and also Farming Stock et of Ben. Wright. Sold 10th October.

Sep.25 Harry White elected relieving officer in the room of Mr Fisher.

Oct 1st Church first lighted up with Gas.

> Thos Wallace 1854 Sep 27th Loss of the United States Mail Steam Ship "Arctic" Cap. Luce. She sailed from Liverpool on the 20th inst for New York—with 185 Passengers—and Crew 130—The "Arctic and the "Vesta", a French iron steamer coming in collision with each other off Cape Race.
>
> Mr Thos Wallace (who formerly resided here) was one who was drowned in the "Arctic" (See under August 6 1850)
>
> (14 Passengers saved and of the Crew 31—Made Broad Cove 20 Miles North of Cape Race—after padling their Boat 44 hours Lloyd's weekly Messenger)
>
> 1854 Sep 27th 1854 Loss of the United States Mail, Ship "Arctic" Cap. Lace for New York from Liverpool—she sailed on the 20th with 185 passengers and 130 Crew.—Mr Wallace with many more was drowned off Cape Horn—The "Arctic" came in collision with the French iron steamer "Vesta"

Cutting October 19 1854. George Bond, tea dealer, fined for assaulting Charles Spurgeon, police inspector (both of Southwold) by town magistrates. (Aug 7 1855 Bond to Beccles Jail for an Assault upon Mr Goldsmith Fined 2s 6 paid next day and discharged)

Cutting Monday evening, October 23 1854, meeting held in the Town Hall to raise £20–£30 for the Patriotic Fund to help the widows and children of soldiers, sailors and marines killed in the war.

> 1854 October 25th—Drowned on his passage from Sierra Leone, on board the African mail Steamer "Forerunner", Paul second son of Mr Thos Vertue of Deptford—late of Woodbridge.

Cutting Loss of the "Forerunner" off St Lorenzo, sailing from Sierra Leone to Plymouth. Mr Vertue was of Sierra Leone.

Cutting Meeting held at Southwold to establish branch of the Blything Hundred Savings Bank. Alfred Lillingston re-elected mayor. (Nov 6 1854)

Cutting Notice from Eastern Counties and Haddiscoe, Beccles and Halesworth Railway announcing opening of line from Haddiscoe to Halesworth on Monday, December 4, 1854

Cutting November 22 1854. Robbery of barn at Wrentham

Notice List of Members of the Corporation, 1854–5

77

1854 Oct 2 Sale at Wrentham Foundery.
This Month—Ringing (after the lapse of several years) renewed.
Oct 7 Sale at Sotherton, Mr Green Haylock's dec. Furniture et.
Oct 9 Mr Crisp's sale at Wrentham
. . 12 SoWold Market Wharf et
Oct 15th Primitive Methodist Chapel (new) opened. They have been here about [   ] yrs.
Oct 16th Infant School, established.
Nov 2d Mrs Goff's Sale, who is gone to reside in Beccles.
Nov 13th Mr David Green's Sale—
Nov 11th A branch Savings Bank—
Nov 21st Mr Jas White—Watchmaker Sale "Under a Bill of Sale" to Alfred Lillingston Esqr. leaves SoWold Nov 22. 1855.
at Frostenden—1854 Dec 2 Sale of C.Harbour's Furnr by instructions fro Wm Stockdale.
1854—First with the Herrings caught by the "Half and Half" Boats and the Cod fishing—such a fishing is not remember'd by the oldest Inhabitant living. The crews of the 3 "Half and Half" Boats shared upwards of £20 a man—and fro 120 Li to 170 Li and 180 £'s have been paid weekly for the catch of Cod Fish.
1854 Decr 20th—Fish first sent fro here to Halesworth Railway.
Dec 21st Fisher's clothes Sale at "Red Lion" Sowold
1855 April 5   also   also.
Dec 30th Geo Bond, Tea Dealer fined by the Magistrates of the Boro' 10s/– for breaking the Peace
1s/– for breaking window, King's Head, Wm Goldsmith.
5/– for getting drunk
6/6 expenses—pd and discharg'd
                          Charles Spurgeon   P.C.
Insertion   Demand for Southwold Fee Farm Rent of £11..12..4
                          dated 27 Nov. 1854,
Visiting Cards To Mrs Bartlett, Brook Street   Captain and Mrs Henry Phillips
                          January 1st
1855 Strong Wind and High Tide. Haven Marshes and enclosed allotments flooded. Breakwater & Gun Hill, much damaged—2d Heavy swell—Tide 3 inches higher in the Blackshore House—than on the 3d Febr 1790
1856 Aug 17–18–19 Wind E & E.N.E. High Tides
Jany 16 Sutton Wm Jnr in "Hue and Cry" deserted fro 85 Reg. foot at Sunderland gave himself on [   ] at Springfield Essex.[15]
Jany 16 News of the death of Henry son of Isaac Welton—died June 10 1854 of Fever on Board the "Majestic" on his passage to the Baltic fleet.
Jany 30th To Halesworth with Mr J.R.Gooding
Jany 31st Died at Brundish Mr Edward Coote—agd 72.

---

15. Chelmsford goal was at Springfield but the barracks may have been intended here.

Feb 1 Jas. Johnson Clark to Georgianna Palmer—
Feby 8th To Ditchingham & Harleston with Wife to daugr Eliza's—returned
on 9th my b.d
1855 Febry 10th Sale of Wreck et. Covehithe and Easton.
Feb 12.Harbor nearly blocked. Men raking a Channel.
Feb 13th Wrentham d. Mr. Thos Girling.
Mar 11   Do   —d. Susan his relict.76
Feb 20th Sale of Mr Rt Smith's effects who goes to reside in London
Feby 21st Revd J.R.Crowfoot, Incumt Jas.Williams and Hy.J.Debney—
Trustees to Mr.John Sayer's legacy.
Feby 22d Sale of Jo Aldred's effects.
To Wenhaston to serve Copy of Writ of ejectment up Mr.Geo Butcher in re
Mrs Dowson's property Blkshore.
Feb. 24 To Lowestoft wt J.R.Gooding who proceeded to London.
Feb 27th News of the loss of "[   ]" Wm. May, Masr at [   ]
Crew saved.
Memorial Card for John Snell, of Wangford, who died April 19 1855 aged 71.
Cutting Wharf and premises at Black Shore Quay to be auctioned at the Old
        Swan on April 25 by George P. Freeman of Halesworth and
        Wangford. By order of the executors of William Dowson.
1855 Feby 28th Wm Butcher charged of stealing a Bed and pair of Stays the
property of Eliz. relict of Wm. Chapman—tried at Beccles Sessions 12th
March, and acquitted.
March 1st Mr Hugh Lawrence, takes Beer House of Mrs Elizabeth Gold-
smith, Green lane.
March 2d Sale of Elizth Goldsmith's Furniture et.
March 5th. Sale of Rt Land's wreck.
March 6th. Sale of Tubby, Norman and Martin's effects—Wrentham.
March 8 Sale of Admiralty Droits.
March 21 National Fast or Thanksgiving day.
March 22 Sale of Mrs Elizth Chapman's Furnr.
March 28 Sale of Wm Bunn's Furniture—Wrentham
1855 Apr 2d Sale of Jas Farrow's Effects—Wrentham.
Apr 3d Newman, Ventriloquist here.
Apr 6 Good Friday—To Lowestoft and Belton with Mr Ed. Gray of Reydon
re the late Mr J. Ives estate et.
Apr 5 Ed Fisher's sale ready made clothes et
Apr 7 To Yoxford valuing Meadow Land for Mrs Nash et.
Same day Mr Saml Gayfer of Reydon, dies—agd 45.
19th Mr John Snell of Wangford died agd 70.
23d [   ] Cleaveland succeeds Hugh Lawrence (vd Mar 1/55) to the
"Bell" Inn Walberswick.
26th I sold Furnr et of H. Lawrence and Wm Haken
30th I sold Furnr et of Wm Barnaby of Henstead
(Quay cts not Sell)

79

May 4 P.Palmer and Self—sells Fish (lt. Button) to William Major
. . . . £45 recd £10
1855 May 15th Sale of Furniture et. of Mr. Jo. Mealing—Wrentham—who is gone to reside in London.
21st To Wangford—Met Mr Bradbeer re—Rolf's rent for Attoe of Litcham
23d—Mrs Jermyn's Land & Cottage, Reydon, put to Auction by Mr. Robinson of Hadleigh at the Old Swan—Not Sold.
26th Mr Jas Woodard, Landlord of the "Pilot Boat" Pub, Ho, removes with his License to the Butcher's Shop in the Market place.
Commenced takg down July.
29th I—Mr. P.Palmer,D.Fulcher,Geo.Gayfer and several others dined at Mr Hugh Lawrence's—Geo Gayfer's b.d.
June 4th Witness'd Mrs Eeeles, Mr. & Mrs Smith—signature to deed of Assignment of Life interest.
7th Sale of Furniture et of Mr Wm Smith (son in law of Mrs Eeles—at Southwold.
1855 June 12th. Died at Yoxford Sir Chas. Blois, Bt 62.
June 14th Sold Crops of Grass et upon Marsh Walls et £15.
June 20th Geo: Child order'd by J P to pay 2s/– a wk—for a Child—its mother's name [   ] of [   ]
June 21 Water Cart—new, commd
June 28 Sale of Mr Jo Soans' effects.
June 30 Ed. Palmer, convicted in a penalty of £1 15s 0d—and his Boat seized by H.M.C. for bringing a bottle brandy on Shore from the "Louisa Elizabeth" Barber.
July 9 Apprenticed Wm Chapman to Hy Ladd, Boat builder for 7 yrs fro. 21 May last.
Aug 20th Met Sir Jo Walsham—Poor Law Commis with all the Overseers & Surveyors of the Union re- poor rates et.
Cutting Halesworth Brewery owned by Thomas Cracknell, who is retiring, to be sold by auction with all its properties at the Three Tuns, Halesworth on June 13. Includes the "Crown" and the "Fishing Buss" at Southwold. B. Rix the auctioneer.
Cutting Maggs to auction two messuages and a cottage in Southwold, late the property of William Chapman, deceased, at the Old Swan on June 21. (Purchased by Wm Woodyard of Bramfield for Betsy Packe of SoWold for £118) One of the messuages has been for 25 years the "Horse Shoe" beer house and both are in the High Street.
Cutting The Southwold Brewery to be auctioned by G.P.Freeman at the Griffin Inn, Yoxford on June 21. The property of G.E.Gayfer. The malting etc were immediately adjacent to the High Street.
1855 July 17th.Halesworth Times first published—
I have No 3—4—5—6 & 7   J.M.
Cutting Maggs to auction messuage in the High Street belonging to John

Flatt, a bankrupt on August 2 at the Old Swan. Occupied by
Frederick Mayhew, cabinet maker
(Purchased by Mr P. Palmer £160)
Notice relating to duties at Southwold Harbour. September 8
Handbill announcing the fall of Sebastopol the news received by Electric
Telegraph at the office of the Yarmouth Free Press.
September 10 1855.
1855 Aug 23d Sale of Furniture et of Geo. Bond who has left the Town.
1855 Aug 26 Mr Geo. Mayhew to London.   returned [   ]
This Month *Infant School*—Enlarged—Rev J. Rustat Crowfoot, Minister
Augt 29 Sale of Jas Woodard's Boats Fish Ho & Fish Gear Sep 1st
Fish House bought by Edwd Palmer—£40.
Same day A Lillingston to House upon Gun Hill—built by Mr. D.
Fulcher—Mr L had been residing in Mr Ewen's House, High Street—the
time of its building
Aug 30 Regatta
Gayfer T. W. agd 17 (Son of Mr S Gayfer dec. vd Apr 7 inst) died of Fever on
the 15th inst. in the Bospherous—on board the "Midlothian"—Rt Phillips.
Sepr 6th Sold Life Boat Ho to F.W.Ellis for £62 together with its site.
Same Day Taylor. Solor comes to reside here. In partnership with
J.R.Gooding. Solor.
(Oct 16 1855 J.R.Gooding Clk to Commissioners of SoWold Haven)
Sworn Coalmetres discontinued
1855 Sep 26th John Wells apprenticed to B.H.Carter for 6 yrs from 6th July
1855.
Sep 27th Mrs Raven's sale at Wrentham—
Sep 27th Married Jo. Johnson Goff to Ellen daugr of J. Johnson Goff of
Wrentham—dec.
Sep 27 "Neptune" Fishg Boat & the "Julia" Fishg Boat launched, built by
Henry Ladd in the Fish office yard.
Sep 29 Died at Lowestoft Mr Thos Balls—Auctioneer et
Oct 4 Geo: Lanham's Sale.
. . . . Jas. Tooke's Sale, Harleston
. .   9 Jo Vineyard's Sale Frostenden
. . 10 Jo Williams & others Sale.
        Lot 1 Geo Rawlinson   £152 10
        Lot 2 W.W. Bardwell   37
        Lot 3 —Same—   48
                                 _____
                                237 10
List of lectures to be given at Southwold School to establish an Adult School
and Evening Reading-Room. October–December 1855
Cutting Notice by Commissioners of Southwold Harbour dated October 10
1855 announcing meeting to elect a successor to Jonathan Gooding
their retiring Clerk.
(Mr. J.R.Gooding elected Clerk in the room of his Father)

Cutting Freehold investments upon Bartholomew Green to be auctioned by Howlett and Lenny at the "Crown" on October 13 by orders of the executors of James Andrews. House occupied by George Rawlinson and Richard Skinner, two cottages occupied by John Took and Thomas Wright.

1855 Oct 15th "Venus" prepared Bill of Sale from Geo Butcher of Wenhaston to William Ayliffe, 2 Russell St, Blackwall, London for £70. Sailed following day.

Cutting Fearful gale on the South East Coast. November 3 1855. "At Southwold, a short distance lower down the coast, several vessels met a similar fate. While the gale was at its height, the Hylton Castle and the Emma, both of Sunderland; the Ocean and the Cape Horn, of Whitby; and the Nelson of South Shields, were driven ashore but the crews were saved."

1855 Novr Mr. J.R.Gooding (See May 20 1852) leaves the Bank—succeeded by Mr George Adamson—who left 2d Sep 1856. went to Saxmundham Succeeded by Mr Roberts.

Cutting Peremptory sale of stock belonging to Daniel Fulcher, carpenter and builder. By auction on November 6 1855 at Southwold to be conducted by Mr Baker.

Notice List of Members of the Corporation, 1855 – 6
1855 November 3d Gale.
Nov 7th Sold by Auction the Hull and all her Stores of the Barque "Cape Horn" of Whitby— Wake—173 tons reg
. .   . .   The Brig "Nelson" South Shields [   ] sold by Private Contract as she now lies.
Nov 9th Sold by Auction, the brig "Ocean" of Whitby and all her stores.
Nov 13th At Misner, Dunwich, Sold by Auction the brig "Pilgrim" and all her Stores—of Sunderland—163 tons regist—Geo Howe, Masr
Nov. 14th at Southwold, Sold by Auction the Brig "Emma" of Sunderland and all her Stores—Glen, Masr 232 tons reg. purchased by Mr. J.J.Goff for getting off—but became a Wreck.
Same day the Brig "Hylton Castle" of Sunderland also all her Stores—215 Tons reg.
28th & 29th Sold the Wreck of the Barque "Cape Horn" and Brigs "Ocean" and "Nelson"
Dec 6 Sold part of the Stores, Copper, Iron et from the "Cape Horn" Ocean & "Nelson".

82

.. 19 & 20 Sold the Wreck of the "Nelson"
.. 21 & 22 Sold at Misner, Dunwich the Wreck, Copper, Iron et of the brig "Pilgrim" for Mr Geo Dix
1856 January 16 & 17 Sold Wreck of "Hylton Castle" for E.Child
.. .. 24 & 25 Sold by Mr Goff wk of "Emma" for his son J.J.Goff

Plan showing position of ships wrecked off Southwold on November 3 1855

1855 Oct 20th Mr Dnl Fulcher assigns for benefit of Crs: to Farrow of Bungay and Jellicoe—Southwold.

1856 Jany 29th, Sent to Ipswich Gaol
.. Feb 6th   Bailed Out.
.. Mar 14th Passed Co Court : Ipswich.
   June 25 All his Houses put to Sale—many Sold
   July 10 Forty five pound Gas Shares put to Sale

Oct 22d To Bramfield. Arthur Cupper's—took A/ct of Sale. Sold 29th following.

Oct 29 School for Adults—opened here by Revd J.R.Crowfoot & others

Nov 2 Sale of the late S. Gayfer's stock in Trade et at Southwold—and on the 3d at Walberswick

Novr 3d Gale

Five Vessels on Shore & wkd. Crews Saved. see draft.

Novr 18th Rt Arnup's   sale. Wrentham
     22d White Jas. Watchmaker, leaves SoWold

Cutting 20th Inst. at Halesworth, aged 74 years, Mr Thomas Tippell, for 50 years bookseller and printer in the above place.

1855 Nov 22d "Old Swan" put to Auction—No offer—

Nov 24 At Wenhaston—Sale of Mr Jas Peek. Furniture Stock in Trade et Wheelwright

Nov 30 Mr Geo:Butcher (Wenhaston) to Ipswich Gaol for Smuggling.

Dec 6th Heavy fall of Snow. About 10 A.M. John Rogers Jnr. Wm Waters and his Son—were off in their boat—when by some cause came in contact with a Brig in the bay—and immediately Sunk—every effort was made by the Crew of the Brig to save them—but they went down *to rise no more* before they could get to their assistance

Rogers has left a Wife and 6 children and Waters the same

Dec 21.22 Sold Wk of "Pilgrim" Dunwich

30th Life Boat "Harriett" brot home. Built at Yarmo by Mr Beecham.

vd March 26/56

Cutting Maggs to auction stores from the "Cape Horn", "Ocean" of Whitby and the "Nelson" of South Shields at Southwold on December 6 1855.

Cutting Sudden death at Lowestoft of John Burgess, shoemaker, formerly of

83

Southwold. He had been an inmate of Melton Asylum a few years previously. January 15 1856.

Cutting New lifeboat tried out at Southwold. Built by Beeching (not Beecham as above) Miss Harriett Sheriffe entertained the crew at the Swan and held a party at Centre-Cliff House. (January 25 1856)

1856 Feby. 1st. Married at [   ]

[   ] Rabbett Esq. to Louisa eldest daughter of the late Jos.Shrimpton—Southwold
(Augt 6 1856 Mrs R. here returned 20th
Dec 18 1856 of a Son

Cutting Henry White appointed relieving office for the Halesworth District in succession to Mr Anthony Fisher. (Feb 23 1856)

Order for Insolvent Debtors Hearing at the Shire Hall, Ipswich, upon Daniel Fulcher. February 2 1856
Directed to Mrs Sophia Gayfer, executrix for Samuel Gayfer of Southwold and Reydon. Hearing March 14.

1856

Jany 16.17 Sale of Wk.*Hylton Castle* for E. Child

Jany 11 Sale of Bows of "Nelson" for Joseph Blowers & C.Fisk

Jany 19 Sale of Adam Fisk's Effects. Wrentham.

Jany 30th (vd May 1846) "Reliance" company serves a Writ upon *"Swiftsure"* for costs of repairs for damage.

Feb 2d John Ling—committed to Beccles Gaol for Stealing a pair of Oars fro the "Swiftsure"—Bailed—March 10th Tried and sentenced to 3 days imprisonment.

Feby 18th Sold Stores of "Glenmoriston" wkd on the 6th upon the Bar crew savd

. . 20 Sold Wreck of "Glenmoriston"—

Cutting Marriage at Southwold of S.C.Wayth, master of H.M.S. Sparrowhawk to Eliza Emily only child of the late George Frederick Souper of the Inner Temple, barrister, formerly of Trinidad. February 28 1856.

Mar 6. Sold Deals at Southwold for Mr. J.Chapman of Gt Yarmouth.

March 19th Henry (agd 22) Son of Mr Hy Botham of this Place, Tailor, accidentally drowned fro falling overboard fro the "Harlequin" Steamer on his passage fro London to Southwold—where he was coming on a Visit to his Parents.

1856 Mar 19th & 20th Harbor block'd up. 20th The London stage coach "Blue" Rous, attempted to drive across on his way to Ipswich—prevented by a small channel at the South or back of the S. Pier

20 & 21 dug out 21 & 22 Two "Billy Boys" and "Vigilant" Geo Magub came in—9 ft Water.

20th Good Friday. The "Active" Wm Taylor—fro London with Goods delivd by Boats on to the Beach Nr. Gun Hill.

29th Manby Revd E.F. here, took Instructions for Surveying Lot 11 and to sell it for £180. see particulars.

2d April. To Halesworth with Elizth widow of Rd Bye and her 3 children. Mary Ann 12, Emily Clara 8, Caroline 6. who were residing here to prove their settlement. May 5th removed them under Order of Removal to Workhouse Wickham Market belonging to the Parish of Chillesford, Plomesgate Union. Where they belong.

Notice   Order of proceedings at the laying of the foundation stone of Southwold Infant School by the Earl of Stradbroke. March 25th 1856.

Programme   for the presentation of a portrait of the Provincial Grand Master at Southwold. March 26 1856.

1856 March 20th Surveyed Harbor. Beach up River viz from Pier end—300 ft. across or width from Pier to pier 115 ft. depth of beach 8 feet— giving 10,222 Tons of Beach and Soil—at 1 ton per yd ob 3½ ft Beach or Soil above Zero level—being 5 ft. below Zero level giving a depth of 8½ ft. Jas Fisk Senr

1856 June 5.6.& 7 a great number employed in digging out inside of Harbor since be excavating with ditches and crafts

Middle Cliff. Southwold. Suffolk

Cutting "This pretty little town enlivened" during the past week by the laying of the foundation stone of the new infant schoolroom; the marriage of the daughter of Captain F.W.Ellis R.N. to the nephew of Agnes Strickland; and the presentation of his portrait to Sir E.S.Gooch M.P., Provincial Grand Master of Suffolk. (March 25 1856.)

Cutting Robert Alexander Strickland, eldest son of Major Strickland of Raydon (sic) Hall and Lakefield, Douro, Canada West, married to Caroline Charlotte, eldest daughter of Captain Ellis and niece of Major-General Ellis, C.B. at Southwold on March 25, 1856.

Cutting Presentation of portrait to the Provincial Grand Master in the National School Room, Southwold. March 26 1856.

Cutting Jonathan Robert Gooding of Southwold, solicitor, married to Elizabeth, fourth daughter of the late Snelling Drosier Roper of Colby, Norfolk. At Colby on April 3 1856.

(Mrs Gooding Born Feb. 18/34 Jany 17/62 of a Son Dec 28 1856 of a Son.May 4/58 of a Son)

April 14 Sale of Mr Geo Cobbs Furniture et at Wenhaston.

April 9 Repository Sale at "Old Swan", including Wd Jo. Bye's effects—decd.

April 16 Sale of part of Wreck Brig "Odin" (George Gardner) 180 TonsWkd on Barnard. Sold at Easton & Covehithe—

(May 1 1856 W.Gooch Sale Wangford)

May 7th *Cobbold's House* in the occupation of Robt Winter on beach partly washed down—High Tide—Gale N.E. House totally unoccupied—Beach so washed away—No room for Boats Houses & Fish houses in great danger. No person living ever saw the Beach in the state it now is. 18th The bottom of a Well discovered at the foot New York Cliff.

Aug 17 18 & 19 High Tides Cobbold's Ho washg down by degrees Herringtons and Simpsons Houses in danger. Cliff much gone opposite Miss Sheriffes

May 8th Sale of Wreck "Odin" at Easton

May 10th Sale of Geo Else's effects Walberswick

May 12 Sale of Wreck—Wm IV at Walswk. Edmund Stanley—Masr.

May 13 Greens let (Alexander) 7 Li 15 s - d 16 Walls (Gray) 16 10 0

May 16 Sale of Wm Ruthen's effects. Wangford.

May 15 Sale of Stores fro brig "Odin".

May 22 To "Bear" Inn—Reydon—J.Gillings and settled for Sales of "Odin"

May 29 Peace—celebrations of. about 620 children and 40 poor Widows treated with a dinner of Plumb pudding and Beef upon the Common.

1856 June 5th Launched "Half & Half Fishg Boat "Norwich"—built by Mr Henry Ladd.

June 8—News arrived of Francis Geo. Son of Francis Wayth being drowned in attempting to get on Board the "Curlew" Ed Archer Wayth at [   ] up the Miderteraen—May 28th—ult.

86

June 19.Henry Woodrow's Sale—Wrentham—

June 27 Fulcher's House Purchasd by Thos Reeve Li 400

July 24 Body of a Man unknown brought on Shore and Interred.

July 25 Mary Hall's sale, Frostenden

Aug 6 Rd Haken to Mary Ann Lincoln

Aug 28 Sold A Johnson's and J.J.Goff's Pleasure Boats. Hy Wrights Nets &
Boat for F.W.Ellis.

Aug 28 Saml Balls breaks his Leg at the "Red Lion" Inn.

Aug 28 Elected Collector of Rates for the Surveyor of Highways—

30th Mar 1857 appointed deputy Surveyor of Roads.

Sep 15   Court. Watchmaker came to reside here.

Sep 25 Philip Catchpoles sale Sotherton.

Sep 26 Wm Lane's Sale, Frostenden

Sep 30 Jonthn Button to Ipswich Gaol. dischargd Oct 24/56

Notice of a vestry to be held on August 28 1856 to appoint a Collector of
Highway Rates. (Jas:Maggs appointed Collector)

> *On reverse* Sep 4th 1856 Sold the residence of the late Mrs
> Thompson in Park lane to Mr. J.R.Gooding for
> 350 li. for Jane Strickland, Reydon

Cutting Public Meeting of the inhabitants of Southwold at the Town Hall on
June 30 1856 to protest against the "present state of the harbour".

Cutting Another report of the same meeting. July 5 1856

> 1856 July 30 The Inhabitants Memorialize to the
> Board of Trade for a loan to lengthen the North
> Pier and Improve the Harbor—reply—Have no
> power in advancing money for such purpose.

Cutting Maggs to auction the household furniture of the late Mrs Betsy
Thompson of Park Lane on October 8 1856.

(Purchased by Jane Strickland 350 £)

Cutting Meeting held at the Town Hall on October 3 1856 to promote a
branch of the East Suffolk railway line from Halesworth to Southwold.

Cutting Jonathan Button, master mariner, of High Street, an insolvent
debtor now held in the Debtors Ward at the County Gaol at Ipswich.
His hearing to be held at the Shire Hall on October 24 1856.

Leaflet   "C.M.Marsden, Miller, Corn and Coal Merchant,
Southwold, respectfully informs the Inhabitants of
Southwold that he has entered upon the Mills lately
in the occupation of Mr Goff and earnestly and
respectfully solicits their patronage, support and
recommendation. October 29 1856."

Cutting Death announced of Sir Edward Sherlock Gooch, M.P. of Benacre
Hall, on November 9 1856.   Long obituary

Cutting Case in Halesworth County Court. Captain Ellis fails to get more
than 5s. of the £7 he claimed from Mr Goff for the use of a "crab"

when the brig "Emma" of Sunderland was stranded on November 3 1855.

Cutting Patrick Nolan, Inland Revenue Officer, attacked by two "ruffians" just outside Southwold on November 15 when he was returning home to Halesworth.

Notice   List of Members of the Corporation 1856–7

1856 Oct 1st Half & Half Fishing Boat "Charley" launched—built by H. Ladd.

Oct 7 Mrs Aldis' Sale—Wrentham

Oct 8 Mrs Betsy Thompson's Sale at Southwold for John Cole Downing of Earl Soham.

Oct 9 John Johnson Goff's Sale at Southwold vd Nov 11 1851. Goes to the Wrentham Mills—Oct 11/56. Succeeded to the Southwold Mills by Charles Marmaduke Marsden 11th Octob 1856.

Oct 10th Samuel Baldry's Sale—Henstead.

Oct 15 I sold Yawl "Swiftsure" to Geo.E. Gayfer—£9. Stores £9.10.

Oct 26 Mr Jellicoe's Son leaves home for Newport—to go to Sea.

Nov 9th   Sir Edwd Sherlock Gooch Bt. dies at Benacre Hall.

. . 22   Revd— Patch commenc'd Curacy.

(Leaves Nov 20 1858. . . . .)

. . 27   Ed Brown Snr   Sale of Furniture

Dec 10   Wm Bartley's sale—Park Farm, Wrentham.

. . 11   Repository Sale—Southwold.

. . 28   Mr Garnham Fisher of Heveningham died.

1857 January 3d Sold Je Jarvis' Nets Lines et.

Cutting Occultation of Jupiter by the Moon (January 2)

(1857 Witness'd it   J.Maggs)

4th Alfred Lillingston Esq   Banns of Marriage—published in this Church.

22d Married to Miss Mason at Edinburgh.

January 7 Sold a Bottom of a Vessel—at Covehithe £30.   15th Sold the Wreck.

. .   7th Bark "Cheverell" 318 Tons. Reg   Thos Caygill Masr of Whitby went ashore or rather aground off Misner—Dunwich—became a Wreck—Crew saved—14th I sold her and Stores—Hull sold for £48—Purchas'd by Joshua Chard & Company—12th I sold part of Wreck—at Dunwich. 18th To Dunwich—Settled Sale March 25th the Bottom of "Cheverell" ashore S of Mr Jo Robinson's House and N of Misner sluice   see Ap 16/57

Ap 23/57 To Dunwich Settled sh   £3 6s 6d

Jany 7th Elizabeth, daughter of Mr James Woodard—of a lb Son by her own Brother, child Died on the 10th inst—12th inst the Son leaves Home. His name is James.

Cutting Maggs to auction hull of the Barque "Cheverell", 318 tons, of Whitby at Dunwich on January 14, 1857. Stranded at Misner.

Cutting Maggs to auction wreck on the beach at Covehithe, January 15 1857.

1857 Feby 2d Beccles Monthly Advertiser first
Published by Read Crisp. Beccles. afterwards
weekly. I have Copy No. 1.

Cutting Jasper Wright, broker of Peasenhall, brings a case in Halesworth
County Court against Joshua Chard of Thorpe and James Maggs,
auctioneer. March 19 1857. Compensation sought for loss of time
and expenses incurred in attending a sale of wreckage at Dunwich on
February 12, when part of the goods had previously been sold by
private contract. The wreckage was from the "Cheverell". The judge
found for the defendants, wishing the public "to understand dis-
tinctly that there was not the slightest imputation upon Mr Maggs as
auctioneer at the sale"   March 19.

Cutting Maggs to auction household furniture belonging to Mrs Mary Goff of
Southwold who is "changing her residence". To be held on April 6.

Cutting Maggs to auction household furniture and boarded workshop at
Wrentham belonging to J.Lambert on April 7 1857.

Cutting "Extraordinary Murder in London". Mr James Scott of the
Caledonian Road, Islington, stabbed to death by Robert Robinson
Tripp, aged about 63, his lodger.   (April 7 1857. see June 18)

1857 Jany 13th   Revd [   ] Huntsman to [   ] daughter of the
late Charles Lillingston Esqr

Jany 22 Alf Lillingston to [   ] Mason—Son born Oct 30/57.

31st To Reydon valued personal Estate of the late Philip Moss.

The "Lamb" of Portsmouth—Marchant—Masr on Shore at Dunwich, got
off by Joshua Chard & Men—taken into Lowestoft. £40—

Feby 9th The Brig "Pensher" Bellass Masr of Sunderland—struck on
Sizewell Bank, leaky, taken to Lowestoft by the Southwold Life Boat—
Reward £200 . Life Boat took £40.

Feb   19.Mr J. Barnarby's Sale. Wrentham

. .   25 Mr J.G. Cooper called re G.Fisher's Houses.

March 3 Mr Earl's Sale at Benacre.

. .   6 Enter'd with execution or Bill of Sale upon Mr Fulcher's Furniture
—by authority from Messrs Lillingston, Palmer et.

March 10th Earl Sherriff's Officer here—with execution upon the effects of
Mr Disney—baker—matter settled on the 13th.

March 10th Valuation of Personal estate of Mr Robert Drewell.

    18th Sale of Mr D Fulcher's Furniture,Plate,Linen et.

    20th Sold Sundries.

1857 March 19/57   Wright v Chard and Maggs

March 23 "Norfolk" half & half.built by Henry Ladd—launched.

25th To Dunwich wt Mr Gooding. The Sea much encroached there—from
East end of Church to edge of Cliff 45ft   several feet of Churchyard gone—
Human bones continually falling out of the Graves into the Sea—at the
bottom of the Cliff at low Water is the bottom of a Well about 3 or 4 ft
deep—the top of it was on the top of the Cliff and was at the least 50 ft

deep—Mr Dix's summer House which stood at least 100 yards from the edge of the Cliff is now only 7 yards.

March 26 Mr.Henry Martin of Newmarket to Jane daughter of the late Mr John Magub of this place.

March 27 To Westleton & Theberton wt Mr P. Palmer in re Rous' property.
                                    Wright pd expences 4.8.0

March 31st Died—Mr Odell—"Saracen's Head" Inn agd 53—1867 Jany 7th Mrs Odell, Died

1857 Apr 2d Mr Esau Spall's sale at Sotherton "Cross Bow"—

Apr 3 Mr Geo Gray's sale at Hinton

Apr 4 Mrs Lucy Warne's Sale of Furnr et.

Apr 6 Mrs Mary Goff's sale of Furniture et

Apr 7 Repository Sale at Wrentham.

Apr 13 Thomas Naunton elected Verger in the room of Jas Wigg resigned

Apr 14 To Saxmundham—Cloth Sale wt Mr Frd Wade Denny.

Apr 18 Sale of Wm B Miller's Furnr under distress for rent.

April 7.Robert Robinson Tripp

May 6 Mr C.Fisher Clk to Mr Baas, Solor Halesworth. leaves—

1857 May 10 Walter Cable to Eliza third daughter of Mr. Rt. Allen.

                    May Pilot Boat "Nil Desperandum". *Never Despair*
                    built   W Warnes T.P. 1st put off to a Steamer by
                    Her

May 14 Times News ppr announces the death of Thomas Rawlingson of the "Excellent" of [   ] June 1856 at Shanghae—China— (Thos son of Geo Rawlingson of this place) Sarah his Wife died May 26/75.51.

May 16th Mrs Mercer comes to "Crown" Hotel—commenced business 20th inst.

                    1861 June 6 Married to Geo Vincent.

May 19th "Angel" Inn—Wm Atmer Halesworth—Sold by Auction by Messrs Howlett & Lenny—purchas'd by G.P.Freeman for £2180—Oct 11th Mr Atmer leaves succeeded by Mr Newman lt. of Lowestoft.

May 28 John Fryett apprenticed to Mark Carter for Yrs.

June 4 Sold Mr Disney's effects at Bake offe et—succeeded by Youngs

June 18th Robert Roberson Tripp was chargd with the wilful murder of Jas: Scott at Pentonville on the 17th of April last—Verdict manslaughter—sentenced to 8 yrs penal servitude.

Cutting Auctions by Maggs wreck of the "Cheverell" on Dunwich Beach
                    on April 16.
                    household furniture of Esau Spall at the "Cross
                    Bow" inn, Sotherton, April 2.
                    household furniture of George Gray at Hinton,
                    near Blythburgh, April 3.

Cutting Suicide of Samuel Hengeston Bloom, aged 52, formerly of Reydon.
                    Bloom had been an agent for Harvey & Hudson's bank at Fram-

lingham but for the last sixteen months he had been unemployed and had lived with his family in Ipswich at Mr Green's, Berners Street. He hanged himself on May 5 from a tree in Dale Hall Lane after failing to find work. An Inquest at the "Greyhound" St. Margaret's returned a verdict of temporary derangement.

Cutting William Upton is to auction a brick and tile cottage in Southwold High Street occupied by William Stammers, on May 7 at the "Old Swan". Also the adjoining cottage called "Croker", occupied by James Wright.

Cutting Mrs Mercer announces that she is taking over the "Crown" Commercial Inn and Family Hotel "decorated and furnished throughout with entire New and Elegant Furniture from the first houses in London".

Trade Card Mrs Mercer "Crown Commercial Inn, Posting House and Family Hotel"

(Mrs Lucy Mercer—commencd May 20/57)

Cutting Marriage of the Earl of Stradbroke of Henham Hall to Augusta, widow of Colonel Bonham and second daughter of the late Sir Christopher Musgrave at St Peter's, Eaton Square. May 26 1857, Fete at Henham Park on the following day.

Cutting Sale of wine belonging to Mrs Bokenham, who is retiring, at her premises, the Old Swan. Auction to be conducted by George P. Freeman on June 18.
On the same day a farm at Walberswick belonging to the late William Borrett to be auctioned by Freeman at the Swan.

Cutting Howlett and Lenny to auction Reydon Grange farm, occupied by John Bicker, at the Swan on July 16.
(Purchased by Mr John Crabtree £3310)
1857 June 25 Sold Mrs Newberry's Furniture & effects.
June 26th Put Schooner "Welcome home" to sale at the"Old Swan"—
June 27 Apprenticed Rd.Pashley to Jo M Marsden—premium £25.
June 29 Apprenticed Thos. Muttett to John Banks.
July 16 Peremptory Sale
July 25 Chas Spurgeon Jnr. leaves home to go to Sea
Augt 3 Died at Blythborough Mr Jo Pattman 76—
Aug 6 Wm Smith to Beccles Gaol(for an Assault upon his Wife) for 6 Months—bailed out Nov 6/57.
Aug 12 Thos Reeve leaves for the Diggings—& W Fox's Nephew for Sea.
September 1st Jas Grayston Esqr. Railway Director—here
Sepr 1st Hudson Anthony Esqr. Banker—Died—at Norwich agd 75
1857 Sep 11th
1857 Sep 3d Sold the late Mr Ed Syer's effects et:
From 4 to 6 A.M.
Sepr 18th Intelligence of the loss of Edwin—Son of Mr T.H.Jellicoe who was

drowned 16th July ult on his passage to Bombay from the "Walcorn Castle" London Cap St Croix.

Sep 26th "Alice" Half & Half Fishg Boat launch'd built by Hy Ladd.

Sep 30 Mr Rt Denny's Sale—Wrentham who quits his Farm

Oct 1 "Ellen" Half & Half Fishg Boat launch'd built by H. Ladd.

Oct 2 Stockdale's Sale Wangford.

Oct 2 C.Spurgeon P.C. to London brought Geo. Denny down refusing to support his Wife and family. paying what the Parish had orderd he was discharg'd—order to pay—5s/– a week in future—

Oct 5 Mr. T.Langley Sale Frostenden

Cutting　Fearful thunderstorm at Southwold. Sepr 3 1857. Norwegian bark northward bound to take in coals was driven ashore. Got off safely due to the exertions of the yawl "Reliance". The master was asked for £150 but he gave £7 more.
(She proceeded to the North.Neilson Masr)

Cutting　Public Demonstration on Blythburgh Heath on September 11 to honour the Earl of Stradbroke and his new Countess. Mayor and Corporation of Southwold present.

Cutting　The High Steward,Mayor,Aldermen and Councillors of Southwold present address to the Earl of Stradbroke at the Swan. September 17.

Cutting　G.P.Freeman to auction corn,coal, chalk,lime at Walberswick at the premises of George Gayfer on September 21.

Cutting　Auction at Walberswick of property of Mr Borrett, deceased, on October 6.

Cutting　Edmund Child, ironfounder, of Southwold married to Mrs Elizabeth Bokenham, "late mine hostess of the Old Swan Hotel", on October 1. The next day a peal of eight bells rung from St. Edmund's on the occasion of their return from Norwich.

1857 Oct 1st "Union" and "Friendship" Half & Half Fishg Boats built by H.Ladd launched.

1857 Oct 19th Thos Thredgale's Sale Westleton. J.R.Gooding Solr—

Oct 20 Jo Beet's Sale Wangford. Under distress for rent

Nov 10th Henry agd 18 Son of Mr John Page—accidentally knock'd of the deck of the Fishg Boat "Norfolk" F.Denny Masr and drowned about 6 Miles off Southwold.

Nov 12 Mary Ann Ladd to Union House—Insane—17th to Melton Asylum and 22d Decr I went to Melton & took her home.

Dec 7th To Westleton in re Mr Manuell's Sale—

Dec 10th Sale of Wm Downing's Jnr Tools et under distress for Rent Mr W.W.Bardwell. Landlord.

1858 Jany 15th A letter recd announcing the death of Mr Dellis.

Jany 20th Sale of Jas Bullard's & Fish's effects—

Cutting　John Bayes of Liverpool married at the Wesleyan Chapel, Wenhaston, to Mary Charlotte, eldest daughter of Charles White of Wenhaston, relieving officer. On Feb 25th 1858.

Jany 21st The "Winds Bride" W. Walker.

Cutting Henry White, relieving officer, of Halesworth, married to Sarah, youngest daughter of John Dunnett of Cratfield, farmer at Cratfield. (March 5 1858.)

Jany 31 Wm Sutton came home. He left again Feb 15th inst

Feb 4th Sale of Fishg Boats. Walswk

Feb 15th Sale of Mr. W.H.Neale's Furr he leaves to reside at Walton on the Naze.

Feb 18th Sale of Mr W Sutton Snr Furniture et. Mr.S.died 21 Jany 1858.

Mar 1. Harbor blocked—Feb.27–28 foot passengers & Carts to and fro open'd on the 10th, cost upwards of £60.

Mar 1st Heavy fall of Snow—persons employ'd digging out the Roads. Post in for 3 days 4 P.M. usual time 7 A.M.

Mar 8 Between 1 and 2 A.M. we were visited with a dreadful Hurricane much damage to the Shipping in many places—little damage here.

Cutting Awful Catastrophe at Southwold. George Ellis, only son of Captain Ellis R.N. of Southwold, John Henry Ord, only child of John Thomas Ord Esq., of Fornham House, Bury St Edmunds and the Reverend Robert Hodges, assistant curate of Wangford, drowned when the lifeboat capsized at Southwold on February 27 1858 during a practice run. They had joined the crew of fifteen as passengers but refused the lifebelts that were offered to them. The boat was launched about noon, the wind being easterly but the sea was not heavy. The shoal was crossed and the inner tideway reached when the sails and masts were lowered and the crew performed the routine exercises. In returning the boat was caught by the heavy sea and crossing the shoal about 100 fathoms from the shore with foresail and mizen set, mizen sheet aft, her keel struck the ground and she capsized. The yawl "Reliance" was launched and witnessed by hundreds on the shore, many of them relatives, ten of the crew were brought to shore. The remainder, although exhausted, also managed to reach safety. Ord, aged 17, was dead when picked up by the yawl, though he was taken to the house of Mr Crowfoot, the vicar of Southwold, whose pupil he was, where resuscitation was tried for hours, though in vain. George Ellis was washed ashore just below Gun Hill, where he was found by his own servant. Aged 18, he was about to join his regiment at Chatham before sailing for India. Mr Hodges was discovered under the upturned lifeboat after the young lady to whom he was engaged had directed the search there. He was 24.

The Inquest was held on the 29th Witnesses:—Benjamin Spence, mariner, William Critten, mariner, John Skelton, mariner, Benjamin Herrington, fisherman (all members of the crew), William Cragie, fisherman and eyewitness, Francis B. Cooper, head coxswain of the lifeboat, Lieutenant William Cress Simmons R.N. (secretary of the local branch of the National Life Boat Institution and an eyewitness), William May, sailor and eyewitness, Charles Sturgeon, Inspector of Police, Henry Lanham, servant to Captain Ellis, Benjamin Crisp.

Coroner listed possible causes as :—defective state of the pads or buoying power, the nature of the ballasting, sailing rather than rowing across the shoal. A verdict of accidental death caused by the inefficiency of the pads and the quality of the ballast was returned.

Notice   List of Members of the Corporation 1857–8

Letter   Janary 28th 1858
                                Brightleasea
Mr Maggs Sir,
    your Being the secertary of the Albion Society, I William Walker Being a member of that Society having to Inform the Society of my Bad misfortune of Losing of the Schoner Winds Bride of London Belonging to Daniel King & Co on a Voyage from Seaton Thence towards London on the East Barrow in the Swin wich the Ship Became a total Rack Losing all My Effects Brought in by the Smack Magnet of the Port Landed Janary 22th 58 Ship Ricked Jan 21st 58.
                    I Remain your unfortunate
                            William Walker
        (Obverse)
    Brightlingsea   Jany 27th 1858
            I hereby Confirm the within statement to be quite correct
                    J.W.Christopher   Tide Surveyor
                                             H.M.Customs
Cutting Letter to the Editor of the "East Suffolk Mercury and Lowestoft Weekly News" in response to a letter to the Editor of the Ipswich Chronicle by "An inhabitant of Southwold".
    Dated April 26th and from F.T.Palmer,builder,of Southwold it defends the crew of the lifeboat from the charge of seeking their own safety first and leaving their passengers to drown, the East Cliff beachmen for not launching their own boat and coming to the rescue (their number was small, the Life Boat itself took 15 of their best hands, some of the others were not present, some were already assisting, the "Reliance was already afloat and coming to the rescue).Nor were the beachmen holding back until they found how much they would be paid for their services[16]
Cutting Letter to the Editor of the Suffolk Chronicle from the same and to the same effect.   Dated April 26.
Cutting Letter to the Editor of the Suffolk Chronicle from "Another inhabitant of Southwold" and dated April 27.

16. F. T. Palmer was presumably Frederick James, a son of Peter Palmer.

The first letter (from "An inhabitant. . . .") was written as the result of a report of the tragedy in the April number of the "Fishermen's Friendly Visitor". The present writer finds it largely borne out by information gained from "several authentic quarters" The Crew of the "Reliance" gave their services very tardily. F.T.Palmer appears to have a decided leaning towards the beachmen who are generally "a very irreligious and ignorant class of men and require the aid of some devoted missionary of the Cross to lead them to a knowledge of the truth. . . " Churches and chapels would be better attended, Sunday fishing would cease, ". . . . . . . a more generous and praiseworthy effort would then be made to assist one another in the hour of extreme peril, and which was so fearfully lacking on the late trying occasion."

Cutting Letter to the Editor of the Ipswich Journal from "Narrator" and dated April 27.

The tragedy "threw the town of Southwold and its neighbourhood into the deepest gloom". The coxswain of the lifeboat was to blame in that "either to save trouble or heedless of consequences, or wholly devoid of nautical skill, ordered out nearly the whole of the water ballast." Did he order those with lifebelts to help those without ? "One young gentleman, a good swimmer, the only surviving son of Capt. F.W.Ellis R.N. made towards one of the crew kept afloat by his lifebelt. This man called out and begged him not to approach or lay hold of him lest both should sink, and the noble youth obeyed rather than imperil the life of another." A yawl and other boats were on the beach and at hand and on the cliffs were beachmen and others who refused to help.

Cutting Letter to the Editor of the Ipswich Journal from Lieutenant W.C. Simmons R.N.,local secretary of the R.N.L.I. Dated May 3. Extra pay had been given to the lifeboat crew on the recommendation of Admiral Thomas Hardy and Captain Ward R.N. who came down to investigate the whole affair.

Cutting Letter to the Editor of the Suffolk Chronicle from T. Henry Jellicoe. Dated May 10.

The writer lives about 100 yards from the cliff. "On the day alluded to, while sitting in my room, I heard several shrieks and one man running past, exclaim "The lifeboat is upset" I *immediately* ran to the cliff and the first sight I saw was the "Reliance" afloat and her gallant crew of noble-hearted fellows using every exertion to reach the men immersed. . . . . . It must also be stated that from the long prevailing north-east winds, the beach where the yawl lay was so bad that she had to be *carried* to get her afloat at all. . . . . . .I have been in many of the sea ports of England. I never saw a more civil and obliging body of seafaring men than those belonging to Southwold."

Cutting To the Editor of the Suffolk Chronicle from "A third inhabitant of Southwold" and dated May 10.
    The general feeling in the town does not support Mr. Palmer (letter of April 26) but rather the views of "Another inhabitant" which "completely answers and overthrows" Palmer.
Cutting George Henry Nutt of Aldeburgh, eldest son of James Nutt, Esq of Worcester, married at Southwold to Amelia Alexandrina, youngest daughter of the late Joseph Shrimpton Esq of Southwold by the Reverend Dr. Sketchley, vicar of Deptford, the uncle of the bride. on March 17 1858.
Cutting Maggs to auction at Wrentham on March 29 the household furniture of Mrs M. Goff, who "declines housekeeping."
Cutting Sale of Geldeston Brewery at the White Lion, Beccles on March 31 by B. Rix. Includes the Lord Nelson, Southwold, bought by J.Cobbold Esq. for £380.
Cutting Death by drowning of Mr. R. Oswald auctioneer and estate agent at Beccles.(May 4 1858.)
Cutting Death at Covehithe of Edmund Cottingham Esq, a "practical farmer" after a few weeks illness.
(May 14 1858 aged 46)
1858 March 26th I went to Rushmere "Tuns" Inn. Valued Elizth Blowers *out* and Saml Turner *into* the said Inn. From thence Mr Chas Fisk (my clerk) to Mr John Warnes, Carlton Colville and spent the afternoon.
Apr 5 Thunder Storm & heavy fall of Hail.
    Mrs Goff's Sale, Wrentham Mar 29/58
    7 Harbor blocked up
    9 Mr Geo Dix's waggons 2 (came here with Barley) went to Dunwich across the Harbor—being 175 yards of dry beach—fro inside to outside—19 Harbor opened.—
    28 Aldrich W. to reside in *Orford*
May 5 To Dunwich & Willingham with Mr J.R.Gooding—*Swain's valuation*
    6 Boniwell's R.R. Sale   26 he leaves "SoWold Arms" public Ho—to reside at Lowestoft.
    20 Mary Church's Sale of Furnr et.
    22 Female Child wash'd on Shore. suppos'd to be Born dead.
    23 Michael (Son of Saml Sayer) of this town—upon ascending the "Blue" Coach (Hartridge proprietor) lost his hold, fell and *killed* upon the spot—at Benhall—where he is Interred.
1858 May 24 Stamped Cheques of 1d came into operation.
May 27 Jos. L. Pashley's Sale
 . . 29 Barber Jo goes to reside in Gloucestershire
June 23d Sale of Deals at Blkshore for Mr Alexander Cumming, Ipswich
July 7th Sale of Phoebe Gilbert's effects Wrentham
July 6 W.C.Simmons appointed Harbor Master pro. temp in the room of F.W.Ellis, dec. Sep. followg elected Harbor Masr.

July 28th Mr Jas Welsh et leaves for New Zealand.
Aug 5th Died at Beccles Leonard Chas. Son of Mr Hy. J Debney agd 10.
Sep 15 Kent Charlotte,Uggeshall, Sale of Furniture et.
Sep 16 Housegoe Ketwick   Frostenden—Sale of Furniture et.
Sep 30th Mr Roberts vd Sep 2/56 leaves this Bank, to the Bank at Stow-
market—Succeeded by Mr Bedwell from Halesworth

Leaflet August 26–27 1858   Fancy bazaar in Southwold Town Hall in
    aid of the Wesleyan chapel and schoolroom

Cutting Maggs to auction household furniture late of Joseph Legatt Pashley
    Esq of Park Lane on May 27.

Cutting Chimney fire at the farmhouse of Mr Lincolne of Cookley on June 5

Cutting Severe storm at Halesworth on June 5. House struck by lightning.
    Jonathan Robert Gooding of Southwold made a Commissioner of
    Oaths.

Cutting Halesworth Petty Sessions, July 21. Overseer of Southwold makes
    application for James Jillings, landlord of the "Bear" at Reydon, to
    maintain his aged father and mother. He is the owner of three
    freehold houses in the borough. Maggs succeeds in obtaining an
    order for 1s 6d a week for the mother and 2s 6d for the father.

Cutting Southwold. August 29. When a Russian steamer "hove in sight
    between four and five o'clock in the evening and signalled for a pilot"
    two boats in straining to reach her got locked together and collided
    with the steamer. One boat carrying 13 men was capsized.
("Cricketer" & "Teazer" Teazer or part of was afterwards picked up at
Sea   Crew saved)

Cutting The Bishop opens new schoolrooms. Lecture by Mr. Blackburn, an
    architect who has recently partly restored the chancel and built the
    schools. (9th Sep 58)

Notice   List of Members of the Corporation 1858–9
1858 Sep 30th   Bicker's Mrs Sale, Blythbro'
.. Oct 5   Rackham Geo Sale, Wrentham
.. .. 6   Barber Jo. Sale, Uggeshall.
.. .. 29   Died—Warwick St. Pemlico—Wife of Rowd Jermyn v.
                Sept 4 1851
.. Dec 3d   Wm May, succeeds Wm Aldrich, Snr Trinity Pilot,
                resigned.
.. Dec 14   Mary Sherwood's Sale. Cove
.. Dec 17   Mr Groome's Sale. Westleton.
.. Dec 21   Died at Bulcamp House John Soans, belonging to this
                Parish
.. Dec 26   John Aldred of Reydon dies—I sold his Effects.

Cutting Maggs to auction shipwreck at south end of Gun Hill, near the High
    Road on December 30.

1859

January 12th	Penny Wm. Excise Officer—Died in Norwich—Buried here.
January 4th	Barber Wm to Betsy Stammers
January 4	Mr Wm Adams of Reydon—died—buried at [ ]
Jany 14	John Aldred's Sale, Reydon D: vd Dec 26/58
March 25	Jo Magub & family leaves to reside in London.

April 1st   Mr T Rundell, Ex Offc removed to Halesworth—succeeded by Mr.George Peacock. v.February 3 1853.

April 11th   Sale of Furniture et of Mrs Esther Mills, Wrentham.

Cutting Maggs to auction household furniture of the late John Aldred at Reydon on January 14

Cutting Maggs to sell shipwreck of the brigantine "Jubilee", 100 tons, at Minsmere Sluice on February 14 1859.

Cutting Maggs to auction household furniture of the late John Lambert at the King's Head, Beer House, Wrentham including brewing plant. on February 23.(Succeeded by Wm Carter Feb 29/68 Followed by Mr Waters)

Cutting Carter, a bricklayer of Southwold, claims 2s 4d from Wright a farmer and innkeeper of Uggeshall. This was because of damage caused to Carter's shop window as the result of a collision between Wright's wagon and three horses and Carter's pony and cart. The judge dismisses case as "trumpery". (Feb XXIII 1859)

Cutting Maggs to auction wreck of the brigantine "Jubilee" of Guernsey, 100 tons, at Minsmere Sluice on March 4.

Cutting John Rockhill, farmer, of Stoven, hangs himself.(March 11/59)

Cutting Maggs to auction modern household furniture of B.Palmer,builder, who has declined housekeeping, opposite the Crown, on March 17.

Cutting James Grinling Cooper Esq of Unthanks Road, Norwich and late of Westwood Lodge, Blythburgh, has died aged 61 at the home of his son-in-law, John Read of Halesworth. April 27

Cutting Obituary of Cooper. A simple eulogy without details.

Cutting Maggs to auction crops of grass belonging to the Corporation upon the Greens and Marsh Walls. April 27. (George Edwds   13 li 2 s 0)

Cutting Report on the East Suffolk Election.(May 7th 1859)

Tenders For the erection of the parsonage house at Stoven.

Robert Carter of Southwold and John Cross of Wangford	£1636 17 0
Benjamin Palmer of Southwold	1278 0 0
Darby and Bull of Bungay	1250 10 0
Redwall of Bury St. Edmunds	1250 0 0
Woodroffe and Son of Beccles	1160 0 0
Artis of Frostenden & Marsden of Wangford	1118 0 0

Carter £518 17s above the lowest.   April 1859.

Cutting Robert Hugman, draper of Halesworth, cuts his throat.(May 29/59)
Train times Ipswich–London   Halesworth–Yarmouth

Cutting Maggs to auction shipwreck of the schooner "Patriot" of Sunderland, 95 tons, at Easton Broad on August 9. Her stores on the beach at Southwold.

Cutting Maggs to auction a messuage occupied by Robert Lowe and — Harvey in Westhall at the Angel Inn, Wangford, on July 21. (£80)

> 1859 July 19 at Asylum, Melton, Michl Barber, lt. of Reydon
> 1859 July 21st at his Son-in-law's Halesworth
> Mr Robt Wilkins Haylett formerly Schoolmaster in this Town.

Cutting Maggs to auction the fishing property belonging to Messers English, including fishing boat "Messenger" of Southwold, on the Quay at Walberswick on August 31.Built at Aldeburgh in 1857. Maggs to auction wreck of the schooner "Patriot" at Easton Bavents on September 1.

Cutting Maggs to auction wreck of the "Patriot" at Easton Bavents on September 1.

Cutting Daniel Forman, late clerk to the Guardians of the Blything Union, has died at Halesworth on September 11, aged 62.
Letter to the Editor of the Halesworth Times from "Veritas" of Southwold on September 3. At a Vestry Meeting held at Southwold on Thursday September 1 held in the parish church and adjourned to the infant school-room the incumbent asked for a church rate to pay for repairs to St. Edmund's, for which £1,000 was needed. He did not have the support of the churchwardens and it was voted down by 12 to 48. A poll was asked for and this 50 to 71 against. If other voting methods had been used as allowed by law it would have been 88 to 132 or 31 to 130 against. The determined effort to enforce a rate has so offended voluntary subscribers that they would do so no longer.

> Samuel Cooper Wayth. 1859 March 28th
> Died from the effects of fatigue and over exertion on the China Station on board the "Princess Charlotte" transport, on his passage home, Samuel Cooper (Son of Mrs Samuel Wayth of this place) Master. R.N. late of H.M. gun boat "Surprise" aged 33.

1859 May 7. Went to Election of M.P. at Hales(worth) Kelly & Ld Henniker elected

July 1 Cooper F.B. hand injured by accidentally being drawn into a Block in the Haven.

July 31 Schooner "Patriot" B.Skipsey of Sunderland, ashore at Easton—leaky—*Crew saved*

Sep 9 Burgess J. Sale at Sotherton

Sep 13 Consecration of the newly enclos'd part of Chyard by Bishop of Nowch,

Cutting Auction at the Old Swan on September 14 of a freehold messuage in two tenements occupied by Maryanne Mayhew in Pinkney's Lane with stable, wood shed etc. approached from entrance in East Street. Worth £11 p.a.

(Purchas'd by Jo Rogers)

Cutting Large Prussian brig wrecked off Misner Haven. The crew and the captain's wife saved by the Southwold lifeboat, except for one man who tried to get ashore by line before they arrived. September 17. The "Lucinde" of Memel,H.Robert Boctheher,to Rochester with sleepers.

(picked up at Dunwich and Interred)

Sep 18   C.M.Marsden to Emily Bye

1859 Sep 17   Palmer W Henry leaves Dr Crowfoot's, Beccles

Sep 9   Burgess   Sale   Sotherton

Oct 10   Wm Eastaughs   Sale   Wangf.

13   Fish Chas Sale of Furnr.

. . 15   Fish C & family leaves to reside in London. He sells to Jo Sawyer his House adjoing my premises.

Oct 28th "Neptune" of Whitby ashore at the Harbor.

Oct 30 "Ann Emma" of Shields on Shore near Life Boat House—and Nov 1 the "Royalist" of So Shields and the "Silva" of Shields , and Hy Ladd's Fishg Boat ashore at Covehithe.

All (excpt the Fishg Boat) became Wrecks. I sold all the Hulls & Stores et. et. except the "Silva"

Nov 1 The "Hero" of Sunderland ashore at Walberswk—Crew saved. She was got off and taken to Lowestoft and repaired.

Cutting George Rackham solicits the votes of the Chairman and Guardians of the Blything Union for the position of Relieving Officer for the Third District.   Halesworth September 26.

(George Rackham elected Relieving Officer October 10th 1859)

John Turner of Wenhaston, similarly solicits the votes of the Guardians.

Cutting Maggs to auction the furniture of George Newbery, deceased, at his home in Reydon on September 29.

Cutting Maggs to auction the household furniture at a house in Park Lane on October 19. (Norton)

Cutting Medals for saving life presented to John Cragie and Benjamin Herrington, coxswains of the Southwold Lifeboat, who came to the assistance of the Prussian vessel "Lucinde" sailing from Memel to London on the night of September 17. The lifeboat crew received Bibles "most splendidly bound". A procession from the boat house to the Town Hall carried a silk flag with the town arms upon it that had been presented some years before by Miss Sheriffe.

Cutting Local Intelligence.(Sept 26 1859.)Charles White of Wenhaston elected Clerk to the Blything Union in place of the late Daniel Forman. He received 31 votes, Read 20.

Blything Union Contracts.Flour—Union House, Mr Goffe of Wrentham 28s per sack. 1st District, Mr Skoulding of Kelsale, 29s. 3rd District,Mr Goffe, 28s, Beef, at per stone, 7s 3d. Mr Chase jun. of Bungay; Mutton, 8s. Best beef suet 7s 6d. Good pork 7s.

Notice List of Members of the Corporation 1859–60
1859

1859 Nov 3d "Anna" of London—Smith Masr—Mr S. Bullard Owner—put to Sale at the Old Swan. *Not Sold*

11th & 12th I sold Wreck of "Lucinde" at Dunwich for Mess Easy, Dix & Co

15th Barber Amos to Everrard

. . Child G.E. to Lawrence

19—Herrington to Smith

Dec 2 "Raven" wk of, Sold at Dunwich—

Dec 17 Sold Broadside of "Anna Emma" for W Bagott.

Decr 18 Heavy fall of Snow & 19–20th

Dec 31 I valued Fishg Boat "Rook" and Fishg Nets for Cross—Leverett £91 *Cross* gives *Leverett* a Bill of Sale for £

1860

Jany 6th 1860 Mr T.B. Bedwell, Bank Agent buys House—premises of Mr Edmd Child.

Jany 26 Sold Wk for John Skelton.

Jany 26 Brig "John & Isabella" of Shields founder'd off here—Crew saved.

Feby 4th Sold—Deals et. at. Walbsk Sluice

Feby 9th (my Birth day) Planted Pear tree in my Garden.

Feb 10 Fishg Smack "Ralph Barnel" of London Malch [   ] Ross Masr wkd at Easton—Crew Saved —22d I sold it again on the 21st March. I sold it in Lots.

Feb 15th Mr Eardley Norton leaves SoWd

Feb 19th Goff & Leishman Millers of Wrentham Assigns for the Benefit of Crs.

Feby 25 a remarkable heavy Gale of Wind—much destruction and loss of life at Sea.

March 9th Samuel Mallett, dro on the North Coast,(Flambo Head) fro the Albion of this place—And Brown, Masr

Mar 15th Sale of Furniture at Wenhaston for Mr. Jas Lay.

March 25th Winter Benj.—broke his leg at the piers—in assistg the going of a Vessel to Sea.

April 24 Sale of Mr W. Moore's Furniture, Wrentham.

Notice To establish a Rifle and Artillery Corps to be drilled at Southwold.

Committee to meet at the Town Hall on February 3. (Issued January 30 1860)

Rules of the Blything Hundred Rifle Corps.

Adopted at a General Meeting at the Corn Hall, Halesworth on January 12)

Notice   Meeting to be held at Southwold Town Hall at 2 p.m. January 2 1859 to establish a Volunteer Artillery or Rifle Corps. (Issued by J.R.Gooding, Town Clerk)

Notice   Dissolving partnership between Robert John Debney and Henry Johnson Debney, grocers, drapers and general shopkeepers. April 23 1860. Firm to continue under the latter.

Cutting   Maggs to auction fir baulks etc at Walberswick Sluice on February 4 1860.

Cutting   Maggs to auction shipwreck near the Lifeboat House on February 16 1860 (Property of John Sawyer)

Cutting   Inquest held at Wangford on February 29 1860 upon the Reverend William French, incumbent of Wangford and vicar of Reydon, aged 51.

Walter Jones Hanner, chemist of Southwold, stated that French came to his shop at five o'clock on the previous Saturday and bought an ounce of Scheele's Prussic acid to remove marking ink from linen. He was warned that it was a deadly poison.

Horatio Girdlestone, surgeon, of Wangford, had been French's doctor for the last three years. In the last four months he had become so depressed as to be at times completely deranged, stating that he had ruined many persons. He did church duty as usual however.and was better on last Saturday morning.

When he did not return home in the evening Girdlestone joined in the search of the neighbourhood, finding the body of the clergyman in Green Lane lying on its face at about 10 p.m. There was a distinct smell of Prussic acid.

The Reverend J.R.Crowfoot of Southwold was visited by French on the Saturday when he seemed a little better. He took a glass of wine and a biscuit at the vicarage at five and then left, refusing an invitation to dinner.

A verdict of suicide while suffering from temporary insanity was returned.

Cutting   Maggs to auction wreck from the oak built vessel "Ralph Barnal" of London near the Lifeboat House on March 21.

Cutting   Maggs to auction household furniture of Mrs Robilliard, who is moving, at Belle Rue Place, Southwold on March 27.

Cutting   Long account of the storm on May 28
(A Tremendous Gale Feby 20th 1860 but not such loss of life & property)

Cutting   Appeal on behalf of wives and children of mariners lost in the late gale,

issued by the mayor of Yarmouth and the vicar of Lowestoft. 192
men lost on May 28 leaving 76 widows and 192 children. Issued on
June 10.

Cutting Case of Henry Watson, the fraudulent rate collector of the parish of
St. Nicholas, Ipswich. Sentenced to 18 months hard labour. August 2
1860.

W.H. means Westminster Hall.

May 23/60 To London—Lodged at Mr Crutchlows
—Coach & Horses, Northumberland Alley Fenchst.

24 To court W.H. saw daughter Sarah 57 Gt. Suff
St P.Ho "Moon Raker" to T. Smiths 183 Oxford
St. thence to Fenchst

25 To Westminster Abbey—Sydenham Palace et.
et.

26 To court W.H. London & Westminster Bridge

Sunday 27 To St. Michael's Church A.M. Aldgate
Ch—P.M. and to White Chapel et. saw scenes of
drunkeness

28 Terrific Gale went to Haywood's Lower E.
Smithfield—called upon Fountain Hartley—thence
to Crooked Billet Tavern—Tower Hill—called
upon Mr Horder 5 John St. Minories—thence to
Lodgings Fench St.

29 I drank 10 A.M. at the Fountains Whitechapel
Church—to Jo Magub's Inn Wards—Horders
Blkwall Greenwich—London Bridge to Fenchst.

30 To Court—Ho of Lords—sat on the Woolsack
saw Geo Child saw Geo Magub in Fenchurch Street
Thos Stall 9 West cottages Wellington Road
Stockwell or the Ho of Lords

May 31 To Court G.Child met me 4 P.M. smoked
cigar in change—To Bank of England 5 P.M. to
Fenchurch St.

June 1 to Court W.H. Notice of Trial coming on
next day. Went to Wild's Globe.

2 To Court W.H.—Case postponed to next term. 3
P.M. took Train and came home

Inn opposite W.H. "Magpie and Horse Shoe"

Writ To James Maggs, George Todd and Thomas Durrant to appear in the
Exchequer Court, Westminster Hall on May 23 in the case between John
Leverett (plaintiff) and Benjamin Masterson Bradbeer and James
Mercer,(defendants).

1860

1860 May 23d I went to London with Mr Thos Durrant & Mr J.R.Gooding, we
were Subpoen'd to Westminster Hall as Witnesses—Leverett v Bradbeer

respectg the illegality or informality of a Bill of Sale—given by Cross of Walberswk to Mr Leverett of a Fishg Boat "Rock" part of Nets et.

We returned 2d June—Trial post-poned to [   ]

May 28th Terrific Gale—

June 22d Jas Jillings from "Bear Inn" Reydon—succeed Saml Baker to the "Southwold Arms" Southwold. Baker took it on the [   ] day of [   ] 18 [   ] after being unoccupied from the [   ] Rd Bonwell was last Tenant prior to Baker.

July 28 To Wickham Market U.Ho with Wd Meadows & 2 Children under an Order of removal fro Eyke

at SoWo

Aug 9 Chas E Stewart, Douro, Canada West, to Charlotte Mary Jane Ellis

1860 Aug 13th Mr Thos Penny leaves after nearly 35 yrs occupancy the "Lord Nelson" Public House and is succeeded by Mr Hugh Lawrence—who has purchas'd it of Mr J. Cobbold—Ipswich—Since which the House has gone under considerable repair & alterations & re-opened on the 8th of Decr 1860—

Cutting G.P.Freeman to auction two tenements and a cottage in East Street, occupied respectively by Henry Simpson, John Palmer junior, and the widow Major,at the Swan on August 11.

(Lot 1 & 2 Henry Simpson 3 W. Baggott)

Cutting August 1860—Southwold. Presentation of £85 to the Reverend J.R.Crowfoot upon his removal to Wangford from Southwold. A Sedan Chair owned by Mrs Martin of the "Lion Inn" while being repaired disclosed the autograph of the Duchess of Manchester and the date 1770.

Cutting Incendiary fire upon premises of Mr Benjamin Pipe of South Cove attended by fire engines from Halesworth, Bulcamp House and Southwold. A tramp is suspected (Septr 1 1860) (5 He was taken and . . . . . .)

Cutting Letter to G.S.Yallop,Academician, Belvidere College, Southwold from "Veritas" and dated September 25, 1860.
Yallop, who had composed a poem on the occasion of the marriage of Miss Ellis to Mr Steward on August 9, was accused of plagiarism from a hymn by a Cambridgeshire clergyman called Berridge in Rippon's Selection of Hymns.

Cutting Proposed Southwold railway to Darsham or Halesworth. November 1860.

Cutting November 1 1860. Fishermen present G.S.Yallop with a handsome church service at his final lecture at the Boat House.
Report upon borough elections

Cutting Southwold—Electric telegraph to be laid between Dunwich and Amsterdam.—three year old Jane Jarvis, left in the care of her 12 year old brother by her fisherman father, dies after drinking from a kettle of boiling water—malicious damage to the Southwold lifeboat.

Cutting Maggs to auction household furniture, two houses divided into nine tenements and a "genteel cottage", all belonging to J.S.Spall at Holton on December 17 1860.

Cutting Maggs to auction the lugger "Andrew" of Lowestoft, lying in Southwold harbour,on March 4.

Cutting Southwold. March 1 1860. Election of auditors and preparation for the fishing season."The last few months have been excessively dull and many have had a hard struggle."

Cutting Maggs to auction fishing property and household furniture belonging to William Doddington (who is removing to a distance) on March 7.

Notice   List of Members of the Corporation 1860–1

1860 Sep 29th Revd S.M.Barkworth Succeeds Revd J.R.Crowfoot to the Incumbency of Southwold Oct 7 Mr Barkworth "read" himself into this Church.

Oct 16 Mr Jas Smith London called upon me with his Uncle Eddy Smith
1861

January 19th My Wife's Brother John Roberts Died at Broome, Norfolk AND July XXIV Sarah his wife.agd 62   1862.

18th Died at Wenhaston.Mr John Youngs.

March 18 Second delivery of Letters—commenced

May 7th Commenced lengthening North Pier.

June 6 Married Mr Geo Vincent to Mrs Lucy Mercer—Crown Hotel May 16 1857

June 8th Geo E. Gayfer—drowned at the Harbor, for particulars—see Death Journal

July 8th—Sale of Mrs Gayfer's Furniture—who left Walberswick. 1st inst.
> June 6 1861. Mr Geo Vincent married to Mrs Lucy Mercer . Mr Vincent continues "Crown" Inn to 11th Octr 1869 Succeeded by Mr Sage—who left 11 Oct/74—then Blunderfield.

Cutting "Balloon Ascent Extraordinary" at a fete at Cremorne. July 24 1861

Cutting Fire on the premises of Elizabeth Palmer, occupied by James Scarlett, farmer, after children had set light to touchwood. Put out by the Southwold fire engine. August 30.

Three cottages close to Mr Wigg's farmstead destroyed at Walberswick after a child of under six had been playing with matches in one of the cottages, occupied by a labourer called Knights. Hiding itself under a bed in an attic it was only discovered just five minutes before the thatched roof fell in. The lives of others were also in peril due to the cheapness of lucifer matches. September 2.

Visiting Cards   Mr William L. Mayhew and Mrs William L Mayhew.

Aug 14/61 Mr Fuller. Drugt takes late Jos. Arthey's shop.

Sep 5. Barber Wm. leaves Southwold to reside in London

Sep 6 Mr Clayton's Sale—Wrentham

. . 17 Mr Alp's Sale—Holton

. . 26 Mr Joshua Gray's Sale—who leaves Southwold

105

Oct 8 Jonathan Peck's Sale—Henstead
(1861 Aug. W.L.Mayhew to Annie Knott   )
1861 Oct 24th To London read particulars (pencil note re Baldry)
Cutting Maggs to auction furniture of George Drake Esq. of Reydon Cottage,
　　　　who is changing residence, on October 3.
　　　　Maggs to auction at Wrentham Mills the household furniture etc.of
　　　　John Johnson Goff, who is changing residence, on October 7
Cutting Funeral at Henstead of the Reverend Thomas Sheriffe, before an
　　　　attendance of 300, including clergy and gentlemen of the neighbour-
　　　　hood.
(Died Oct 10/61 71)
Cutting Maggs to auction the household furniture etc of George Meering,
　　　　who is changing his residence, at the"Five Bells" Inn, South Cove
　　　　on October 10.
Cutting John Penny, of Southwold, butcher, assigns for the benefit of his
　　　　creditors, Frederick Wade Denny, of Southwold, grocer and draper
　　　　and Henry Johnson, of Wrentham, butcher. October 12.
Notice　　　　　　　　　List of Members of the Corporation 1861–2
Trade Card Queen's Arms. Commercial & Family Hotel. 70 Newgate Street.
　　　　London. Joseph Gibson. Side entrance 30 St Martins Le Grand,
　　　　opposite General Post Office.
Cutting Prisoners. Mary Ann Crisp (32) sentenced to 12 months hard labour
　　　　for theft of a black bugle fall from H.M.Sutton, draper, of Botolph
　　　　Street.
(of Southwold. Norwich Oct 15/61)
Cutting William Atmer, junior, commits suicide. Temporary insanity.
(Oct 18/61 ag 26)
Cutting Thames. Captain William Burwood Baldry, master and part owner
　　　　of the "Shantung", now at St Katherine's Dock, charged with the
　　　　wilful murder of John Riley, ordinary seaman, on the high seas.
　　　　Riley had refused to work because of illness and had been repeatedly
　　　　beaten by his captain. He died on September 12. Charge denied, bail
　　　　refused. (Oct. 1861)
Cutting Central Criminal Court. October 24.
　　　　The charge against Baldry has been reduced to manslaughter.
　　　　Evidence given that Riley had actually died of dysentry, that he was
　　　　dirty and lazy. Because the beating given him by Baldry had
　　　　accelerated his death the latter was found guilty and sentenced to
　　　　nine months hard labour.
　　　　　　　　　　Myself (Maggs) Mr J.R.Gooding, Mr H.J.Debney
　　　　　　　　　　and Mr Rt. Warnes at the Trial—to speak to his
　　　　　　　　　　previous good character. Oct 24/61
　　　　　　　　　　To　　　London to Trial of W.B.Baldry.
　　　　　　　　　　　　1861

Oct 23 To "Queen's Arms" 70 Newgate St.
. . 24 To Trial Old Bailey—thence to "Queen's Arms" Hotel
. . 25 To Fenchurch St—"Coach & Horses"—called upon Mr Horder—Jo St. Minories
. . 26 returned Home
Mr Gooding & Mr Debney went with me
(24 I walked quite round St Paul's Church Yard 8 A.M.—the clock struck)

Funeral Card In memory of the Prince Consort. Died December 14 1861.

Cutting Death of James Williams, M.D. from a sudden attack of bronchitis. He had planned to leave Southwold for a tour of the south of Italy. (Jany 1862)
Funeral of Peter Palmer on the 4th. A large congregation. "In all his business transactions he was extremely methodical and exact."

Cutting The Brewery, Southwold. S.H.Fitch is prepared to supply genuine ales in fine condition at 8d, 10d, 12d, 16d and 18d a gallon.
Also Barclay and Perkins' London Porter.
Benjamin Palmer, Estate & House Agent, Contractor, Appraiser and Builder. East Street, Southwold.
Dwelling house with a good Sea View to be sold by Benjamin Palmer, House Agent. (Purchased by John Cragie 152 £ March Jany 1862)

Voting Paper for two Councillors. January 30. (Wm Money & Thos Doy elected)

1861 Decr 18th To Minsmere—Sold Hull of "Content" of Sunderland. 23d Sold Stores.

Decr 28th Died my Old Friend Mr Peter Palmer, Builder.

1862

Jany 9 Died Jas. Williams—M.D.
. . 10 . . Rt. Denny, Wrentham
. . 13 Sale of Jas. Jilling's effects.
. . . . Dr. Blackett Dr. Succeeds Dr. Williams
. . 19 Blackett Revd 1st preached here
. . 20 Sale of Effects of S.Tooke, Wangford.
. . 23 Williams Dr. Valuation
Feby 10 Sale of Wreck "Content", at Minsmere Sluice for Mess s Easey & Dix et.
. . 19 Garden House & Land, Wrentham, Sale of—Purchased by Mr. Cottingham for 200 £ J. Winter & Son Solors. Norwich
. . 22 Mr Catchpole, of Blythborough. Grocer. Died.
1862.Feby 24 Sale of Furniture of Mr Wm Carter, Wrentham. Succeed'd by Mr Waters.
. . Feby—Mr. T.J.B.Bedwell, assessor of taxes, (or rather Collector) in the room of Mr P. Palmer Dec.

107

March 17. F.H.Vertue, elected Surgeon—for SoWo & Walswick in the
room of Dr Williams,

May 16 Mrs Williams left Southwod

Mar 17 Ira Thos, Fuller,to Deborah Lucy, Second daughter of Mr.
F.W.Denny, Draper et.

Mar 21 High Tide & Wind—Washed Ho of Jas Simpson Down also
Reading Room (Ellis) (Materials Sold to Jas Woodard) and Life Boat
Ho (new One Built S of Gun Hill) Also part of Saml. Waters Hos. and
other property much damag'd.

April 25 Sale of Rd.Skinner's Fnr.

May 13 Died Mr. Ed. Wigg of Walberswick—Farmer.

June 4 Gooding Wm.(Uncle to Mr.J.R.Gooding) accidentally killed
upon a Buss—returning from the Derby Races to London.

Cutting Letter to the Editor of the Ipswich Journal from Francis H. Maude
of Trinity Parsonage, Ipswich upon the Act of Uniformity. March 6
1862

Cutting County Court (Jan XXXI /62) Blything Guardians v. W.H.Warton
relating to premises in Sotherton.

Cutting Election of Councilmen at Southwold.
Southwold Lifeboat takes five men and a dog off from a small boat
outside the outward shoal. They had come from the "Princess Alice"
of Ipswich which had sank on the Sizewell Bank. January 28

Cutting Highway accounts examined at Southwold and Alfred Lillingstone
re-elected Surveyor.
A severe storm on March 21–22 1862. The pilots' yawls and fishing
boats removed to the top of the cliff. Damage to lifeboat house,
sailors' reading room, the government boathouse and two fishermen's cottages on the coast.

Cutting G.P.Freeman to auction property belonging to the late Robert
Denny at Frostenden, Wrentham and Southwold. At the latter place
a warehouse, granary and coal bin at Blackshore. On March 14 at the
"Eagle" Inn, Wrentham.
Freeman to auction residences and land at Walberswick at the "Bell"
on March 15.

Cutting The Reverend E.L.Blackman, curate of Walberswick and Blythburgh, brings a case against M.Spalding for a "brawl" in Walberswick Church. Spalding fined £5 on two counts at Halesworth Petty
Sessions. July 30 1862.

Cutting Inquest at Reydon upon William, son of Thomas Watson, mariner of
Lowestoft, and grandson of Susannah Watson of Southwold. The
nine year old boy fell from the cart of John Bedingfield, carrier, of
Southwold on the evening of September 5 as they were approaching
the town. The harness had broken and the child had died from
concussion.

1862 June 9th Whit Monday 1st Pile driven at Breakwater—Sep 15th Last Pile driven—Mr Benj Palmer—Contractor. Cost £. [   ]
June 30 Wrentham ~~Geo~~ Hen Gage's Sale.
July 11 Samuel Strange—Town Crier—gives up the Bell to the Corporation —30th inst He and his Wife leaves Southwold. He had been Town Crier from 1831.
August 7th Chas Naunton—Serjt at Mace (fro 1840 to   ) was elected Town Crier.
July 17 Mrs Jane Hawes' Sale. left 21st.
. . 19 Jacobs' & Butcher's Sale. Wenhaston.
. . 22 Smith Jo Reydon Quay. dies—On 16th Sep I took Valuation of his Personal Estate 188 *li* 0 s.6 d.
Aug 24 Andrew Johnston Esq. of Halesworth dies at [   ] Buried [   ]
Sep 6 I embarked on Board the "Dolphin"—P.C. Geo. Wright for Harwich—8th to Ipswch. and Wherstead Park—Lodged at Morley's— Wellington Inn—Harwich—returned the 10th—
1862 Sep 12th Crisp Wm. to U. House.
. . 25   Wenhaston   Sale of Geo Butcher
Oct 13   Wangford   Sale of J. Bloomfield
. . 18   Walberswick . . . . G. Elmy—for Mr. R. Barnes.
. . 20   Wrentham—Mr Roberts   Sale
. . 21   Died at Yarmouth Mr Rt. Warnes fro Injury recd fro the Ship's Tiller at Sea. Interred here.
24   Wm Phillipoe's Sale
Nov 5 Mr Geo Bokenham—Dies in London
Nov/62
14   Robt. Girling—Henham Sale—
Nov. 17   Wreck of "*Harry King*" at DUNWICH
18   Sale of John Penny—Effects—
19   The Bodies of a Stranger and a—[   ] Crabtree *washed on Shore*.
20th Hawk Screw Steamer (of London)—Iron—came On Shore —North of the Town Sold for £40 to Jas. Jillings & Co.
Decr 20   Sold part of Wreck—arisg from S.S. "Hawk"
Notice   List of Members of the Corporation 1862–3
1862   Beccles Sessions. Oct 13th John Leman Ewen,Esq. Qualified to act as Magistrate.
1863 Jany 5. Edward Louth Blackett M.D. took the Oath of Qualification to act as Magistrate for this Borough.[17]
Cutting Maggs to auction the household furniture of Charles Howard, who is changing his residence, at the "Harp" beer house, Wenhaston .

17. Even though the family came from Ireland, Blackett's second name was Ralph, not Louth.

Then the household furniture of James Underwood of Wenhaston. who is removing to a distant county. October 8 1862

Maggs to auction the household furniture of Samuel Pallant of Southwold, who is declining housekeeping, on October 9.

Cutting Maggs to auction a steam engine, wreck and stores from the screw steamer yacht "Fanny" of Newcastle, 25 tons, built at Glasgow in 1861, John McDonald, master. At Southwold on November 7.

Maggs to auction household furniture of Thomas Rounce at Southwold on November 13.

Cutting Average mortality at Southwold from 1824 to 1861 37.5 p.a. In 1862 it was only 24, nearly half of that for the country as a whole. Over 80—5, over 70—6, over 60—3, over 50—1, over 40—2, over 30—2, over 20—2 and three children. One person living in Southwold over 90, 18 over 80, 96 over 70. (Dec 1862)

Cutting Extraordinary high tides and great damage at Southwold. Everything standing upon the beach swept away—beach houses, fish houses, boat houses, boats. (Dec 21 1862)

Cutting Late gales at Southwold. "Sadly altered is the beach where the picturesque old fishing huts and homes of the fishermen clustered under the Cliff, doubtless fondly remembered by many a one, who has come to this healthy place weak and desponding, and left it strong and full of hope, and who will remember the attention and civility of a "Sam Waters" or the long yarns of a "David Simpson" and their neat cottages on the beach. Never again will the yarn be spun at the old cottage door, nor the pipe of peace be smoked in the hut of"Sam". All this is of the past; now all is wrecked and consumed by that never ceasing, ever unsatisfied wave. Nothing is now left between the sea and the Cliff, and even in many places that has also suffered. Destruction and desolation greet you at every step."

Cutting Maggs to auction part of the wreck of the steamship "Hawke" of London, 800 tons, at Southwold on June 26. 1863

January 15th 1863.

15 Sale of Rob. Marsh's Effects Reydon.

22 . . . . Stephen Baxter's Do Wangford

Feby 23 Jo Bloomfields Sale Holton

Mar 9 Ira T. Fuller's accident preparg Fire Works for P. of Wales' marriage.

. . 12 Sold Coals Blkshore for W.Hearnshaw

. . 18 Rd Lord's Vessel on Fire, Blkshore

. . 23 Alfd Wentworth's—laid corner Brick with 2d piece under it—In Stables—

. . 31 Forder Jonas took an acct of his Furniture, Stock in Trade under an Assignment for Crs.

Apr. 4 Sold them by Auction.

Apr 2   Sold Furniture Messs Adams Crisp & Archer.
. . 14   John Ducker executed at Ipswh for the Murder of P.C. Ebenezer
Tye at Halesworth—25 Nov. last.
      14   Sale of Wm Robinson's Effects at Holton
May 5   To Mr Thos Carne Miller's, Surgo, (Wrentham) taking acct for
Sale under Bill of Sale to Mr H.Johnson
. . 13   Sold by Auction. Furniture & Effects.
1863 May 27 Mr. C. Crisp and his Son Joseph fro Halstead, called.
July 4 To Lowestoft to Mr Seago's—re Cox's Sale—Wrentham
14 Cox's sale of Furniture et. One premises Sold to Mr Cottingham £110.
other Not Sold.
July 29 *Henham Review*

Reading Room & Cottage

Cutting Contract for building a reading room and cottage on the cliff at
      Southwold, the property of Mrs Rayley—B.H.Carter £546 4s
      Robert Carter £565 10s G.Child £599 Mark Carter £625 and John
      Artis (Frostenden) £694 17s. Lowest tender accepted.
Mr B.H.Carter, Builder   Opend June 2 /1864.
Octob 9 John Barber to Union Ho
      14 To Toft Monks with Mr Wincop re Mrs Ethridges property—Sold
to Mr Colman for £120.—

1863
July 8th To Ipswich with daugr Ellen met Mr &
Mrs Pain fro Harwich and Mr & Mrs Durrant at
the "*Sea Horse*" Inn Bank St. near Key Church—
thence to the Suffolk Hotel (Mayhew)—Commercial Road—Slept there that night.
9th Pain, Durrant and his Wife—met Ellen and
Myself—Mr & Mrs D. repaired to St Peter's
Church met Chas Durrant and Ellen and witnessed their Marriage July 9/63
We all dined at the Suffolk—Pains and myself took
Boat to Harwich. Mr & Mrs Durrant rode round
with pony to Harwich I slept at Morley's Harwich.
Chas and Ellen to London until the Sunday
10 I returned fro Harwich to Ipswich and Home.

Cutting Baker of Bungay to auction at Southwold the "Red Lion" public
      house on Gun Hill, for the last fifty years in the occupation of the
      family of James Martin. Also the old established chemist's shop next
      door, late of Joseph Arthy and now occupied by Walter Hanner. Also
      a cottage in the occupation of Christmas Stannard and a modern
      white brick and sash-fronted residence adjoining the Red Lion, with
      a full view of Gun Hill, occupied by Charles Carter who is under
      notice to quit. July 23 1863.
      (Sold L800)

111

Cutting Lowestoft. Fatal accident at sea to Edward Palmer, 23, of the fishing lugger "Union" of Southwold, master Ballantine Brown. Both Palmer and Brown were from Southwold. The "Union" with its crew of six was caught by a sudden squall at half past six on Sunday night as it entered St. Nicholas Gat. Her foremast was broken into three, one piece of which struck Palmer on the head. He never regained consciousness and the boat was raced into Lowestoft to get there at a quarter to two, when a surgeon was summoned. Palmer was the master's brother-in-law. Craggy Ashman Hall, William Aldred, and William Peck, also of the crew, joined Brown in giving evidence at the inquest.

(Nov 8th 1863)

Cutting Eastern Counties Asylum for Idiots and Imbeciles. Algernon Philip Vertue of Southwold elected an inmate. Vertue is nine years of age and his father is a surgeon and has another imbecile child seven years of age.

(Ipswich Jan 21/64)

Cutting Fire at the premises of Mr Kett, miller of Wrentham. November 8 1863.

Notice   List of Members of the Corporation 1863–4

Novr 8th 1863

Cutting Alfred Lillingston elected mayor of Southwold for the twelfth time   (Nov.9/63)

Novr 30th   Mary Anne Howse's Sale   Wrentham

Nov 19 David Parker—Bricklayer—accidentally killed at Stepney

Novr 18 1860 His brother Wm—Mariner—killed accidentally at Lowestoft.
See Death Journal.

Decr 15th & 16th   T.N.Palk's Sale of Earthenware et.

1864

January 21 Algernon Philip—Son of Mr F.H.Vertue—Surgeon—admitted into Eastern Counties Asylum

Jany 7 Died in Union House—Mr Joseph Mills (1871 Sep 27 Died Mary his Wife 82 U.Ho.

Mar 31 Mr Jo Herring. Wangford. Died,

April 27 Married Ed. Ralph Blackett M.D. to Agnes—youngest daugr of Wm Gwyn R.N. Tasburgh Lodge, Norfolk.

1864 Apr 27th Revd Wm Hay Chapman came—licensed perpetual Curate

May 11 He succeed Revd Morley Barkworth   May 1st Mr C's first Sermon Luke XXIV v.46–47

May 9th *WatchHo* belonging to H.M.Customs and a portion of the Path opposite Miss Hudson's Lodging Ho washed away—by the Sea.

May 16 To Harwich by "Cynthia" (cutter).

. . 17 Ipswich, Needham Mkt. and Baylham—to daugr Ellen's 19 Left

Baylham and return'd home—Saw Mr Breesdell, *Ipswich*
June 2d Reading Room opened Aug 22d Barometer.

Cutting Halesworth County Court. April 26 1864. John Bokenham of Southwold, North Sea Pilot, sues Thomas Frederick Whitmore, of Reydon, farmer, for restitution of £1 8s 9d. This was the price of a quarter of pork sold by Whitmore to Bokenham. This had been declared unfit by William Bickers of Southwold, butcher, and after condemnation by the Borough Magistrates had been burnt on the Common "amid a large concourse". Evidence of seizure given by Charles Spurgeon, Sanitary Inspector, of the unfitness of the meat by Bicker, George Frederick Drake, gentleman, of Beccles but late of Reydon, Evidence of the good quality of the pork given by Whitmore and his wife, Sarah Ann, by Anderson Boulton, his pig-man, by Robert Howlett, a dealer, by Phillis Button, wife of William Button, who lived in Whitmore's house, by Jane Catton, who kept the Swan Hotel, Southwold, who had bought part of the same pig. Impressed by her evidence, the judge found for Whitmore. Before this the production in court of a large pot containing some of the pork caused a good deal of amusement.

Cutting Fraud committed upon the "Ocean Pride" Lodge of Odd Fellows at Aldeburgh by one of its members. (April 30th 1864)

Cutting Opening of the Sailors' Reading Room at Southwold, the gift of the widow of Captain Charles Rayley R.N.

Cutting Maggs to auction the household furniture and brewing plant, the property of William Smith, who is giving up the business, at the Victoria Street Brewery on June 30 1864.

Cutting Wright of Aldeburgh to auction the hull of the "Andrew" of Hamburg, 529 tons, B.Bohn master, built in 1853 and now lying on the beach between Aldeburgh and Thorpeness. January 21 & 22 1864 (Stores £900 Hull £200 by J.Jillings)

Cutting Celebration at Benacre Hall of the Coming of Age of Sir Edward Sherlock Gooch. (22 Sep 1864)

Cutting Maggs to auction household furniture, the property of the owner of East Cliff House, on November 17 1864.

Cutting Population of Great Britain in 1864.

Cutting Serious inroad by the sea at Southwold. Coast guard watch-house, the path from New York Cliff to Gun Hill, part of Miss Hudson's garden, belonging to the round-house, were all swept away. The northerly part of the town, where most of the fishing boats are placed, has been spared.

> An Original Poem for Recitation by Eliza Cook at the Fete of Odd Fellows and Foresters at Wherstead Park. September 8 1862.
> (I was present J.M.)

113

Notice   List of Members of the Corporation 1864–5 `
1864 Aug 8 Wrights valuation to Cottingham Wrentham—Cottingham's Sale
Oct 20/64
25 Cutt's Sale Wangford
Sep 7 Accident Boy Watson k.
.. 8 Hunt Ed Sale SoWold
.. 19 Cullingford Mrs Blyford Sale
.. 14 Palmer B. dischargd fro Gas Works
      Succeed by—Blowers
      "Bear" Inn (Reydon) Silenced
      Bot by Mr Alefounder
    14 Nov Mrs Charo Major's Sale
    17 Nov Mr R. Firmin's Sale
    22 December—Gale from the East.—Two Brigs rode it Out—But a
Colchester Schooner "William" ran to the Maria—South of the Harbor.
3 poor fellows of the Crew namely Alfred Barrett 26—Jabez Welby 20 &
Lord name unknown took to their Boat—and were drowned. The
Schooner afterwards drove off and arrived at Colchester.
    22 Ellen & Son came—left Jany 12/65
    22 Son-in-law Chas Durrant gets situation in H.M.C. Harwich
    28/64 Sarah—leaves for London

A.D. 1865

Jany 8 Mrs S. Bloom Reydon Dies 88
    5 Uttings Sale Brampton
Feb 4 Mrs Moss' Sale. Reydon.
Feb 5—St Luke Parish—Chelsea Wm. Jos Hart to My Daughter Sarah by
the Revd Frs Syrage
                    Feb 8th Soup Kitchen 1st Opened in this Town.
Mar 16 Mr H. Ruggles Sale. Mr R died 21 Jany at Yarmouth.
Ap 3. Jas Aldred's Sale Uggeshall
.. 21 Simpson's (fro Lowestoft) Sale at the Red Lion Inn SoWold.
May 2 Mr J.R.Gooding—Solicitor and Mr Bedwell, Bank Agent on their
way fro Haleswo—Just as they arrived at Reydon their Horse set kicking and
plunging dashed the Gig to Atoms, ruined himself—But happy to say the 2
Gents but slightly bruised
27 Sale at Wenhaston—Smith, Hubbard & Leggett
Feby 4 Mrs Moss's Sale , Reydon.
.. 17 Mr S.Bloom's Sale , Reydon
.. 20 & 21—Carting Snow out of Streets
Mar 16 H Ruggle's Sale SoWold
Ap 3 J.Aldred's Sale Uggeshall
.. 4 Susan Wales Valuation SoWo.
.. 13 Baldry Wm   Do   Sold
Oct Property purchas'd by Ed. Chapman

114

Letter   Southwold
                                                       Febry 9 1865
                        The Worshipful the Mayor & Council
                        Mr Mayor and Gentlemen
                                              Several efforts have been
                        made to establish and encourge a competent com-
                        pany of Church Bellringers, but without much
                        success chiefly from pecuniary causes. I therefore
                        beg to solicit your kind aid and patronage on their
                        behalf, if reference be made to your records you
                        will find a liberal donation was bestowed upon this
                        object by your worthy predecessors who were as
                        constant in expressing their joy and loyality by a
                        merry peal as the blue tint of our briny ocean
                        fortified by this precedent I sincerely hope your
                        kind assistance will be afforded.
                        The company should they meet with public support
                        purpose making themselves proficient in their art,
                        and to ring on Trinity Monday, Queen's birthday,
                        9th of Nov and at Christmas and on any occasion of
                        public rejoicing. Being aware of a little prejudice
                        against Bellringers, I append their names, as a
                        guarantee for respectability.
                                 I am Mr Mayor & Council
                                    Your Obedient Servant
                                       F.H.Vertue Hon. Treasurer
                        James Wigg
                        Chas Naunton "Cabinet Maker"
                        Jno Allen
                        R. Watson
                        Tho Prime
                        Albert Naunton
                        Edw Barber
                        J King
                        P.S. Since writing the foregoing I have seen the
                        Revd W.H.Chapman who has very kindly promised
                        his support.
Cutting Southwold. Young man called Syer falls into night soil vault on
          Sunday night about eight o'clock on his way home from a beer house
          and saved from death. (Jany 22/65)
          The wife of James Lowsey dies from a fit. Inquest held at the "Lord
          Nelson" (Jany 23/65)
          Lifeboat comes to rescue of the brig "Elizabeth" of Lowestoft,
          Captain Watson, carrying coal from Newcastle to Southampton and
          brings her into Harwich (Jany 24 1865)

                                    115

Miss Eliza Chapman, the vicar's sister, marries Sir John Blois of Cockfield Hall in London. (Jany 25/65)

(Sale of "Andrew" & "Alfred" Nets—Ropes & Stores Sale 379 £ 8s 0   Jany 26/65)

Cutting Exhibition of works of art . . . . . . curiosities etc at Wrentham lecture hall. "Mr Maggs of Southwold, a well known collector of scarce and valuable articles contributed an oil painting of the Old Mill at Eastern Bavents, Stoven Cherry Tree Inn ; and two curious pictures—the Creation of Man and the Creation of Woman. . . . . . Mr Maggs, an anchor dredged up at Southwold . . . . . . Mr Maggs, a curious earthenware bottle." (February 14 1865)

Cutting Inquest held at the "Crown" upon James Fish, 71, a shoemaker, who had hanged himself in a loft on Mr Lane's premises, where he worked. He had left the house of Hannah Taylor, with whom he lodged, shortly after five on Friday afternoon. The body was discovered by William Naunton, labourer, James Pack and Superintendent Spurgeon. Dr F.H.Vertue gave evidence of previous mental and physical ill health while William Fish, boot and shoe warehouseman of 90 Paddington Street, Islington stated that his father's sister and father had suffered from insanity. Deceased " appears to have been much respected and was a local preacher of the Wesleyan denomination".

(1865 19 June   Hanged himself June 16/65)

1865

July 17th To Ipswich Election for East Suffolk. I was upon the Hustings called upon R.Epling, Town Brewery upon Custom House Inn   Saw Randell. Took Boat to Harwich to my daughter Ellen

    20 To Ipswich by Boat with Mr S. Spicer   21 left Harwich by the Pilot Cutter "Providence" of SoWold Jo Wright Masr with Mr B Patman Shopkeeper (Mr Simon Spicer & Crew arrive home 9.30 P.M. During my Stay at Harwich Saw Mr. N. Youngs—Pain and Visited the Church et et Went on board the Pacific and Zealand Steamer—laden with Cattle et. Saw Frs Wayth.)

Cutting Two young men named Butcher, aged 15 and 21, drowned off Dunwich when their boat capsized. Their father was in Middlesbro' burying another son who had just died.

(July 28 1865)

1865 Ap 21 —Simpson's Sale, Lowestoft.

.. .. 26 Sale of Primes—at the Crown

.. .. 28 Mrs Osborne's Valuation, Walswick

.. May 9 Severe Thunder Storm 5. A.M.

.. .. .. 26 Eliz Boyden's Valuation

.. .. 27 Hubbard's Sale, Wrentham

.. .. 28 Exceeding heavy Rain & Wind

.. .. 30 Strong gale fro the W.

116

.. June 1 Heavy Rain
.. .. 1 Died at Haleso Mr. T Cracknell
.. .. 7 Do   at Leiston Mr Rd Debney
.. .. E Magub's Valuation
.. .. Sold Shares of Vessels—E Magub
.. July 3 Elizth Drake's Valuation—Wangford
.. .. 12 Prisa Syer's Valuation SoWo
.. .. 17 To Ips (Election) and to Harwich—returned 21st
.. .. 21 Wm Cragie's Valuation
.. .. 26 Fishing Boat "Sole Bay" Launched
.. Aug 16 Geo Stannard of this place Fisherman—Drowned off Easton
         by the upsetting of his Boat fro a Sudden gust of Wind and
         being quite alone.
         about 10 Wks after his body was wash'd on Shore at Lowestoft
         —and Interred

1865 Sep 4th I first had a knowledge of Sir E.S.Gooch met him at the Old
Swan Hotel—SoWold with Mr J.R.Gooding and Mr Cobb—I have in my
possession a Cigar given me by Sir Edwd—I here Shew you his Autograph
19 & 20 To Yoxford, Darsham and Wrentham with Mr John Fisk re Harley
Markham's Estate
Sep 21 Sale of Wm Cragie's House East Cliff—Purchas'd by Mr George
Magub for 330 £—
22 Ann Smith's Sale ,Wrentham
25 —Rumsby Benacre
29 —Dawson Cove
★

Oct 3 J Cole, Wenhaston
.. 4 J Garrod, Wrentham
.. 10 Mrs Ballentine, SoWold
.. 9 N Rackham Reydon
★ In the Month of Sep/65 Mr Wm Hotson purchases Mrs Souper's property
  South Green £700
Cutting An exhibition of curiosities and antiquities at the New Hall, Market
         Place, Southwold. September 13–20. In aid of the Church restora-
         tion fund.
Label   Mr Maggs Southwold I Hare I Brace Part
         E.S.G.   (Sep 25/65)
Cutting Maggs to auction household furniture of Mrs Ballentine, who is
         changing residence, at East Cliff House on October 10. 1865
Cutting Maggs to auction household furniture of the late Mrs Elizabeth
         Magub on November 28 1865.
Cutting Meeting of Southwold Life Boat Committee
Cutting The brig "Billy" of Whitby, 119 tons, laden with coal, driven
         aground by the gale opposite the centre of the town, 180 yards from

the beach. The crew of six lost in spite of the efforts of the lifeboat. (Jany 9 1865)

Cutting Letter to the Editor of the Ipswich Journal from "An Inhabitant of Southwold" January 17 1866.

In spite of all its amenities want and starvation stalk the streets of Southwold. These have become unfit for decent people after dark due to the language and danger of molestation from "low, profane youths". Drinking, gambling and the desecration of the Sabbath are the cause.

Letter Crest and motto of the Gooch family. "Benacre Hall, Wangford. Sir Edward S Gooch is very much obliged to Mr Maggs for his exceeding handsom present of a Codfish.

Oct. 31st 1865 To Mr Maggs."

1865 Oct 25 Sale Mr John Laws
.. .. 27 Mr Harley Markham's Sale Darsham
.. Nov 10 Cap. Bevan's Sale at Mrs Firmin's Ho
.. .. 12 Schooner "Curlew" E.A.Wayth lost Crew Saved
.. .. 20 Son of Mr Jas.Simpson fell from his Ship—Drowned
.. Dec 2 Mrs Kett's Sale

1866

Jany 13 —"Billy" of Whitby and Crew lost on the Shoal off here 2 of the Crew pick'd up at Easton and Buried here.
.. 18 To Dunwich. Mr J.Dix Valuation
.. 19 I sold the Wreck of the "Billy" to Mr J.Jillings.
.. 29 —Curdy alias Alexander & [   ] King of Walberswick Dro off Dunwich by the upsettg of their Boat.
Feb 28 I sold Furniture of Mr I.T.Fuller Druggist
Mar 31 Mrs Mole's Sale, Shadingfield
.. 14 Frost do So Cove
.. 15 Alexander do Reydon—gone to London
Ap 5 Hezekiah Warne's Sale at the "SoWold Arms"
1866 Ap 9 Mr Legett's Sale Reydon at the House formerly the "Bear" Inn
Ap 24 Sold Oil Factory and Fishing property of Messs Davis & Thorneycroft situate leading to the Harbor Bot.by Richard Grand
May 7 Calver's Sale—Wangford
.. 11 Jo Cooper's Sale at Jo Spoore's of this place Cooper leaves for London
17 Smith's Sale Wangford
June 19 Sold premises late Mr Wm Sutton.
Augt 4 Thos Wales to Boyton Alms Houses
Oct 19 Mr Rt Howlett late of Wangford—Innkeeper. Died at Bungay
Decr 7 John Magub Seaman on Board the "[   ]" of "[   ]" drowned.

Cutting John Crickmore junior and a boy called Thomas Rogers escape drowning when their boat capsized in a squall while going through

118

Kessingland Gat. Saved by Thomas Welton in his boat. Many visitors to Southwold during the last month. Confirmation held by Bishop of Norwich at St. Edmund's, Francis Henry Vertue appointed a magistrate.
(July 7 1866)

Cutting Girling and White of Peasenhall and Rendham to auction farms, lands and marshes belonging to the late J.B.Edwards Esq in Reydon at the Swan Hotel on July 26.

Cutting Sir Edward Sherlock Gooch married to Ellen Emily, eldest daughter of Major R.A.Hirst of Tattingstone Place and Down Grange, Hants at Tattingstone. October 9 1866.

Cutting The Reverend William Hay Chapman to move to the living of Doveridge, Uttoxeter, Derbyshire. Testimonial presented to the Reverend C.J.Hamilton, the curate, who is joining his father at St Michael's, Chester Square. (Decr 15 /66)

Cutting During the gales along the coast the sails of Mr Baggot's mill fell off owing to want of repair. Loss of the "Guardiana" (John Magub, junior aboard) on the Winterton Ridge,
A meeting held in the Town Hall to further the Blyth Valley Railway.

> Roper Emma B. Palmer at St James's Piccadilly
> Revd H. Ward Oct 5th
> (Aug 31 Mrs P—of a Son)

Cutting Southwold. Thomas Hurr and two brothers named Barber drowned when a gust of wind capsized their fishing boat when two miles from the coast and in the lee of the schooner "Mary" of Perth, Wain, master. A man named Watson rescued by the schooner. Hurr left a wife and twins, the Barbers were young and unmarried.
(January 5 1867 24th One of the Barbers washed ashore at Dunwich. Interred here)

Cutting Examination in bankruptcy of George Edmund Child, ironfounder and contractor of Southwold. February 23.

Cutting The Rector of Filby refuses to read the burial service for an ex-soldier, William Walpole, because he had not attended church.
(Feby 23 1867)

Cutting Disastrous fire at Henham Hall. (Feby 26 1867)
Wyatt's building of 1793–7 destroyed.

Cutting Opening of new organ at Reydon (June 2 /67)

Cutting Suspicious death of an infant child of Rebecca Spence.
(June 22 1867)

Cutting William, aged 16, the son of Crisp John Plant of Southwold, drowned at Tobago, West Indies. Washed from the deck of the barque "Mary" of London, John Spicer, master.
The Reverend C.M.Rouse appointed to Southwold. (Aug 10/67)

Cutting A sudden gust of wind between one and two o'clock p.m. coming

119

from the N.W. removed the sails from the Black Mill on the Common, occupied by C.M.Marsden and the property of W.W. Bardwell of Sotherton. Considerable damage was done to the round house.

(Sep 24 1867)

Cutting Restoration of the chancel roof of St. Edmund's. Medieval painting carefully restored and the old wooden east window, that had rotted, has been replaced. Southwold tradesmen carried out most of the work—stonework, Messers Allen, carpenter, Naunton, joiner, Prestidge, plumber, Strowger, glazier, Forder. (1857)

1867 Jany 2 Rt. Wake leaves SoWold.

. . Jany 8 Mr Rt Carter Married to Mrs Cross in London.

. . Feby 18 County Election, Henniker Major & Corrance, Elected

March 6   Mr Brufton appointed Superintendant of Trinity Pilots.

. .   . . T.I.Fuller's Sale Chemist et by me under an execution.

March 17th Died at Norwich Mr. Rt Mills 77

May 23rd Sold to Thos Reeve, his Houses for £ 335 £.

. . 27   Mr John Palmer appointed Harbor Master, in the room of W.C. Simmons

April 16   Married at Norwich Hugh Lawrence to Rhoda the Wife of— Battram ! !

May 4   Mr Jellicoe receives an account of his son's (   ) death Oct last.

. .   . . Mr Crutchlow Died. . . . .

June 2   Mr Wm Rockhill Uggeshall. Dies 65

. .   . . Married R.P.Critten to Kate Lowsey

Sep 24   Sudden blast of Wind—3 Sails blown from off Black Mill.

Cutting Charles Foster appointed a magistrate (Jan 7 1868) Low mortality (1.377 %) at Southwold in 1867, less than at most resorts.

Cutting Maggs to auction houses of the late Edward Mills in High Street (occupied by Robert Pattman,shoemaker) and in Park Lane (occupied by John Magub,Mrs Syer,Mrs Simms and Mr Crisp John Plant) at the Crown on May 21 1868.

Cutting To the Editor of the Ipswich Journal. A letter from "Old Antiquity". "How Corporation Records are Preserved". Leaf out of book once belonging to the corporation of Dunwich and dated 1796–7 picked up in Southwold High Street. October 31 1868.

1868

Jany 21 Mr Saml Strange died in London

Feb 12 Mr Jo Read of Wrentham, Grocer, drowns himself near the Bound Post upon this beach.

May 21 Sold Mr Edward Mills' Property to John Skelton & John Sawyer in Park Lane and Ho in High Street to Robt Pattman who sold it to B.H.Carter

Mr Ed Mills, died

Nov 9 Died at Beccles, Mr W Wallace Bardwell, late of Sotherton.

Cutting Results of the Southwold municipal election (1868)

Cutting Consecration of the extension to Wangford churchyard (Nov 3/68)

Cuttings Queen Anne's Farthing—Storm—Tithes.

January 1869

Cutting The Reverend Nathaniel Wilson of Reydon College (sic) reads the Gospel, at the recent ordination in Norwich Cathedral, an honour given to the best candidate in the examination. He is to become curate at Southwold.[18]

Cutting Inquest at the Walnut Tree, Benacre upon Forster Bokenham, 53, of Southwold who was drowned with James Taylor and George Baxter when William Doddington's fishing boat was sunk just below Southwold on January 24.

Cutting The "Lord Coke" of Middlesborough stuck on the Sizewell Bank. Her crew of four rescued by the Southwold Lifeboat.

> Muttett—formerly of Walberswick—Master
> Jany 15 1869.

Winter Evening Entertainment at the New Hall.

Cutting Rescue of the crew of the"Lord Coke", loaded with a cargo of bricks, a schooner.   (Jany 6 1869)

Annual Meeting of Odd Fellows.

March 1869

Cutting Attempt to recover the treasure of the "Lutine"

Cutting The vicar (R.C.M.Rouse) gives a dinner to his church officials etc.

Cutting Farewell address presented to the Honourable and Reverend E.V.R. Powys (April 19 1869) by the Vicar and Churchwardens of St. Edmund's upon his leaving Southwold to become Vicar of St. Nicholas, Warwick.   (May 27 1869)

Meeting of the Dispensary Committee at the Town Hall. Patients on the books—32 at the beginning of the quarter, 48 admitted since, cured 42, relieved 18, dead 1, remaining on the books 17

Five windows on the south side of the parish church to be restored during the summer, two given by Mrs Rayley, one by the Mayor, one provided from funds raised by the churchwardens and the last given by Allen, the stonemason and Strowger, the plumber.

Cutting Peter Gray, labourer of Southwold, before the (Beccles) magistrates for making a false declaration so that he might marry Sarah Emma Gray, his niece. Gray, was a widower of 28 who had been living with his father at Reydon. Sarah Gray, 21, had shared the house with them and "happened to fall in the family-way" (July 8 1869)

Cutting The case resumed and dismissed by the magistrates. However the

---

18. For 'College' read 'Cottage', Jermyn's old home.

prosecution demands that Gray be committed to the next assizes, the Reverend S.B.Westhorpe, Vicar of Reydon, pledging himself to continue the prosecution. (12 July /69)

Cutting Bazaar to raise funds for restoration work at the parish church. The latter included the *insertion* of *six* new windows on the south side, at a cost of £20 each. The brickwork in the lower portions of some side windows still to be removed. New East and West Windows have been made. (Aug 19 1869)

1869 July 14 Died at Darsham—Mr Dan Warren—Buss-Driver—50 agd

Cutting Maggs to auction the wreck of the "Elsinore" of Elsinore, 600 tons, at Walberswick on December 30 1869.

Cutting Charles White of Bulcamp concussed as the result of falling from his horse and cart at the watering between Blyford and Wenhaston. (Apr 5 1870)

Cutting Double cottage close to Walberswick church inhabited by an old woman called Pearson and a man called Bloomfield and his family burnt down. Belonging to Sir J.R.Blois it was old and thatched and the outhouses were chiefly built of furze faggots. Another fire at St Helena farm, occupied by Mr Briggs, destroyed some wheat stacks and was caused by children playing with lucifer matches.

Cutting Death of Lord Henniker
(1870 Apr 16th No 6 Grafton St London)

Illustrated letter heading, Hospital for Consumption, Brompton.
(From Mr Chas Carter June 30/69 Returned) Manver's Ward
London July 29th/69

Cutting Tea party for the aged poor given by Mrs Rayley at the Elms for seventy aged over 70.
New East Window at St Edmund's by Ward and Hughes to the memory of the late Miss Sheriffe.

Postcard To Mr.H.J.Debney, Draper, Southwold giving printed list of prices for crapes from Ellis, Howell & Co. St Paul's Churchyard, London. (Issued 1st Octr 1870)

Parish Magazine of Cawthorne, June 1870.
"Collected in the Parish Church of Cawthorne for the inhabitants of Southwold, in Suffolk, towards their losses of £4000. Collected the sum of 12s 6d, the 28 August, 1659—Entry in Parish Register."
(With Rev R.C.M.Rouse Comps:)

1870 Apr 22 Wm Catton and Wm Child to Australia—by the "Sussex".
June 30 at Halesworth Found dead in Bed John Crabtree Esqr Solicitor
July 30 Harvey, Banker, Norwich. Shoots himself.
Aug 29th Old Swan Sold—to Mrs Jane Catton 1550 £. Town Hall to the Corporation—Cottage £150 to Mr Jas Jillings
Aug 25 I sold Furniture of Mr Tharmes at the"Red Lion"Inn who left this Town on the 27 inst. Succeeded by Mr Jas. Jillings.

Octr 18th Telegraph—Wires first worked from here.

Nov 17 Dr Blackett leaves to reside at Wangford.

Nov 22 Lord Mahon called upon his Voters in this Town

Nov 24 Rev A Ritchies property sold by Auction. See particulars of Sale.

1871 Jan 1st News of Geo Son of Mr John Bokenham T.P. killed by a fall from the rigging of his Vessel at Falmouth.

Apr 29 Died at Lowestoft Mr S. Tymms Printer.

October 1st R.P.Critten to Isabella Woodard

1871 March 16th Loss of "Charles" Geo Eves & Crew on the Kentish Coast

Cutting The schooner "Robert Cottle" of Ipswich, from Sunderland went aground coming through the Standford Channel off Southwold. Becoming leaky it hoisted distress signals. Because of the heavy sea the lifeboat was unable to reach her. The vessel broke up in a few minutes. Stephen Fisher, the mate, Henry Hacon of Aldeburgh and John Crickmore, a boy were drowned. James Leggett, master, Charles William and Ernest R.C.Fulcher were saved on the floating wreck. The disaster occurred at nearly the same spot where the "Billy" of Whitby was wrecked. Two of the crew were carried to the Red Lion Inn, the other to the Old Swan. Miss Bawtree sent blankets and brandy down to the beach. The wind was S.E by E. and the ship was 114 tons, registered in 1864 and owned by the master.
(Sunday Novr 5 1871)
(Sold Coke on the 11th Vessel repaired & taken to Goole Jan 7 1872)

Cutting Suspension of Fincham and Simpson's Bank, Diss. October 7 1871.

Cutting Lenny and Smith to auction the household furniture of the late Mrs Rayley at the Elms, Southwold on 9–11 August 1871.

Cutting The billy-buoy "Friends" of Goole, Mapplebeck, bound from London to Southwold with 30 tons of cake parted from her anchors while riding in the bay and came ashore about 9.15 p.m. The crew was saved though the boy broke his wrist falling from the rigging. A gale was blowing from the E. A mainmast was brought to land by the lugger "Faith" of Southwold.
(Dec7 1871)

Cutting Massive stone coffin-lid found at Icklingham All Saints, followed by finding of coffins and skeletons. (Dec 12 /71)

Cuttings Death and funeral of Sir Edward Sherlock Gooch at Benacre. (June 3 1872).

Cutting Report upon the Hon. Arthur Birch, born in Southwold and acting Lieutenant Governor of Prince of Wales Island. The son of the Reverend H.W.Rouse Birch and grandson of the sister of the first Earl of Stradbroke his brothers are respectively a Canon with a living near Manchester, the head of a Spanish mercantile establishment in London, an ex-master at Eton and now a clergyman at Bridgewater, a judge in India.

123

1872

Feby 13th Mr Geo Magub—buys premises of Mr Marshall Twaddell
March 19th Died Mr Edwd Gray—Reydon.

Cutting Excursion of the Suffolk Institute of Archaeology and Natural History to Butley Abbey and Orford Castle. (1872 July 13)

Cutting Thomas Freeman of Ipswich sues George Philip Freeman of Wangford, auctioneer, his brother, for negligence in making a valuation. (Assize 25 Mar 1870) Thomas Freeman, former agent to Lord Stradbroke, awarded £2,000.

Cutting George Philip Freeman of Frostenden, auctioneer and farmer, adjudged bankrupt. March 21 1870.

Cutting Meeting of Freeman's creditors—debts between £10–17,000.

Cuttings Relating to Freeman's case, including a defence of the character of Frederick G. Freeman, Agent of the Henham Estates signed by Lord Stradbroke and a large number of others.

Cutting G.P.Freeman convicted of obtaining money under false pretences, sentenced to four months hard labour. (Oct 15/72)

Cuttings G.P.Freeman dies of small pox in Springfield Gaol. (January 1st 1873)

1873 I sold for him this was his last sale of Hay Walls Halesworth.

Cutting The Ballot Act (July 1872)

Cutting Large iron paddle steamer "Eiderstedt" of Tonning, Captain Clausen, driven ashore at Covehithe Point. Homeward bound from London, she was originally built to run the blockade during the American Civil War. The sea is breaking right over her and one paddle wheel is severely damaged. (Oct 16 /72)

Cutting Abolition of toll gates at Wenhaston, Blythburgh, Melton and Rushmere by the Ipswich and Southtown Turnpike Trust, which has "expired". The gate house at Benacre has been bought by Sir Francis Gooch. (Nov 1 1872)

Cutting The Reverend Claude Cecil Thornton M.A. licensed to Southwold (Nov 2 1872)

Cutting William King and Jonathan Norton of Aldeburgh drowned off that port near the Napes buoy. (Dec 5/72)

Sold Novr 1872 for Breakg up.

Cutting Two smacks, the "Coronella", property of Mr George of Southtown and the "Thomas and Edward", belonging to Mr Hawes of Gorleston, rumoured lost in the North Sea gale of November 10–16. (Dec 6 1872)

Cutting Inquest at the"Anchor", Walberswick upon James Marsh, labourer, who had been found dead in bed, after being an invalid for many years (Dec 7/72)

Cutting The schooner "Celeste Maria", Jean M.L.Verez of Ile Daiz, from Grimsby to Dieppe, laden with 150 tons of coal, stranded by the gale upon the Barnard Sands, the crew being rescued. Lifted off by the flood tide she settled off Covehithe, near the wreck of the steamer. The wreck of the schooner was sold at Lowestoft for £32 (November 30 1872)

Cutting Frederick G. Freeman of Park Farm, Henham, to auction two brick and tiled cottages in Victoria Street, occupied by Christmas Stannard and Goodwin Hurr with a workshop occupied by George Taylor. Also two brick and slated cottages on East Green, facing the National School, occupied by Henry Boyce and Isaac Warnes. At the Old Swan on December 12 1872.

Freeman to auction a brick and tiled residence in two dwellings in the High Street, occupied by William P. Spence and Samuel Powditch and a double cottage with shoemaker's shop and back yard in Wangford in the occupation of William Howeld and John Bickers. At the Old Swan on December 12. These properties were owned by the late Mrs Margaret Terry, the others belonged to the late Garnham Fisher.

Cutting Church well decorated for Christmas but the vicar exhibits a "tinge of sadness in his expression. . . . . .and tone of voice which imparts to some persons a sense of depression.—Communicated"

Cutting Bibles presented to Mrs Charles Stewart, formerly Charlotte Ellis, who had established a gospel class for the fisherfolk in the old Lifeboat House on the beach. When, ten years ago, this was swept away during a severe gale, the Sailors' Reading Room took its place. Mrs Stewart now lives at Acton, Middlesex. (January 1873)

Cutting The "I.O.U." of Ipswich, owned by Frank Christie, coal merchant, rumoured lost between Cardiff and Lisbon. Seven hands aboard. Report on the weather.

Cutting Maggs to auction the hull of the brig "Mary Russell" of Dundee, 200 tons, now stranded at Dunwich, on February 3 1873, together with oats, part of her cargo, now lying near Mr Dix's warehouse.

Cutting The Sailors' Reading Room, the best in the town for public meetings etc. had been built by the late Mrs Rayley for the use of the sailors and fishermen. Now there was a difference of opinion between the Vicar and the non-conformists over the running of the services held there. These had been in his hands alone, although the foundress, though a churchwoman, was the daughter of a non-conformist minister.

To the Editor

Sir—In looking through the local papers I can only find one place that appoints officers who reside at a considerable distance from the parish.

The Vicar of Southwold has appointed a gentleman who resides in London as his churchwarden, the Mayor of Southwold also resides in London, and one of the Borough Magistrates resides in Norwich. The borough has four magistrates, but only one lives in Southwold.

It was rumoured that the Vicar was about leaving and there was a suggestion that his successor should reside in London and his curate in Norwich. There is one policeman only and as at present he frequently walks up and down the High Street, it is proposed that his successor, in common with everyone else, should reside in London. The inhabitants of the town will be free from the annoyance of the presence of any of their officers. It is in contemplation to establish a co-operative store in London where the town will be supplied with every requisite. The little town will then rid itself of all trades-people and be regarded as a most desirable residence for widow-ladies and aged spinsters. Undoubtedly after mature consideration, other towns will follow its example. I am, dear Sir, yours respectfully,

Southwold,April,1873   JOHN HONESTY

Cutting   SOUTHWOLD—A Haunted Town.
                    To The Editor

Dear Sir—What "John Honesty" says of some of our town officials is true; they have indeed a "local habitation and a name" but that is all that can be said of them for about nine months of the year. But though absent as regards the body they,like Margrave in Bulwer Lytton's "Strange Story" seem to have a marvellous power of projecting their shadows on every important occasion. Should a railway to Southwold, for instance, be talked of—these dusky phantoms flit about and confer in mysterious manner with some of the grand old Tory lords and squires to be found in this region, whose ideas are so thoroughly out of date that they seem to be ghosts of the antique past, condemned to live again on earth and retard its progress on account of their former sins. The result is, that the thing collapses; railway promoters being but men, cannot contend against shadows and spirits. Is a tramway set on foot ? It is wonderful the commotion these ghosts and shadows make in every gloomy hall and dingy vestry along the proposed line. Southwold did very well, say the ghosts, in their day without any such new fangled contrivances, and so it ought now; while both declare that as they can glide along without troubling either train or tram, they will oppose both with all the power and authority that belong to them as occasional visitants from another world. Does any man of enterprise, in or out of Southwold, intimate a desire to hire town land for building ? These shadows and ghostly figures fill the Council Chamber, pervade the streets, lurk in the empty houses of their owners (which chill the beholder as he passes them) and so gibber and shriek and predict such doleful things about the vulgarity that will surely flood the town if it is enlarged, and moreover, threaten in such a frightfully earnest manner that they will take their flight from the town for ever if only a single brick is made for such a purpose, that the resident members of the Corporation are quite scared and are glad to let the bold intruder out of the Town Hall by any back way, and beg him never to come again.

It matters not, indeed, what new scheme may be started; if it is at all of a progressive nature, down swoop the shadows and thickly gather the shades and between them they generally manage to burke the matter in spite of the convictions and protests of the few remaining shopkeepers.

The last building which these shadowy beings have begun to haunt is the Sailor's Reading Room, whether they will be dislodged is yet uncertain: most likely not, as some of them are of an obstinate turn of mind.

Dear Sir, what shall we do ? Pray inform

                Yours very truly

                    AN ANXIOUS INQUIRER.   (1873)

Cutting Letter to the Editor of the Ipswich Journal from "Thomas Sincerity" referring to the letter from "John Honesty" which has been the topic of conversation not only in Southwold but in the neighbourhood "I hope it will bring the influential inhabitants to a sense of duty and justice that Southwold may not be held up to derision in future as at present. Admitting there are many widow ladies and aged spinsters residing in the town, there are sufficient men of business to fill the offices of the town" Southwold May 1873

Cutting Maggs to auction the household furniture etc. of Mrs Mary Lillingston, deceased, of "The Lodge" in July.

Cuttings James Watling Knights, auctioneer of Hasketon, bound over to keep the peace by Woodbridge magistrates after threatening his wife, Mary. Sent to gaol for want of sureties. July 23.

Cuttings Suicide of Knights, aged 53, by hanging himself in Ipswich gaol

Cutting House of Edward Chapman in Park Lane, Southwold, struck by lightning during a severe thunderstorm. (Aug 25/73)

Cutting Harvest Festival at Saxmundham. Sermon preached by the Reverend Claude Thornton, Vicar of Southwold. (Sepr 1873)

Cutting New lifeboat launched at Dunwich (October 9th 1873)

Cutting Sailors' Reading Room may have to be closed. Mrs Catton has offered one of her large rooms at the Swan in its place. Work has begun on the public pump in the Market Place. Results of municipal election. "The present Mayor—J.E.Grubbe Esq.—is a gentleman both in manners and position, an acute man of business, and an old and tried friend of the town; and it will, we think, be some time before his equal is found. Like all men, he is not quite perfect. His chief drawback as Mayor is that unfortunately, he is not in favour of a railway (liking the present quietude of the place) but at the same time , it must be remembered to his credit; that though he was not personally desirous of a tramway, he not only did not oppose the project, but yielding to what appeared the general wish, exerted himself to forward it." (Nov 9 1873)

Cutting Alderman Prestwidge lays the last brick on the first course of brickwork for the town pump at 9 a.m. on November 13. (1873)

Cutting Incipient Ritualism. Because of the isolation of Southwold and because the living was in the gift of the Simeon Trustees, St. Edmund's had been spared "the absurd antics of ritualism". However, though the vicar declared himself a thoroughly Evangelical Low Churchman and no ritualist, he had scarcely settled into the parish than church bells were being rung for Saint's days and early communion, "obscure utterances about the efficacy of baptism to wash away sin"were accompanied by "dark deeds" of plundering the non-conformist Sunday schools and he showed himself unwilling to meet or work with dissenters. Now he proposes raising the floor of the chancel upon which the communion table stands, introducing gas candelabra within the sanctuary and cementing over the tombstones there so that the whole area could be tiled.

At this, the staunchly Protestant people's warden, who had borne with the changes already made and had "tolerated the announcements that on Christmas-day the services would be musical" convened a meeting of churchgoers at the Town Hall on December 4. The vicar, taking the chair by right, declared the meeting informal and not legal and suggested a vestry be held in a week's time. Mr. Ewen argued with Captain Powell, holding that the surplus from the "steeple fund" should not be devoted to relighting the church. Mr Sawyer declared that when he signed the application to the bishop for the alterations in the chancel, he had no idea that anything like an altar was to be set up. Mr Marsden asked whether it was legal to apply for a faculty without the agreement of the parishioners was told by Captain Powell that it was not. Mr Fitch in "a bold and capital speech" stated that if the High Church proceedings were persisted with, they would split the congregation. Major Ward, on the contrary, thought that to raise the table a few inches was "but a little thing" but Mr Debney urged that the difference was between a Protestant communion table and a Romish "altar". "After this several warm conversational discussions were carried on, especially by some ladies at the lower end of the room."

Since this meeting several handbills have been mysteriously distributed about the town. On Saturday night it was one headed "Popery v. Protestantism" and on Sunday evening "Questions for old St. Edmund to answer" The author of these is not known but "that the good steady-going Church of England folks of Southwold should be scandalised at anything approaching to Popery is not to be wondered at." . . . ."great credit is due to Messrs Sawyer, Debney

128

and Fitch for the zeal and courage with which they have opposed this Ritualistic innovation."

Cutting Vestry Meeting held on December 11 at 11 a.m. at which the vicar defends the proposed changes, they have the bishop's assent and are thus not open to a vote. They are however in accordance with the rubric and not Romish or Ritualistic.

On the evening of the same day a crowded meeting was held at the Town Hall. The vicar obtained a vote in favour of raising the chancel floor and introducing candelabra, while the fate of the tombstones was left to the bishop. (Decr 1873)

Cutting Letter to the Editor from "Gallio" urging disestablishment. Both parsons and parson-mongers must be muzzled "We certainly do, occasionly, get periods of repose when the parsons leave us (which they do, upon the average every two years or less if the "call" be very loud) for which we must be grateful. But no sooner does a new one come into possession than he endeavours to make a clean sweep."

Cutting Southwold lifeboat escorts the German schooner "David", bound for London from Burghead with barley, into Lowestoft, after she had sprung a leak. (Decr 16th 1873)

Adjourned Vestry Meeting. A nondescript assembly at the Town Hall on December 11 of those who had a right to be present (the rate-payers) and their wives, sons, daughters and servants, who had not. The vicar, in a carefully studied address, said that if we made our own dwellings beautiful "we ought much more to beautify the House of God". Concerning the chancel step, this was not a ritualistic act, it had been done at Beccles by the rector, "one of the lowest Churchmen in the county." Would the Bishop of Norwich, "the lowest Churchman on the Bench", have sanctioned it ?

Mr H.P.Jellicoe stated that though only one step was asked for "that one would be a step towards Rome". Mr Debney hoped that the vicar would not call for a vote that would divide the parish. Mr.E.Moore said that he had attended with pleasure ritualistic services at St. Mary le Tower, Ipswich and St. Alban's, Holborn and had noticed similar steps in these churches. The vicar asked how the Reverend W.Hay Chapman had been able to introduce three steps at the restoration of Lowestoft parish church. A motion to elevate the table was proposed by Mr.C.Foster and seconded by Mr.Debney. "A number of those who had no right to vote and some who had having held up their hands" the vicar declared the measure carried. Its opponents, holding it and the meeting illegal, for the most part abstained. A vote to accept the candelabra presented by the widow of G.V.Blois Esq was passed but the cementing over of the tombstones was rejected, not referred to the bishop as previously reported. The vicar then proposed that a curtain should be placed across the reredos, which he considered " an unfinished work and unworthy to form part of so beautiful a church". This move was abandoned, amongst the objections being the claim that the tablet in memory of the three young men drowned when the lifeboat capsized would be covered up.

"It would be needless to make any remarks upon the feebleness of the Vicar's reasoning . . . . . while loudly asserting by his voice that he is a Protestant of the Protestants . . . . by his acts . . . . he declares himself to be a follower not directly of the Papists but of the "apists", the Anglican Ritualists."

Notice POPERY VERSUS PROTESTANTISM—THE TRIAL

Of Old St. Edmund will take place on THURSDAY next, the 11th instant, at Eleven o'clock, when every Householder, both Male and Female, are respectfully requested to attend. December 1873. (C.C.Thornton Vicar Frederick Graham Powell, John Sawyer Churchwardens)

Handbill QUESTIONS FOR OLD ST EDMUND to answer

Is Preaching in the Surplice—a custom of Ritualists?
Is Reading Prayers from the Chancel   . .
Is Responding by Music and Singing   . .
Is Early Communion, fasting   . .
Is Special Celebration for
Departed Saints   . .
Is Special Prayer   . .
Is the Altar elevated upon Stones   . .
Is the Lighting within the Communion   . .
Is teaching Charity Children to Bow
at the Name of Jesus   . .
Is teaching them to Stand when the
Clergy approaches   . .
Is teaching them to fall upon their
Knees when he enters the Pulpit   . .
Is the word RMEN loudly pronounced   . .

Cutting Letter to the Editor from "Veritas", dated Southwold, December 17. and headed "Light for those in darkness".

"On Thursday, the 11th inst, Old St. Edmund (church) was put on his trial and found sadly wanting. It was proved on inquisition that the poor ignorant people of Southwold had been satisfied with a communion table (the Vicar told them they were a century behind the times.) Now forsooth they must have an altar with a glaring, queerly shaped covering. They rested easy in their stupidity, without lights in the communion; now they must have candelabra. They have heretofore respected the burial place of the dead, now, with their new light, the memorial stones to the departed, within the communion rails, must be chipped to form a resting place for a covering of cement—of course, Roman—and this to be overlaid with encaustic tiles. Before the year 1873 they foolishly imagined vestry meetings were legal if they consisted of ratepayers only. Now they find an agglomeration of husbands and wives, parents and childrens, boys and girls, called a vestry meeting. Well may the people heartily pray "Lighten our darkness, we beseech thee, O Lord"

Cutting Halesworth County Court, December 22 1873. East Suffolk Tramway Company sues George Magub, pilot, of Southwold for £10, payment for two shares. The Board of Trade had given permission for construction from Halesworth to Mr. Ewen's house, and it was hoped to extend it to the Swan. Magub and other Southwold shareholders claimed that payment was not due until the tramway was commenced from Halesworth to Southwold. Judgment reserved.

Cutting Public readings of the Mutual Improvement Society, Mr Jellicoe in the chair. Already 54 members.
Low rate of mortality at Southwold, 37 deaths in a population of 2,155 last year. One inhabitant is 94, two 90, twenty-eight 80, "Southwold is too healthy for doctors to live and too healthy for patients to die." (Jany 1874)

Cutting A sailors' reading room to be opened in the parish committee room at a penny a week on January 19 1874. The room presented by Mrs Rayley is to be closed because the present owner will not give the committee power to exclude the "clerical element".
The Mutual Improvement Society, recently formed, meeting with opposition because of the unfounded rumour that it was hostile to the Church of England. The first meeting was held at the New Hall. The committee is equally composed of conformists and non-conformists and Tuesday evenings have been chosen as less likely to clash with other fixtures. (January 10 1874)

Cutting Halesworth County Court. January 26 1874. Judgement given against George Magub, but only for about half the amount claimed, as the tramway from Halesworth to Southwold had not been started or given Parliamentary consent.

Cutting Loss of a North-German barque laden with petroleum on the Long Sand off Harwich. (Feby 25th 1874)

Cutting Norwich Ecclesiastical Court. April 7th 1874. The Vicar and Churchwardens of Southwold v. T.H.Jellicoe and M.Marsden and other parishioners. The latter oppose the covering up of certain tombstones in the sanctuary and their representation by brass facsimiles. These commemorated Judith Nunn (died in 1677),Mary Rich (who also died in 1677) and two members of the Robinson family. R.J.Allen, stonemason, deposed that the removal of the stones was of no consequence as they did not lie over the bones of those whose memory they perpetuated. The vicar stated that no representatives of Mary Rich could be found and the representatives of the Robinsons were agreeable to a faculty being granted. The great-granddaughter of Judith Nunn, now over eighty, alone objected. It was agreed that the stones be moved elsewhere in the church and not covered.

Cutting Fire at Reydon destroys two wheat stacks , a waggon etc. belonging John Chilvers, farmer. The fire was discovered by a neighbouring farmer, John Wayling, as he retired for the night. (Ap 17 1874)

Cutting Wreck of the Norwegian vessel "Alma" laden with ice upon the Sizewell Bank. The Ipswich lifeboat stationed at Thorpeness and the Southwold lifeboat rescued the crew of twelve and the pilot.
(Apr 15 1874 I Sold her Wreck for £30 May 1 1874)

Cutting Letter to the Editor of the Suffolk Mercury from Benjamin Morse Spalding, whose wife was descended from Judith Nunn. Other descendants named are Mrs Purchas of Cambridge and her sister, Miss Mills; the wife of Dr. Drozier of Caius College, and Miss Spalding. Mrs Drozier is the daughter late Reverend John Purchas of Brighton and Mrs Purchas, the latter the great grand-daughter of Clement Rutland Church, formerly of Southwold, whose mother was the only surviving child of Thomas, son of Judith Nunn. "Who can feel surprised at the indignation and resentment shown by the parishioners of Southwold at proceedings having no higher nor better aim than to force symbolic Ritualism on the people without their concurrence." Walberswick April 15 1874.

Cutting The "Albion" running to Yarmouth, will stop at Southwold when the weather allows. John Cragie is the boatman appointed to land passengers.
Chimney on the premises of Mr Child, ironfounder, struck by lightning. (June 1874)

Cuttings Railway Accident at Thorpe.(Sep 10/74)

Cutting Attempted murder at Clenchwarton. March 30

Cutting Programme of Mutual Improvement Society
Municipal Election. The Mayor (J.E.Grubbe) has sunk his preference for a quiet town in promoting the building of a new terrace of houses. (Nov 2/74)

Cutting Mr Harrison of the Lion Inn injured by the upsetting of his vehicle near the Five Bells, South Cove, while coming from Lowestoft last Tuesday and the next day William Moore, coming from Saxmundham fell out of his cart and injured his face. (Nov 24 1874)

Cutting The Reverend Mr Eger replaces the Reverend Bruce Cuming B.A. as curate at Southwold. January 17 1875.

Cutting Suffolk Lent Assizes. Robert John Allen, stonemason, of Southwold, found to have obstructed the highway to Blackshore close to the gate leading on to the Common. Maggs gave evidence that he had known Southwold all his life. He had been the Collector of the Corporation

Ground Rents since 1840. He had never regarded the ground in question as part of the highway. He had collected rent from Mr Jermyn and from Mr Allen and his father as tenants of the spot.

James Wigg had known the spot for sixty years. From 1819 to 1826 while he was an apprentice to John Burcham, wheelwright and carpenter, his master used to lay wood there. George Rawlinson, 78, said that when he first went to Southwold in 1814 the piece of ground in question was a slough. Henry Ladd, 77, of Southwold, said the ground in dispute was always a swamp in wet weather and impassable. James Lay, 72, had been 30 years in Southwold and had rented the premises occupied by Mr Hind, the complainant and used to enter them from the Common. There was no entrance from the front part where the stones now lay. Joseph Artis, builder, built the premises now occupied by Hind. There was no opening to the premises from the road in dispute. John Marsden, James Jillings,59, William Gooding,74,farm servant to Joseph Wigg in 1814, gave confirmatory evidence.

Richard Francis Hind had stated that in June 1857 he, with two others, had bought the property next to the highway to store fishing gear. There had been a few stones then but there were now so many that they blocked the footpath on the north side. The Jury found that there was an encroachment. (Ipswich 29 Mar 1875)

Cutting Hind and Others v. Allen. The Corporation of Southwold were virtually the defendants in the case, Allen was their tenant. There was evidence from 1648 that this was a highway. There was now 200 tons of stone and the complainants were unable to occupy their premises as fish merchants. This was of great importance as near this spot was to be the proposed terminus of the railway from Darsham to Southwold. Mr Hind bought the property from Mr Borrett Gooch of Yarmouth. He had six fishing luggers and used the buildings for stores. There are four fishing seasons and eight times a year he had to move the heavy gear to and from his premises.

Daniel Butcher, building surveyor of Lowestoft lived in Southwold from 1818 to 1858. When in 1853 Allen brought stones from Benacre Hall, Butcher, as mayor, gave him permission to put them on the site. There was a swampy place nearby, caused by cattle in the summer standing under the trees to get the shade.

Joseph Blowers "old enough to be better than he was" had known Southwold for sixty years, the road in question was formerly quite open, there was a footpath on both sides and a furze fence on the north side. The footpath on the north side was a good one and he and others used it to go to chapel. When he first knew the place the cattle used to come from the common into the town.

His son, Joseph, 50, master mariner and manager for Mr Hind confirmed his father's evidence.

133

Alfred Wentworth remembered the road twenty eight years. In 1847 it was a public high road and all open excepting that a gate was put across. William Stammers, 52, also proved the road open. He had seen small pools of water in the road where the cattle had stood. He was a carpenter who had worked for Mr Hind (April 8 1876)

Cutting Court of Queen's Bench. April 22 1875. William Smith had been sent to the county gaol for six months hard labour by the Southwold magistrates. He had asked a friend of his in the town lock up how he liked it when the constable came out and seized him and a scuffle ensued. Asked by the judge if the lock up was like a pound, counsel for Smith said it was a very primitive place. It had only one policeman and although it was a corporate town, the gentleman who held the office of mayor had been so for many years because no one else would accept it. For the magistrates it was stated that after striking the head constable Smith ran off to his mother's house. There he brandished an axe and threatened the constable with violence. However as the summons was served in his lawful absence fishing aboard his lugger the Lord Chief Justice quashed the conviction.

Cutting William Smith, described as a fisherman and stonemason at Lowestoft, sues the magistrates for unlawful imprisonment. He claimed that Joseph Heddington, late constable of Southwold and now deputy-governor of Hertfordshire County Gaol, had tripped him up outside the lock-up and threatened to run him in. He had not threatened the constable with an axe. Asked if he had suffered in health during his twenty two days in Ipswich gaol Smith replied that he did not fare so well in as he did out. Mr Bulwer, for the magistrates, hoped that that would be very widely known.

Heddington told the court that George Barningham had been put in custody at the Town Hall on suspicion of robbery and Smith had been very drunk. He had pursued him with Naunton, a special constable, and Lambert, one of the county police.

Lydia Smith of Southwold, the plaintiff's mother, said that she had sent the summons on to Lowestoft by Wentworth the carrier from where her son had sailed on the smack "Hope". The jury awarded Smith £16 and costs.

Cutting Southwold surprised by the news that Sidney Smith, headmaster of the National School for twelve years, had been dismissed without explanation. A native of the town he had been educated at the school and distinguished himself at Training College. He is of blameless character and has brought the school to a high standard of discipline and efficiency. He had quarrelled with the vicar over teaching the doctrine of baptism but that was a thing of the past. However he had recently applied for an increase in salary, though he had withdrawn this request when he found that the funds were not available. This incident will make people want to have a Board School in which they

134

can have a share in the management.

Cutting Monument to Agnes Strickland by John Allen, stonemason, in Southwold churchyard, not a gift from the Queen but beautiful enough to be so.

Cutting Mr Barker of Halesworth, who is staying at Southwold, thrown out of his gig while driving by the river side. His little son broke his arm. "B" a widower of Southwold advertises for a wife. A hoax is suspected.

An Etonian writes in praise of Southwold.

Cutting Charles Woods, over 70 and weak in intellect, who had moved from Southwold to Dunwich, drowned while returning from Walberswick. Banks, the bootmaker, had taken him to the Blue Anchor public house, when he found him wandering there the previous day.

Cutting Accident on the Great Eastern Railway at Oulton Marshes(June 1 1876)

Cutting Halesworth County Court. January 24 1876. Walter Harrison, inn-keeper of Southwold v. Robert Folkard, carrier of Southwold, for 16s 4d., the value of a box of cod-fish.

Edward Thomas Coe, veterinary surgeon of Wangford v. Robert Moore fishmonger of Southwold to recover £20.10s on a warranty of a horse.

East Cliff Villas, Southwold, Suffolk

Cutting Fire at Baggott's Mill, recently hired by C.M.Marsden but unoccupied at present. Mr Marsden is believed to be insured. Dinner of
the Peri Club. at the Victoria (Feb 2 1876)

Cutting Halesworth County Court. Harrison v Folkard re. the lost box of
cod.

Robert English, fisherman of Southwold,
v. Walter Harrison, innkeeper of Southwold to recover £4 4s the value
of some cod.   George Cady, dealer of Yoxford v. Thomas
Naunton, dealer of Southwold in an action to recover £16 4s 6d the
balance of an account. (Feb. 21 1876)

Cutting Declaration of the Poll in the East Suffolk Election. (Feb. 22 1876)

136

CALENDAR OF INSERTIONS IN VOLUME II OF MAGGS'S DIARY

The Insertions for Volume I (up to 1836) are calendared at the end of the Diary for 1818–1848. These, for 1836–1848, are noted in the transcript of the Diary if sufficiently important, though briefly. Those, after 1848, when they become more important and eventually take over the narrative, are transcribed in full or summarised as they occur.

Rates of Commonage 1836–7
Notice announcing a bazaar to be held by the Ladies of Southwold on the Bowling Green of the Swan Hotel in aid of the New Independent Chapel. (July 7 1836) ("and 8th. Took upwards of £190")
Notice of Sermons to be preached by the Rev. J. Sherman of the Surrey Chapel, London, by the Rev. S. Davis of Needham Market and by the Rev J. Alexander of Norwich at the Opening of the New Independent Chapel. (July 6 1837) ("Collected £108..5..0")
Notice of a Sermon to be preached by the Rev. H.H.Norris M.A., Rector of South Hackney and Prebendary of St. Paul's and Llandaff in aid of funds for erecting a new gallery in St. Edmund's that will provide 100 more free sittings. (October 9 1836) ("Collected £16:4:–")
Cutting Delays to the mail coaches caused by snow.
Notice that Mr Palmer is to auction the tolls or wharfage rates at Black Shore Quay for the next three years . December 9 1836)
Rates of Commonage 1837–8
Notice that Mr Palmer is to auction the grazing on two marshes in Southwold (March 30 1837). Amended in manuscript to read that Benjamin Palmer is to auction the grazing on four marshes in Southwold. (March 22 1838)
List of the Council for 1837–8 Manuscript notes of the names of the Treasurer, Town Clerk, Auditors and Assessors and against the name of Councillor Benjamin Palmer, butcher, "Died 27th Dec 1837 1838 3 Jany Mr Jo Gayford Shipowner elected in his place"
Ticket for the Coronation Dinner at Southwold. June 28 1838 No 41. Signed "J.Maggs" with the note "No of Children Dined on Gun Hill—512"
Notice from the Mayor, William Crisp, requesting shopkeepers to close at 4 on the afternoon of the funeral of Mrs Caroline Acton. (Notice dated September 26 1838, the funeral on the Friday following.) On the reverse "Lines on the Death of Caroline Acton—by Miss Agnes Strickland—in M.S.

> In that dread day; when Prince and Peer,
> And all who sleep in dust,
> Must yield account of wealth and power
> Committed to their trust.
>
> How many then who sternly sent
> The wretched from their door,
> And basely hoarded or mispent,
> On selfish pomp, their store.

Awakening from the graves brief thrall
To meet their Judge divine
Shall vainly wish their stewardship
On earth had been like thine.

For thou wert of that blessed train,
Who meekly here below,
Perform their Heavenly Master's will
In soothing human woe.

Thy gentle heart and liberal hand
Dispensed to all relief;
Thou hadst a gift for every want—
A tear for every grief

And tears unfeigned are shed for thee,
In many a mournful cot,
Where long thine honored memory
Shall flourish unforgot.

Yet we who knew thy virtues best
Forbear for thee to weep,
The ripened ear must bow to earth—
The full of days must sleep,

And Death is to the guileless heart,
A calm and welcome guest,
The shadow that must pass o'er all
Who join the ever bless'd.

Farewell we will not mourn for thee,
For thou hast humbly trod
The paths of purity and peace;
And such shall see their God.

List of the Council for 1838–9 By the name of Councillor James Boyce, builder "Died 19th Jany 1839—Joseph Arthy Elected 28 Jany 1839 Druggist"
Rates of Commonage 1839
List of the Council for 1839–40
Notice of a Public Dinner to commemorate the Queen's marriage. At the Crown on February 10 1840. "Tickets,to include a PINT of WINE, 5s each to be had at the BAR of the HOTEL"
Blank tickets for beer, beef (directed to Mr Oldring, butcher) and bread. The beer ticket redeemable at the Police Station House.(February 10 1840.)
Cuttings "Recollections of a smuggler" by "An old man of eighty four" "Alarm that two others and three soldiers from Southwold had made a seizure of 500 tubs of gin in a vault under his (Sherwood alias Clear Cupboard's) hog stye near the sea" (at Sizewell Gap, about 1780)

Notice announcing publication of Maggs's "Vessels of the Port of Southwold" ("1840")

Rates of Commonage 1840

Cutting The Auctioneer—a satirical description

Cutting Annual Meeting of the Subscribers to the Southwold Life Boat at the Town Hall. The Society had been founded in 1840 ("Nov 11th 1847")

List of the Council for 1840–41

Cutting The carrier pigeon that was found in Maggs's garden. Maggs includes the pieces of paper that it carried. (September 26 1841)

List of the Council for 1841–2

Statement "of all monies received and expended on account of the Mayor Aldermen and Burgesses of the Borough of Southwold" (Year ending 31 August 1841) Printed.

Rates of Commonage 1842

Particulars for the lease of the Town Farm for 8 years. To be auctioned at the Town Hall by Fulcher and Maggs on March 17 1842.

Cutting Cutts, a shopkeeper of Wrentham brings an action against Goldsmith, a carter of Southwold for damage done to the horse of the former when in collision with the cart of the latter at Wrentham. £8 12s awarded.

Cutting Bazaar for the benefit of the infant schools. Held on Gun Hill with Howlett's band from Norwich in attendance. £300 raised. Poems by Agnes Strickland "Seaside Offering" and her autograph on sale.("Aug 26–27 1856") Auction (*by Jas Maggs)

Cutting Queen Adelaide, the Queen Dowager, has sent twelve embossed cards with texts from Scripture in her own handwriting to the Southwold bazaar.

Lines on the death of James Martin, C.G.O. killed by the firing of one of the cannons on Gun Hill at the celebration of the Prince of Wales' Birthday, November 9 1842. Printed.

Cuttings Abraham Girling, aged 43, killed in a scuffle at the Cliff House at Long Island. A pilot, it was found that in a fight with Foster Bokenham, Girling had fallen over the cliff. "The case had caused much excitement in the town."

Subpoena To John Sutherland, Charles Edward Bird and Joseph Arthy to appear at the Assizes at Bury St Edmunds on March 25 1842 when Forster Bokenham is tried for manslaughter.

List of the Council 1842–3 Against the name of Edward Charles Bird, Alderman, is written "Died 8th Aug 1843"."Thomas Hen Jellicoe Grocer Monday 21 Aug 43".

Cutting reporting death of Francis Robinson Esq. of Cliff House, Dunwich, aged 91.

Handbill announcing that Frederic W. Denny is to take over the business of Mrs Abbott, draper, grocer and tallow chandler, High Street, Southwold. Notes "Mr Abbott died Sep. 1 1852 1853 (Mrs Abbott) June 15th leaves the Town" (Southwold May 2 1853)

Cutting "In thus publishing the following letter of apology from the Rev. H.W.R. Birch, of Southwold, Dr Wake deeply feels the painful but imperative duty which has been imposed upon him. He is aware it exposes him to misconstruction, but feels that the circumstances to which the letter refers leave him no alternative.

"SIR—I am perfectly satisfied that any statements made by me, affecting either your moral or Professional Character, or your Character as a Gentleman, are entirely without foundation. I have, therefore, no hesitation in retracting them, and in expressing the regret I feel that I should have for one moment given you any pain or annoyance. I need scarcely add that, under such circumstances, I shall not again make any statements whatever injurious to your character, but on the contrary make a point of contradicting such statements as far as I possibly can. As I desire that the vindication of your character should be as complete as possible, you are quite at liberty to make such use of this letter as you may think proper.

I am,Sir, Your obedient servant, H.W.R.BIRCH
London, October 3rd, 1843. To Dr. Wake."

Trade Card O.J.Boyce, Tobacconist 137 Waterloo Bridge Road, London

List of the Council 1843–4 Against the name of Councillor James Martin, inn-keeper is noted "Dd July 29 /44 George Edmund Child Iron Founder Elected Aug 6/44"

Cutting The "Sally", Welham, of and for Ipswich, was driven on shore at Walberswick in a gale on its way south from Goole laden with coals. The master was washed overboard and drowned. The Southwold lifeboat went out to two ships aground on the Barnard Sand but was too late to rescue the crews. (November 3 1843)

Charity Ticket Southwold Medical Dispensary directed to Mr Hammond, Medical Officer, on behalf of Sarah Brown. The ticket to be given to Mr Arthy, druggist, with the first prescription. (1843)

Cutting Ann Manning, 32, charged with having set fire to a dwelling belonging to James Ruthen at Wangford. Ruthen had caused her husband to be sent to Beccles gaol for non-payment of rent and she and her six children were due to be sent to the workhouse. ("2 Years")

Cutting The Southwold Brewery auctioned on behalf of the late William Crisp and realised £2,892. (Brewery £410, King's Head Public House £330, East Green Maltings £870, dwelling house £350, home malting £500, garden £33, Black Shore granary £80, coal bin £74, lease of marsh £5, shares of vessels £240—brewery, some of the maltings and dwelling house were bought by Mr Woodley of Cambridge.)

Circular announcing dinner at the Crown (tickets 12s 6d) on May 29 1844 in honour of Joseph Berry Edwards, who is leaving Southwold

Notice announcing performance by Hylton's Royal Menagerie (September 16 1844)

Lines upon death of young man (note—"named Lyons") killed on Wangford

Hill, July 15 1844, in an accident involving a cart. By Mary Smith of Wangford.

Cutting Mills v. Goff. Mills, a labourer from Wrentham, sues Goff for trespass in making an illegal distraint,

Cutting Letter from the murderer, Yarham, to Sarah, his wife, just before execution.

List of the Council 1844–5

Card of Robert Clark, late butler of Mrs Sheriffe of Southwold and now of the Angel Inn, Wangford. ("Jany 6th 1845. Took")

Cutting The"Princess Alice" of Newcastle, George Manderson, master, run down by the "Voyager" of South Shields off Southwold. Abandoned by her crew she came ashore on Walberswick beach, half a mile south of the pier. Now in Southwold harbour, most of her cargo of coals having been discharged.("Jan 13–14 1845")

Cuttings The collapse of the suspension bridge at Yarmouth.

Lines written upon the death of two young men, named English, drowned while fishing near Walberswick. ("1st July 1845") by Mary Smith of Wangford ("Daugr of the late John Lowsey of this Town")

Notice Maggs to auction the eight years lease of the Gate House at the Town Hall on June 19 1845. With the garden and piece of arable land belonging to it, now occupied by William Chapman or his under tenant. Crops of grass growing on the marsh walls to be auctioned at the same time.

Cutting Letter to the Editor of the Ipswich Journal from "a learned author with a Greek signature." (Suwald July 1 1845)

Better provision should be made for the Assistant Curate of Southwold.

Cutting Letter to the Editor of the Ipswich Journal from "A Churchman" replying to the above. (July 8 1845)

The income of the incumbent is £180 p.a. and not £50 as stated.

Cutting Letter to the Editor of the Ipswich Journal from the first correspondent.(July 15 1845)

The vicar of Reydon still has parochial rights at Southwold, the income from the endowment of the chapelry is under £50.

Cutting Letter to the Editor of the Ipswich Journal from "A Churchman" replying to the above. ("26 July 1845")

Detailed refutation, the real value of the perpetual curacy is £180 p.a. This agitation should never have been begun.

Notice Exhibition of Royal Wax Figures by James Ewing, Artist. Includes Queen Victoria and Prince Albert, the Finding of Moses in the Bulrushes, the Last Moments of Anne Boleyn etc etc. ("Septemb 15,16,17, & 18th 1845")

List of the Council 1845–6

Gaol List 10 William Safford Bobbit 41 Committed February 25th 1846 (r. & w.w.) by F.W.Farr,esq. convicted of a breach of the peace, to be imprisoned six calendar months, unless, &c. ("1852.Feb 26—For 14 days—as a Vagrant.") (Jarman, Printer, Beccles)

Cutting Thomas Rounce of Southwold married to Catherine, fifth daughter of Samuel Plant, of Easten Bavent.

Cutting Maggs to auction three brick and tiled freehold cottages at Wangford on the High Road from Southwold to Beccles with 50 rods of garden ground adjoining at the Angel Inn, Wangford on March 18th 1846.

Rates of Commonage 1843–7

Certificate issued by Jonathan Gooding, the defendant's attorney in the case between Robert John Debney and Henry Johnson Debney (plaintiffs) and James Easey that James Maggs, auctioneer, has been paid £6 for his attendance at Suffolk Assizes. (Four guineas for four days, the rest mileage for 36 miles)

Subpoena to Maggs to attend the Assizes at Ipswich, July 28 1846. Easey is described as executor for John Easey.

Cutting The case above brought to recover £6 3 10 for goods delivered. Verdict for plaintiffs

Cutting Letter to the Editor of the Ipswich Journal from Orlando Whistlecraft on the "Notably Hot June of 1846" (Minerva Cottage, Thwaite, 1846)

Notice Regatta to be held on August 27 1846.

Cutting Southwold Regatta ("Sep 3 1846") Fireworks at 9 p.m. on Gun Hill instead of at 11 p.m. on the bowling green at the Swan as previously, so that they should be seen by more people. A ball at the Town Hall.

Handbill Maggs to sell Birmingham and Sheffield Goods at the Old Swan on September 10 1846.

List of the Council 1846–7.

Cuttings Visit by Joseph Wolff, 35, the chiropodist, to Southwold. Later accused of false pretences, upon Dr Wake and William Charles Fonnerau of Ipswich. The accused "who was dressed in a loose brown coat with a light waistcoat, had a fine intelligent countenance but his appearance was not at all professional" was acquitted, in spite of the evidence of William Blowers, blacksmith, that he had seen him near his father's shop picking up the parings from horses' hooves. These it was suggested he passed off as corns that he had extracted. "During the trial several well dressed persons, apparently of the Jewish persuasion, stood against the bar near the prisoner and took much interest in the proceedings, and on his leaving the dock shook hands with him heartily and left the court with him."

Cutting satirical verses "The Chiropodist". signed L.E.H. Southwold. An attack on the credulity of the lawyer, the physician, the squire, the priest and the lady.

Notice Opening of the Primitive Methodist Chapel at Walberswick on December 25, 1846 with a sermon preached by Mr W. Sapcoat. On Sunday January 3 1847 two sermons will be preached by Mr E. Mollett late of Cambridge.

Printed reply by the Commissioners of Southwold Harbour addressed to the Lords of the Admiralty and defending them from attacks made upon them in the 1st and 2nd Reports of the Tidal Harbours Commission. (Southwold, January 13 1847)

Cutting Case at Chelmsford Assizes in which William Pashley, at one time a farmer at Reydon but now living in Southwold and once a licensed victualler of White Notley, brings a case for slander against his wife's uncle, a Mr Higham. This he loses.

Notice of the appearance at the Town Hall on April 27 1847 of the Ethiopian Singers. Admission,one shilling, reserved seats in front 2s. Children half price. For one night only.

Notice of the second appearance, under the patronage of the Mayor, of the Ethiopian Singers "in consequence of the great applause and the overflow to witness(their) performance". On May 5, when they will give a morning and evening concert.

Cutting Opening of the Norwich and Lowestoft line. ("July 1st 1847") ("See July 15th 1831")

Cutting Tenders invited for deepening Buss Creek. (May 27 1847)

Cutting Terrific thunderstorm at Southwold on August 5 1847.

Cutting George P. Freeman to auction the hull of the pilot boat "Swiftsure" on the beach at Southwold under directions from the Admiralty. (June 9 1856)

Cutting Freeman to auction the "Swiftsure" on October 23.

Reprint from the "Bury Post" of September 8 1847 headed "Marriage at Southwold" and reporting the celebrations in the town at the marriage of John Heigham of Hunston Hall and Miss Lydia Birch, daughter of the Vicar of Southwold.

Cutting recording the same.

Cutting W.C.Fonnerau Esq. of Ipswich has offered £50 towards the repair etc. of St. Edmund's providing the pews in the nave are replaced by open benches, only those in the chancel being retained for those who prefer them. The idea is however warmly opposed by some of the principal ratepayers, who are unwilling to vacate their comfortable pews in the body of the church. ("Dec 19 1846")

Cutting Letter to the Editor of the Ipswich Journal from Fonnerau, dated December 23 1846 from East Cliff House, Southwold.

The opposition to his proposals, which had already been implemented at St. Margaret's, Ipswich (his parish church, he was the owner of the Christchurch Mansion) had been exaggerated in the paper. He had sent papers round Southwold describing the intended changes. At a subsequent parish meeting these were overwhelmingly accepted and a committee was chosen to carry them into effect. A canvass around the town showed 560 in favour, 20 against and the support of Dissenters as well as Churchmen. Only two of the principal inhabitants are opposed. Contrary to the article however, he does not intend that the pews in the chancel should be retained.

Handbill circulated around Southwold containing Fonnerau's proposals. Population of the town—2,700 plus visitors (likely to be affected by the probable coming of the railroad.) Dwelling houses—450. Pews in the church—104. Appropriated pews—85. Occupants of pews—213. Occupants of pews rated under £10—21. The church and chancel will hold 600. On November 15 there were only 88 in the centre portion of the nave, 5 in the north aisle, about 40 in the chancel. Pews mean that some of the congregation have their backs to the minister, the voices of the clergy are obstructed etc etc.

Handbill To the Rate-Payers of Southwold urging them to attend a Vestry Meeting called for July 30 1847 to listen to opponents of the proposal to change the pews for benches. They must not be persuaded out of their rights, once a faculty has been obtained it will be too late.
(Bye & Drewell, Printers, Southwold)

Handbill To the Inhabitants of Southwold from Daniel Fulcher, one of the churchwardens, asserting that the change will add 200 sittings in the church, without any addition to the church rate. July 30 1847.
(Bye & Drewell, Printers, Southwold)

Cuttings Letters to the Editor of the Ipswich Journal.
April 28 1847 from "An old churchman" "Whilst our lodging-houses are preparing for the reception of annual visitors to the town, we are all looking for an increase of accommodation for them in our parish Church" . . . . ."the great fear" is that it "will be made a local job". Already "good taste has been outraged" . . . "by the hideous ostentation of the modern altar piece, and the certainly less gaudy but most obtrusive exhibition of common carpentry-craft in the gallery under the organ" It is unquestionable that there is no builder in the town who has enough knowledge of ecclesiastical architecture to carry out the changes in keeping with the style of the church.
May 5 1847 from Fonnerau. In reply to "An old churchman" the altar piece was the work of the county surveyor and the gallery was also designed by Mr Whiting, who rejected one produced by a local builder that was in keeping with the style of the church. The new benches will be similar to those in St. Margaret's and have the approval of the London and diocesan societies. The work will be done by a competent person. The Bishop supports what is being done.
(May 15 1847) from "An old churchman' If the altar piece and the gallery were designed by the county surveyor and his plans were correctly carried out, then the danger that the pure style of the church will be violated is even greater. Fonnerau is not in a position to know but it is likely that the work will be done by one of the churchwardens, who as employer and at the same time employee should be disqualified for the contract.

Cutting "The Rage for Benches" Southwold. August 5 1847

> Open benches ! open benches !
> Is the cry all up the street;
> Down with pews, each pew entrenches,
> On your neighbour's right of seat.

See my Lord, with rule in hand
And four hundred pounds to pouch;
Marshalling a rabble band,
Before his silver mace to crouch.

"A FACULTY ! A FACULTY !
A FACULTY !" says he;
"A faculty full easily,
Shall be obtain'd by me."

"Lordly Warden, big in pow'r,   (Dnl Fulcher
Who resists my lordly *rule*   Churchwarden)
Shall be branded from this hour
And be deem'd an arrant fool."

"For no faculty, no faculty,
No faculty has he;
Who does not see with clearest eye,
He'd best be *ruled* by me."

"Wood I've purchas'd, oak and birch,
Poppy heads are all a doing;
To ornament *my* parish church,
And do away the pewing."

"Rods are made,'tis said, of *birch*,
Avaunt ! ill-omen'd fears !
I'll plan and plane it for my church,
And pay up all arrears !"

Cutting Senseless squabbles in Southwold about pews and benches. While it is suggested by some that there are not enough sittings available in the parish church, last Sunday afternoon (the fullest service of the day) there were only 43 persons, including children, to fill 263 free sittings. The pews in other parts of the church were comparatively empty. ("Aug 11 1847")

Cuttings Letters to the Editor of the Ipswich Journal.
August 11 1847 from "An old churchman."
The question of pews and benches has been removed from our brawling vestry to the Consistory Court of Norwich. It originated with a casual visitor to the parish (Fonnerau), the Bishop seems to think that the change is necessary because of limited accommodation in the church but the minister, who ought to be the best judge, does not agree, even though there is a majority in the parish in favour. In fact, up to now there has been no complaint of a lack of sittings and the additional space provided by the gallery built a few years ago has not been fully taken up. If the recent canvass had been accompanied by a request for subscriptions the support given might not have been so great.
August 21 1847 from the same.

The article of August 11, stating that on Sunday August 8 under half of the 263 sittings in the gallery were filled, confirms the opinion of the minister. The same was true on Sunday last. The fact that tenders have not been asked for gives added suspicion of a "job", particularly when the churchwarden who is a builder says that the cost will not be greater than £450. The incumbent urges the poor state of the building, the roof is in a dangerous state, as are the stonework and leading of the windows. To carry out repairs will cost £1,000 to £1,200 and this should take priority over the money to be spent on the change from pews to benches. "It will be, indeed, most fortunate if the mischief ends in the parish in which it had its beginning. ("Aug 21/47")

August 24 1847 from "A parishioner"
Supports "An old churchman" and attacks a grant of £20 made by the Town Council towards the cost of the benches.

Cutting Publication by the Editor of the Ipswich Journal of a copy of a letter from the Reverend H.W.R. Birch, perpetual curate of Southwold,to the Secretaries of the Church Building Society and of the Norwich Diocesan Society on August 17 1847. This was at Birch's request and in support of the letter from "An old churchman" of the 21st.

Birch opposes donations from the societies towards the cost of benches until the fabric of the church is repaired. He repeats that the 270 free sittings are never half filled, that the intention is to employ common carpenters from the town unfit to undertake the decorative work. His own churchwarden supports him. In a postscript he states that Fulcher, the Parish Church-warden is also the Mayor and the main mover and only applicant for the necessary faculty.

Cutting Letter to the Editor of the Ipswich Journal from Fonnerau dated from Christ Church Park, August 25 1847.

The reason that the gallery has not been filled for the last Sunday or two is that the Sunday School children are on holiday during the harvest. If the pews are replaced the church will fill. "I was at Norwich on Monday, and when our application for a Faculty came before the Court, it was postponed, as Mr Birch's Proctors stated that he (Mr Birch) was in London on urgent family business. Now I saw Mr Birch in Norwich myself, and so did two other gentlemen on that day."

Cutting   "The Auto-Faculty of a Warden"   Displayed in a Soliloquy
         "What care I for devastation,   Or WOOD versus STONE, LIME,
         "Crumbling arch or stone decay'd;   HAIR, and Co.
         "Give me but accommodation,
         "And cent. per cent. to be repaid.

         " 'Tis true I've sworn by all that's good,
         "The holy fabric to repair;
         "But then I feel I deal in wood,
         "And not in stone, or lime or hair.

"Things go very queer in S'owld,
"There's little stirring but the spray;
"I'll raise *the wind* and fish for gold,
"And all *my faculty* display!"   August 28 1847

Cutting Letters to the Editor of the Ipswich Journal
August 29 1847 from the Reverend H.W.R.Birch.

The dilapidated state of Southwold Church is confirmed after actual inspection by Mr Bardwell, the celebrated author of "Temples and Churches". It is untrue that the changes have the unanimous support of the population of Southwold. "It is true that I left London on Monday, the 23rd, by the 11½ a.m. train and that I entered the Norwich station by that train and crossed over to the Lowestoft line. Having been detained on urgent family business in London until 11 o'clock a.m. I availed myself of the 11½ a.m. Norwich and Lowestoft train from London, to reach home that evening."

Approximately the same date from "A Proprietor".

This unhappy parish is too prone at all times to engender strife and animosity in itself. Fonnerau defeats his own argument for if the Sunday School children were absent why did those who normally could not find room take advantage of the fact. In fact, in the church which is under his own patronage (St. Margaret's, Ipswich) two of the most respectable families have been driven from divine service by the changes he has brought about. In the narrowness of his mind and in the weakness of his eyesight he has overlooked a more important church, that at Lowestoft. Here he could have tried his hand on behalf of a population of 4–5,000 where the church is under the patronage of the bishop, who is ready to sweep the pews out of every church in the diocese. He has interfered in what concerns him not.

Cutting The first hearing of "Pews v. Benches" in the Norwich ecclesiastical court was on August 2, it dragged on to the 23rd and then to September 6. The faculty will not heal dissension, at the instigation of a stranger an assuming churchwarden and a self-interested and mischievous part of the population are thrusting the proposition on the rest while the objectors are subjected to gross insults and vulgar epithets.

Cuttings Letters to the Editor of the Ipswich Journal
September 14 1847 from Birch submitting the report of Bardwell on the state of Southwold Church (dated from Glenstall Castle, Limerick, September 6 1847) that contradicts Fulcher's claim that it is in a fit state of repair. The report is given in full.

September 21 1847 from Birch attacks the expenditure of £500 upon the interior when £1,200 will be needed for the fabric.

Cutting Vestry held at which the Perpetual Curate and Mr Boniwell, his churchwarden, confront Fulcher, the people's warden, with Bardwell's report, which the latter rejects. 800 persons have signed a memorial in favour of benches and now the majority at the meeting vote that Bardwell's fears are unfounded. A poll being demanded and kept open until 4 p.m. on the following day the promoters of the project muster 69 supporters with a combined rating of £809 in a parish of 436 qualified voters and a rateable value of £5,562. It now remains to be seen whether a faculty addressed to two churchwardens can be carried out by one against the will of the other. ("Oct 9 1847")

Cutting Letter to the Editor of the Ipswich Journal from Birch, dated November 8 1847. At the requirement of the Archdeacon, Mr Fulcher has taken upon himself to employ Mr Stannard, an architect and surveyor from Norwich, who after an inspection of St. Edmund's has issued a report which Birch now asks the Editor to print, together with Bardwell's further refutation.

Report by Joseph Stannard printed with Bardwell's refutation.

Roof of the south aisle—very dilapidated Roof of the north aisle—requires little repair. Lead upon both roofs—in a bad state. Roof of Nave and chancel—generally in a good state. Windows—in a good condition considering their age and situation East window—of wood but well executed and perfectly sound. Flooring of the tower—in a very bad condition. Facing of the plinths of the walls—repaired with brick, not the most tasteful material. Bardwell's reply is detailed authoritative and well argued, criticising Stannard's deductions and proposed remedies rather than his observations.

Cutting Accident at the Eastern Union Railway Station at Hadleigh. ("Sep 16 1847")

Cutting Sudden death of Mr Thomas Grimwood of Woodbridge, timber merchant, aged 65."A sincere friend of the poor." ("18 Sep 1847")

Cutting Charles Harrison, second son of George Kerby Esq., of 43 Lothbury, London married at Southwold church to Eliza, youngest daughter of Mr Debney of Southwold.

Cutting Storm on the 7th (October ?) when some cottages at Henstead are destroyed.

Cutting Maggs to auction two dwelling houses on Church (now Bartholomew) Green with boarded warehouse adjoining, formerly a blacksmith's shop. On October 21 1847 at the Old Swan. Owned by Mrs Mary Oldring.

Cutting Council elections "To so low an ebb have corporate distinctions fallen at Southwold that the day of annual election of town councillors arrived, without a sufficiency of candidates in the field for filling up the four vacancies. Six persons were, however nominated, when a struggle ensued, not for who should get in, but for who should remain out of the office. To wit, a gentleman who was nominated without his knowledge, felt so indignant on being informed of it, that he immediately caused handbills to be posted, and he sent the town crier round the parish to solicit his friends and fellow burgesses to vote against him, and by these active measures placed himself at the bottom of the poll. . . . . if it should hereafter become necessary, either in an obituary notice or on a grave stone, to express the utmost depth of social and civic degradation in any departed burgess of Southwold, let it be said "that he was nothing,—not even one of the TOWN COUNCIL"

Cutting Letter to the Editor of the Ipswich Journal from "C"
Attacks previous article (of November 3). denying the facts given and reserving the greatest degradation for those who slander and libel and stir up trouble.

Cutting Meeting of Southwold Corporation elects Daniel Fulcher mayor for a fourth term, in spite of an attempt to replace him with Peter Palmer, who had previously been a Petty Constable.

Cutting Death at Tattingstone of John Preston Neale, aged 68, late of the General Post Office and author of "Westminster Abbey" etc. (November 14)

Cutting Death at Ipswich of Mr Postle Jackson, printer and proprietor of the Ipswich Journal, aged 69. (November 15) "Mar 6 1855 Stephen Jackson"

List of the Council 1847–8

Cutting Letter to the Editor of the Ipswich Journal from "A Burgess" (November 16 1847)
"C" is in error. The unwilling candidate did send out the town crier and bills were posted in the Market Place and the windows of the Town Hall.

Cutting Letter to the Editor of the Ipswich Journal from "A Burgess of Southwold"(November 17 1847)
That from amongst a council of 16 only one person can be found in four years to fill the office of mayor speaks for itself. There is no difference in rank between Palmer and Fulcher, they are both carpenters, indeed Fulcher was once Palmer's journeyman, at the very time that the former was constable. The latter office is one of utility and respect.

Notice from the Editor closing the correspondence "Municipal Corporations in general and Southwold Corporation in particular, are too contemptible for the public to be interested in the squabbles respecting the honours of a seat at the board. . . . the public are heartily tired of "this puddle in a storm".

Railway Times Yarmouth to London : London to Yarmouth.

Cutting Thomas Wallace, Vestry Clerk, invites tenders for the repair of the roof of the south aisle. (January 7 1848)

Cutting The Hawk, Hutchins, a Rochester barge from London, with deals, enters Lowestoft reporting that the "James and Mary", "More" another Rochester barge, has sunk in a gale with three hands off the Barnard Sand. (January 5 1848)

Cutting Mr John Merrells, farmer of Sizewell Gap, aged 84, has died at the house of his son-in-law, Mr Charles Kersey of Aldringham. (4 Jan 1848)

Cutting Southwold lit by gas on Thursday the 21st by George Child, the engineer of the Gas Works.

Prospectus of Southwold Gas-Light Company. ("Jany 1848")
"Trustees Mr Rt. J. Debney and T. Wallace, Esq. Solor. W.A. Thompson. Auditor for the directors—and W.M.Woodley. Auditor for the Shareholders. Mar. 19th Commenced building the Gasometer. May 1st Commenced excaviting and laying down the Pipes—June Erecting Lamp Posts et. September 21st 1848 Two Strangers Employed namely "Kent" & "Gain" and Fitch the fitter of burners.

1849 Gas Rate 4d in the £ collected yearly 2d in the £ one of 2 rates pd by
the Corporation Gas Rate 4d in the £ collected by me Maggs, Assistant
Overseer. Superintendent of the Works Benj Palmer"

ERRATA ET ADDENDA

The text of this volume has been cleared of obvious error but due to the inexperience of the transcriber/editor, the pressure of time and, perhaps, traps set by the writing of the diarist, the following corrections, mostly insignificant, should be made to the first volume:

page 6/line 19 read Gleaner for Eleanor   21/13 held/holds
22/11 Building/building   23/27 Cancelled/cancelled   24/1 *insert* is made
after no mention   25/20 Vane/vane   25/37 *insert* £5 *after* Watch
House–Corporation   27/24 hires/had   28/11, 13 Betts/Balls
28/17 to/of   28/20 *omit* to   29/17 *omit* part   30/20 shall/that
30/23 less/loss   31/12 Income/I receive   31/17 Paid/paid
32/6 hand/hands   33/9 *insert* Post Mistress *after* Emily Bye
33/11 Naunton/Marsden   36/17 Angier/Aungier
36/21 succeeds/succeeded by/to   36/29 Rbt Barker/Robt Barker
37/2 & 3 *insert in margin* This house was to 1810 Nags Head *after* Pilot
Boat.   37/7 licenced *before* Victoria   37/29 *omit* the *before* Shetland
39/35 Barham/Barsham   43/14 Sand/Land   44/26 Wife/wife
46/20   Top sides/Sep sides   46/30 Elizth and Ann/Elizth-Ann
46/38 East green/East Green   47/34 *insert* Dissolved Dec 1864 *after* 1816
Friendly Society   48/24 S. H. Bloome/S. M. Bloome   50/38 *insert* I
before conducted   50/40 *insert* a *before* Miss Lacey   52/5 B.B./R.B
52/25 roused/raised   52/42 vessel/vessels   53/10 as/of
53/44 55/65 54/2 23/5 54/3 *insert* Aug 17 *before* 1815   54/10 *insert* May 18
after 1818   54/11 *delete* May 18   54/41 taxed/total   55/5 This/New
55/41 Walberswick/Walbers   56/2 26th/24th   59/10 Owen/Dean
59/18 *insert* Esq *after* J. Catton   60/7 *insert* I *before* received
61/2 adjoining/sdjoining   64/12 *insert* 1841 *after* Feby
65/18 Harbour/Harbor   65/24 1805/1808 68/10 *insert* 1844 *after* June 3
68/16 marries/married   71/24 stopt/slept   71/39 Sailed/sailed
73/6 parted/posted   73/40 Incendary/Incendiary   74/14 Pivett/Rivett
76/17 tresspassing/trespassing   79/8 milinery/millinery   79/10 5th/6th
81/7 *delete* the *before* modus   82/36 Howes/Homes
84/9 Intered/interred   91/31 Privilege/Privildge
98/4 reinstated/re-elected   98/31 May/Sep   98/43 3 March/Jan 4/45 *Then*
insert 1844 Dec 30th Died at Bulcamp House Mr. John Norman
ag 74 Interred here Jan 4/45   100/29 the/this
104/34 1841/841 104/35 Mayow/Mayhow   105/37 *insert* 25th *before*
Xtmas   111/37 The number of confirmation candidates refers to the third
confirmation   113/3 61/41 114/43 th/gth   115/42 Mrs./Mr.
118/36 Meshach/Messhach   120/41 Sands/Lands   125/3 & 16 C. A.
Everett/E. A. Everett   127/16 Harbour/harbour

132/13 sprinkling/sprinklin   132/28 Property/Propery   135/12 *insert* Jo *in front of* Parry
135/35 Harvey's/Haweys   135/36 Mr./Mrr.   136/41 Butcher/Butchers
136/45 *insert after* Geater youngest Son of Mr. Thos Geater   137/33–4 Add (not sold. this is the 2d time put up. Oct 15 1856 I sold her) Oct 1 Oct 15
140/4 Swain/Swan
141/6 Blythborough/Blythburgh   143/8 Respets/Regre.

INDEX

References to Volume II are in italics

I. INDEX LOCORUM

School) 3, 58: Demarara *63*: Denham 74: Dereham *24*: Derhend St. Mary (Wilts) 123: Dieppe *124*: Diss 125, *123*: Ditchingham *64, 69, 79*: Douro (Canada West) *86, 104*: Dover 44, 78: Doveridge (Uttoxeter) *119*: Downs (The) *57*: Down Grange (Hants) *119*: Dublin 131: Dudgeon (Bank) 98: Dungeon (Bank) *21*: Dundee 124, *125*: Dunkirk *16*: Dunwich 2, 2n., 43, 45, 52–3, 68, 70–2, 76, 91, 97, 101, 104, 108, 110–2, 132, 147, *2, 10, 14, 50, 56, 69–70, 74–5, 82–3, 88–90, 96, 100–1, 104, 109, 116, 118–20, 125, 127, 135, 139*; (All Saints) 91, 110n; (Cliff House) 119, *139*; (Little Dingle) 118, *54*; (St. James) 67

Earl Soham *88*: Eartholm (sandbank) *31*: Easton Bavents 6, 15, 21, 24, 43–6, 49–51, 56, 74–6, 82, 91, 93, 105, 107, 109–12, 114, 127, 130–1, 137–8, *1, 13, 29, 30, 55, 79, 86, 99, 101, 116–8, 142*; (Easton Broad) *99*; (Easton Farm) 67: Easton Cliff 43–4, *29*: Edinburgh 112–3, *88*: Elsinore *122*: Eltham 77: Ely 76, *24*: Epping 76: Eton (College) *19, 21, 123, 135*: Exeter 38, 48, 62: Eyke *104*

Fakenham *24*: Falmouth 57, *123*: Farnham 98: Feversham (Kent) 8: Filby *119*: Finchley *54*: Flamborough Head *101*: Fornham (House) *93*: Foy 119: Framlingham 3, 55, 71, 115, 138, 142, *90*: France 6: Fressingfield *33*: Friborg 133–4: Frostenden 55, 92, 109–10, 113, 118, 134, 139, *30, 43, 45, 54, 74, 76, 78, 81, 87, 92, 97–8, 108, 124*

Galloper Lights *57*: Gazar 127: Geldeston 84, 100, 108; (Brewery) 96: Geneva 64: Genoa 129: Glasgow *110*: Glemham 51; (Great) 134: Glenstall Castle (Limerick) *147*: Gloucestershire 96: Godalming 73n: Goodwin Sands 41: Goole 46, *123, 140*: Gorleston 106, *16, 124*: Gothenburg 75: Grimsby 101, *66, 124*: Guernsey *33*, 98: Gunfleet 118, *65*

Haddiscoe *24*, 77: Hadleigh *80*, 148: Hague (The) 81, 147: Hales 67: Halesworth 1, 13, 16, 41, 53, 60, 70–1, 73, 77–8, 92, 96, 102–3, 107–8, 112, 115–6, 126, 132, 136, 139, *10–11, 17, 25, 31–4, 41–2, 48–9, 52–3, 55–6, 59, 63, 66, 69–70, 74, 77–80, 83–5, 87–90, 93, 97–100, 102, 104, 108–9, 111, 113–4, 117, 122, 124, 131, 135–6*; (Brewery) *80*; (Bridge) 38: Halstead *111*: Hamburg *113*: Hanworth Hall 104: Happisburgh 6, 64, 110, 125, *1*; (Sand) *75*: Harleston 10, *69–71, 79, 81*: Harlow 134: Harrow 136: Hartlepool *45, 51, 66*: Harwich 13, 44, 46, 125, 127, 135, *51, 75, 109, 111–2, 114–7, 131*; (St. Peter's) *111*: Hasketon *127*: Haslemere 131: Hastings 32: Haughley 139: Heigham (Norf.) 53, 128: Henham 32, 96, 124, 143, *10, 18, 109, 111, 124*; (Hall) *91, 119*; (Park Farm) *125*: Henstead 8, 24, *17, 56, 79, 88, 106, 148*: Hereford 9; (Cathedral) *23, 23n.*; (St. Martin's with All Saints) 9: Herefordshire 23: Herne's Bay 127: Hertfordshire *134*: Heveningham *15, 17, 88*: Higham 66: Hinton *90*; (Hall) *74*: Holkham 61: Holland 41, 71: Holton 64, *56, 69, 70, 105, 110–1*: Home (sand) *65*: Hosenden Hall 19: Hoxne 16, 92; *75*: Hull 43–4, 92, 133, 138, *50, 52, 55, 57*: Hulver 68: Hunston Hall 137, *8, 143*: Huntingfield 67, *7, 53*: Ichalve (Island of) 126: Icklingham, All Saints *123*: Ile Daiz *124*: Ilketshall, St. Andrews 22: India *123*: Indus (river) 98: Ipswich 7, 13, 36, 45, 55, 70, 73, 76, 84, 93, 99n., 100–1, 107, 111, 113, 116, 120–1, 123–4, 129, 132, 134, *6, 10, 16, 19, 23n., 27, 29–30, 45, 48, 56, 62, 68, 83–4, 87, 96, 99, 104, 108–9, 111–3, 116–7, 123–5, 140, 142–3*; (Assembly Room) 56; (Bank Street) *111*; (Berners Street) *91*; (Chantry) 49; (Christchurch Park) *143, 146*; (Commercial Road) *111*; (Curriers Arms Lane) 20; (Dale Hall Lane) *91*; (Gaol) 66, 72, 79, 110, 129, *54, 62, 83, 87, 127*; (St. Margaret's) *143–4*, 147: (St. Mary le Tower) *129*; (St. Nicholas's) *103*; (Stoke) 49; (Town Brewery) *116*; (Trinity Parsonage) *108*: Isle of France 53: Italy 116, *107*

Inns, Hotels, Beer Houses and Public Houses

Anchor, Park Street, Southwark 134: Angel, Halesworth 32, 55, *90*: Angel, Wangford

125, 131, 140–1, *29, 62, 99, 141–2*: Bear, Reydon 62, 134, 136, *4, 16, 21, 44–6, 59, 63, 67, 74, 86, 97, 104, 114, 118*: Bear, South Town 6: Bear, Yarmouth 66: Bell, Walberswick 96, 115, *79, 108*: Belle Vue, The Hague 81, 147: Blue Anchor, Walberswick 1, 2, 6, 11, 56–7, 60, 66, 84, 97, 124, *124, 135*: Brickmakers' Arms, Southwold 28n: Buss, Blackshore 28, 36, 37, 42, 128, *80*: Cherry Tree Inn, Stoven *20, 24, 56, 116*: Coach and Horses, London, *103, 107*: Crooked Billet, London *103, 107*: Cross Bow, Sotherton, 124, 135, *10, 90*: Cross Keys, Beccles 134: Crown, Little South Street, Wisbech 140: Crown, Southwold (= New Swan) 35, 47, 66, 71, 77, 95, 106, 113, 120–1, 123, 125, 131–2, 134, 136, 137, 145–7, *6, 8, 11, 21, 25–6, 29, 35, 42, 45, 50, 56, 67, 70–1, 80, 82, 90–1, 98, 105, 116, 120, 138, 140*: Crown and Angel, St. Stephen's, Norwich 140: Custom House Inn, Ipswich *116*: Dock Inn, Ramsholt 74: Dog Inn, Brampton *50*: Eagle, Wrentham *25, 46, 54, 108*: Five Bells, South Cove *106, 132*: Fleece, Bungay 16: Fox, Darsham *45*: George, Thurton *8*: Green Dragon, Harleston 7, 10, *69–71*: Green Man, Southwold 36: Greyhound, St. Margaret's, Ipswich *91*: Griffin, Yoxford *51, 80*: Harp, Wenhaston *109*: Horse Shoe, Southwold *80*: Hotel de Paris, Cromer 145: Joiner's Arms, Southwold 36, 64: King's Arms, Halesworth 70: King's Head, Beccles 24: King's Head, Southwold 9, 35–6, 35n., 71, 73n., 128, *39n., 78, 140*: King's Head, Wrentham *98*: Lord Nelson, Southwold 35n., 48, 100, 108, 124, *96, 104, 115*: Lion, Wangford *30*: Magpie and Horseshoe, Westminster *103*: Moonraker, London *103*: Nag's Head, Southwold 37: New Quay, Reydon 138: Pilot Boat, Southwold 37, 75, 116, 138, *16, 45, 80*: Queen's Arms, Newgate Street *106, 107*: Queen's Head, Lowestoft 10, 135–6: Red Lion, Southwold 9, 36, 48, 64, 75, 93, 103, 115, 130, 140, 145, *7, 8, 13, 24, 32, 40–1, 48–9, 56–7, 78, 87, 104, 111, 114, 122–3, 132*: Reydon P.H. 23: Saracen's Head, Aldgate 111, *90*: Sea Horse Inn, Ipswich *111*: Ship Inn, Dunwich 101, *14, 74*: Southwold Arms, Southwold 36, 118, 125, 137, *6, 33, 45, 96, 104, 118*: Sportsman's Inn, Hackney Fields 120: Star, Southwold 37: Suffolk Hotel, Ipswich *111*: Suffolk Hotel, Lowestoft, 125, *16*: Sun Inn, Foregate, Clement's Inn, London *56*: Sun, Halesworth *50*: Swan (Old), Southwold 13, 31, 33, 33n., 35, 38n., 40, 42, 47, 61, 71, 75, 95, 103, 105, 110, 112n., 117–18, 122, 124–7, 129, 133, 135–6, 138, *8, 13, 18, 24, 26–7, 34–6, 48–9, 62, 64, 68, 71, 74, 76, 79–81, 83–4, 86, 91–2, 100–1, 104, 113, 117, 119, 122–3, 125, 127, 131, 137, 142*: Swan, Wangford 51, *44*: Three Tuns, Halesworth *80*: Tuns, Rushmere 96: Tuns, Yoxford 113, 125, *30*: Two Brewers, Southwold 35n., 36: Victoria, Southwold 37, 145, *136*: Vine, Bishopsgate Within 111: Walnut Tree, Benacre *121*: Wellington Inn, Harwich, *109*: White Hart Inn, Blythborough *50*: White Horse, Southwold 74: White Horse, Old Haymarket, Norwich 24: White Lion, Beccles 96: White Lion, Southwold 35n, 36: White Swan, Beccles 133
Jarrow 118
Katwyk *29*: Kelsale 67, 132, *101*: Kent *123*: Kessingland 45, 92–3, 110, 131, *2–3, 16, 74, 119*: King's Lynn 91, *24*: Kingston, Upper Canada, 76: Kirby Cane 6, 10, 74, 85, 93, 118, 127, 133, *24, 34*: Kirkley 6, 76, 99: Knock Lights *57*
Latimere Dam *59*: Laxfield *23n.*: Leiston 60, 81, 111, *30, 46, 117*: Lisbon *125*: Litcham (Norf) *14, 80*: Liverpool 84, 100, 140, *77, 92*: Llandaff *137*: Loddon 135, *24*; (Asylum) *132*
London 9, 20, 29n., 43–5, 57, 68, 77, 82, 84, 91, 97–8, 100, 102, 106, 116, 119–21, 125–6, 130–2, *13, 16–7, 19, 24, 27, 29–30, 32–4, 37, 40, 43, 46, 48, 51, 56, 61, 70, 72, 74, 79–81, 84–5, 94, 98–102, 105–6, 108–10, 114, 118–20, 123, 126, 129, 140*; Albany 9, 99, 102, 106; Aldgate Church *103*; All Souls, Langham Place 139; Billingsgate 105; Blackwall *103*; Brick Lane, Whitechapel 105; British Museum 103;

Brompton Hospital *122*; Buckingham Palace 102; Charing Cross 18, 105; Charlotte Street, Fitzroy Square 102–6; Chelsea *37*; Church Street, Manchester Square 9, 82; Covent Garden Theatre 103; Cremorne *105*; Crucifix Lane, Bermondsey 105; Custom House 103; Deptford 77, *96*; Edinburgh Castle Inn 102, 105; Elephant and Castle 105; Farrington Street 105; Fenchurch Street 9, 102, 105; Fitzroy Square 102, Gravesend 9, 82, *12*; Great Russell Street, Covent Garden 138; Great Suffolk Street *103*; Great Titchfield Street, Cavendish Square 102; Great Tower Hill 105; Great Western Railway Station 105; Greenwich 53, 106, *103*; Greenwich Hospital 102; Greenwich and Croydon Railway Station 105; Hackney 134; Sportsman's Inn, Hackney Field 120; Hadlow Street, Burton Crescent 106; Hanover Chapel, Regent Street 102; Hertford Street, Mayfair 66; Holborn 103, 106; (St. Alban's) *129*; Hungerford 106; Islington 100–1, *42*, *116*; (Caledonian Road) *89*; John Street 106; Lloyd Street, Lloyd Square 103–5; London Bridge 105, *103*; London Docks 103; Lothbury *148*; Manchester Square 106; Monument 105; Moonraker Inn *103*; Mount Row, Berkeley Street 111; National Gallery 102; Newgate 108; Newgate Street *106*; Northumberland Alley, Fenchurch Street *103*; Old Bailey 70, *106–7*; Old Kent Road 105; Oxford Market 102; Oxford Street *103*; (Pantheon) 106; Pentonville *90*; Picadilly 82, 105; Promenade, Holborn 102; Providence Court, North Audley Street 111; Russell Street, Blackwall *82*; Queen's Square, Westminster 102; Saracen's Head, Aldgate 105; South Street 106; South Moulton Street 105–6; St. Catherine's Wharf 102–3; St. Giles 102; St. James 101; St. James's Palace 106; St. James's Piccadilly *119*; St. John's Street, Minories *103*, *107*; St. John's, Waterloo Road 67; St. Katherine's Dock *106*; St. Luke's, Chelsea 11, *114*; St. Margaret's, Westminster 102; St. Martin's-le-Grand *106*; St. Michael's, Chester Square *119*; St. Michael's *103*; St. Paul's 102, 105, *137*; St. Peter's, Eaton Square *91*; St. Saviour's, Southwark 134; St. Thomas's Hospital 102; Seymore Place 102; Lower East Smithfield *103*; Staple Inn, Holborn 105–6; Strand 105; Sun Inn, Foregate, Clement's Inn *56*; Surrey Chapel *137*; Sydenham Palace *103*; Titchfield Street 106; Tooley Street 111; Tottenham Court Road 102, 106; Tower 73; Tower Hill *103*, Upper John Street, Fitzroy Square 102; Wapping 127; Warwick Street, Pimlico *97*; Waterloo Bridge Road *140*; Wellington Bridge 105; West Cottage, Wellington Road, Stockwell *103*; Magpie and Horseshoe, Westminster *103*; Westminster Abbey 102, 106; Westminster Bridge *103*; Green/Grey Coat School, Westminster 2, 58; Westminster Hall *103*; Whitechapel *103*; Wild's Globe *103*; Wimpole Street, Cavendish Square 139
Long Stratton 10, *70*: Long (Sand) *131*: Lowestoft 44, 63–4, 72, 74, 79, 81, 93, 96, 99–100, 104–5, 108–9, 116, 118, 121–2, 124, 126, 128, 130, 135–7, 139, 141, 147, *3–6*, *11*, *16–7*, *24*, *29–31*, *33–4*, *37*, *49–50*, *52*, *55*, *57*, *66–8*, *75–6*, *79*, *81*, *83*, *90*, *96*, *100*, *103*, *105*, *111–2*, *114–7*, *123*, *125*, *129*, *132*, *133–4*, *143*, *147*, *149*; (Chapel Road) 6; (Harbour) 74; (St. John's) 76
Maidenhead 99: Maidstone 137, *30*: Maldon (Essex) 7, *13*: Manchester 39, *24*, *123*: Mapplebeck *123*: March 81: Margate 96, *3*: Marlesford 1: Mediterranean *86*; Melton *124*; (asylum) 7, 75, 96, 104, 106–7, 109, 124, 139, *11*, *37*, *46*, *50*, *54–5*, *63*, *71–2*, *75*, *84*, *92*, *99*: Melton Constable 61: Memel *100*: Middlesborough *12*, *52*, *116*, *121*: Middleton *33*: Minsmere 46, 112, 114, *3*, *75*, *82–3*, *88*, *98*, *107*; (sluice) *98*; (haven) *100*: Mutford 101
Nacton (Union House) *49*, *74*: Napes Buoy *124*: Narva *100*: Needham Market *112*, *137*: Newcastle 7n., 43–5, 54, 58, 64, 82, 99, 106, 109, 125, 134, *7*, *12*, *26*, *51*, *66*, *110*, *115*, *141*; (St. Anne's) 118: Newcome (sand) 100, *3*: Newmarket *24*, *90*: New Orleans *29*, *34*: Newport, South Wales 75, *88*: Newton *70*: New York 77: New Zealand 97:

North Cove 73: North Fleet, Thames 98: North Sea 58, *3*: Northumberland *69*: North Walsham *45*: Norwich 10, 55–7, 64, 68, 70–1, 73–4, 77, 82, 99, 103, 106, 108, 112, 115, 123, 125, 128–9, 133, 139–41, *7–8*, *10*, *15–6*, *21*, *24*, *26*, *52*, *91–2*, *98*, *107*, *120*, *122*, *126*, *137*, *139*, *143*, *147–8*; (Botolph Street) *106*; (Bracondale Hill) 84; (Cathedral) *121*; (Unthank Road) *98*; (Victoria Place) *10*

Odessa 127: Orford 44, *96*; (Castle) *124*: Ormskirk *57*; Ostend 41, 110: Oulton (marshes) *135*; (Union House) 139: Oxford (Pembroke College) 19: Pakefield 45, 100, 106, 126: Peasenhall *18*, *89*, *119*: Perth 43, *119*: Peterborough *24*: Petersburg 102: Plomesgate Union *85*: Plymouth 44, 77: Portmadock, Caernarvonshire 75: Portsmouth *89*: Preston 79: Princes Risborough 19: Prince Edward's Island 53: Prince of Wales Island *123*: Putney 7: Pye (sand) *16*

Quebec 71n., 98, 138, *50*

Ramsgate 51: Raveningham 10, *50*, *55*, *70*; (Hall) *63*: Rendham *119*: Rendlesham 1: Reydon 5, 23–4, 34, 40–1, 43, 47–8, 50, 53, 56, 61–2, 68, 71, 74, 93, 104, 107, 108, 111, 113, 118, 128–9, 131–2, 134, 135n., 136–7, 139, *1*, *4*, *8*, *16*, *18*, *25*, *30–1*, *42*, *44*, *45–6*, *52*, *54–5*, *68*, *72*, *74–5*, *79–80*, *84*, *86*, *89–90*, *97–99*, *102*, *108*, *110*, *113–4*, *117–9*, *121–2*, *124*, *132*, *141*, *143*; (Common) 47; (Reydon Cottage) 2–3, 61n., 134, *10*, *30*, *49*, *54*, *106*, *121*; (Grange) *91*; (Green Lane) *102*; (Grove) *23n.*; (Hall) 40, *86*; (Quay) *69*, *109*; (New Quay) 34, *65*; (Wood House) 40; (Wolsey Bridge) 68, *16*: Richmond 73: Ringsfield 122, *69*: Robin Hood's Bay 119: Rochdale (Old Church) 84: Rochester *100*, *149*: Romsey (Hants) *17*: Rostock 101: Rotterdam 79, 92: Rowcliff (Yorks) 98: Rowhedge *59*: Rushmere *96*, *124*: Rye *32*

Salisbury 73: Salthouse 49: Sand Hail (bank) 43, 130: Sand Pan Hole *19*: Sand Pit 43: Savannah 100: Saxmundham 56–7, 68, 71, 93, 110, 123, 138, *53*, *56*, *63*, *82*, *90*, *127*, *132*: Scalloway 112: Scarborough 44: Scole 71: Scotland 19, 58, 85, 103, 116, *13*, *31*, *55*: Scroby Sand *49*: Seaford, Sussex 6, 6n.: Seaham *61*: Seaton *94*: Sebastopol *81*: Seeton sluice 98: Seine *56*: Shadingfield *24*, *118*: Shanghai *90*: Sheffield *142*: Shetland 37: St. Lorenzo 77: St. Malo *70–1*: Shields 53, *100–1*; (North) 44–5, 94, 122, 125, *45*, *65*; (South) 93, 100, 118, 125, *19*, *33*, *57*, *82–3*, *100*, *141*: Shotley *54*: Sibton 2, 56: Sierra Leone 77: Sizewell 46, 100, 114, *71*, *75*; (Bank) 7, *45*, *61–2*, *89*, *108*, *121*, *132*; (Gap) 141, *53*, *138*, *149*: Sole Bay 2: Somerleyton *56*: Sotherton 33, 118, 135, *10*, *78*, *87*, *90*, *100*, *108*, *120–1*: Sotterly 34n., 113, *68*: South Cove *33*, *104*, *106*, *118*, *132*: Southampton 10–1, 85, 91, 109, 131, *6*, *9*, *54*, *66*, *115*

Southwold   Adult School *81*, *83*; Assembly Rooms *11*; Back Street (Victoria Street) 36, *20*; Baggot's Mill 16, *119*, *136*; Baptist Chapel 51, 77n., 137, 146, *8*; Barnaby Green 48, 54, 116, *53*; Bartholomew Green 33, 60, 76n., 139, *36n.*, *82*; Beach 132, *86*, *110*; Belvidere College *104*; Black Mill 42; *50*, *67*, *120*; Blackshore 7, 11, 27–9, 36, 42, 47, 51, 53, 73, 78–9, 81–2, 85, 92, 100, 104, 108, 119, 121–2, 124, 129, 132–4, 143, *8*, *42*, *50*, *52*, *55*, *59*, *62*, *66*, *71*, *78–9*, *96*, *108*, *110*, *132*, *137*, *140*; Bound Post 35, 43–4, 75, *120*; Brewery 61, 122–3, *46*, *80*, *107*; Brick kiln 23, 28, 139; Bridge Gate 76; Buss Creek 129, *65*, *143*; Casino 12n., 47, 47n., 104, 144; Centre Cliff Lodge 8, 104, 120; Centre Villa, Gun Hill 74n.; Child's Yard 51, 101; Church Green 5, 33–4, 38, 114, 120, 136, *148*; Church Lane 73; Church Street 28n., 36; Cliff House *139*; Coastguard watch-house 55, *2*; Cobbold's House *86*; Common 29–30, 40, 42, 54–5, 73, 82, 94, 96, 99, 148, *56*, *80*, *86*, *133*; Constitution Hill 61n.; Dissenting Meeting House *34*; East Cliff 44, *19*, *94*, *117*; East Cliff Green *71*; East Cliff House *113*, *117*, 138n., *143*; East Green 46, *125*; East Green Maltings *140*; East Street 67n., *24*, *100*, *104*; The Elms *122–3*; Fish Office Yard *34*, *68*, *81*; Gaol 25, 28, 56; Gas Works *114*, *149–50*; Gate 42, 76; Gatehouse 26, 42, 54, 127, *141*; Green Bank 56; Green Lane

(Trinity Street) 128, *79*; Guildhall 33; Guinea Pightle 54; Gun Hill 14, 30, 43–4, 47, 47n., 48, 67, 70, 75, 99, 110, 116, 144, *1–4*, *11*, *17*, *26*, *31*, *35*, *49*, *62*, *64*, *78*, *81*, *85*, *93*, *97*, *108*, *111*, *113*, *137*, *139*, *142*; Gun Hill Place 8n.; Guns 38, 51, 55; Harbour 37, 58, 65–6, 120, 124, 126, 130, 135, 147–8; *19*, *31*, *52–3*, *63*, *65*, *68*, *79*, *81*, *84–5*, *87*, *93*, *96*, *99*, *105*, *118*, *120*, *141–2*; Herrington's House *86*; High Street 7, 10, 16, 36, 57, 60n, 61n., 77, 77n., 101, 143, *11*, *20*, *73*, *80–1*, *91*, *97*, *120*, *125*, *139*; Horsebridge 133; Independent Chapel 5, 62, 85, 94–5, 99, 104, 143, *34*, *76*, *137*; Infant School 76, 78, *81*, *85–6*, *139*; Kill Cock *4*; Kill Cock Cliff 7, 7n., 138; Kill Cock Cliff House 72; Ladies' Walk 99; Lifeboat House *81*, *102*, *108*, *125*; Lime Kiln 33, 47; Lloyd's Bank *10n.*; The Lodge, Gun Hill 14, *127*; Long Island Cliff 7, 7n., 35, 41, 67, 95, 132, *2–4*, *17*, *64*; Long Island Cliff House 117, *139*; Manor House 8n., 10, 13, 19, 39n., 113n.; Manor Lodge 19; Market 25, 28; Market Cross 25; Market Hall 23, 32; Market Place 7, 15, 25–6, 42, 78n., 113, 121, 133, 141, *9*, *10*, *20*, *74–5*, *80*, *117*, *127*; May Place 18; Meeting House 95; Meeting House Lane (Lorne Road) 95, *30*; Methodist Chapel 39, 46; Mights Bridge 26n., 41, 113; Mill Lane 5, 39, 46, *9*; New Hall *117*, *121*, *131*; New York Cliff 7, 67, 114, 131, *1*, *2*, *4*, *17*, *64*, *68*, *86*, *113*; New York Cliff House 7, 39, *64*, *68*; North Cliff 45, 131, *3*, *48–9*; North Field 29; North Green 34n., 101n., *44*; North Pier 25, *53*; Park Lane 11, 15, 19, 57, 67, 135, 144, *1*, *29*, *87*, *97*, *100*, *120*, *127*; Park Villa 19; Pinkney's Lane 9, 128, *100*; Powder Magazine 53; Primitive Methodist Chapel *78*; Prison 54; Pump *127–8*; Queen Street 32n.; Sailors Reading Room 16n., *108*, *111*, *113*, *125*, *127*, *131*; St. Edmund's Church 1, 7, 14, 16, 32, 37, 41, 56, 61, 64, 70–4, 81–2, 94, 102, 111, 119, 121, 124, 126, 137, 139, 142–3, *1*, *9*, *11*, *13*, *19–20*, *22–4*, *27–9*, *33–40*, *43*, *46–48n.*, *56*, *59*, *64*, *71–3*, *76–7*, *92*, *97*, *99–100*, *115*, *117–120*, *122*, *125*, *128–132*, *137*, *143–9*; Saint Edmund's Hill 34; St. James's Green 7, 72n.; Salt Creek 133; Saltworks 12, 39, 53, 133, *15*, *25*; Sand Pit 132; Skeleton Field 26, 26n.; Skilman's Hill 33, 105; Skilman's Lodge 105; Sole Bay Academy *10*, *18*; South End 8, 9, 138, *9*; South Green 4, 9, 11, 15, 19, 57, 88, 105, 143, *68*, *76*, *117*; Southwold Railway *104*; Station House 113, *48*, *138*; Tamarisk Villa 18; Thompson's Folly 40, 129; Town Farm 23–4, 34n., 115, *139*; Town Field 22, 28, 30; Town Hall 5, 33, 33n., 82, 104, 108, 137–8, 144, *9*, *14*, *19–20*, *40*, *42*, *62*, *68*, *73*, *77*, *87*, *97*, *101–2*, *119*, *121–2*, *128–9*, *139*, *141–3*; Town Mill 26–7; *49–56*; Two Gun Battery 38, 51, 55, 72, 72n.; Victoria Street *125*; Victoria Street Brewery *113*; Watch-house 25, *113*; Waterloo Bridge 53; Waterloo Mill 27; Wesleyan Chapel 39, 46, 112, 97; Wood's End Marsh *18*; Wood's End Creek 29; Workhouse 34

Spanton Lane *59*: Spexhall 140: Springfield (Essex) 78, 78n., *124*: Standford Channel *123*: Stanfield Hall *15*, *16*: Stanmore (Little) 85: Starston 95: Stettin 106: Stockton (Norfolk) 10, 11, *11*, *24*, *34*, *36*, *54*; (Upon Tees) 45, 82, 93, 110–1: Stoven 15, 101, *20*, *24*, *53*, *56*, *98*: Stowmarket 97: Stowupland 21: Strathfieldsaye 32, 32n: Stratton (Long) 10, *70*: Sunderland 124, 127, *16*, *41*, *61*, *62*, *70*, *72*, *78*, *82*, *88–9*, *99*, *100*, *107*, *123*: Swaffham *24*: Sydney (New South Wales) 75

Taganrag *57*: Tasburgh Lodge *112*: Tattingstone *149*; (Place) *119*: Texel 98: Thames (river) 81, 84, 93, 134, *3*, *12*: Theberton 23, 137, *56*, *68*, *90*: Thetford 133: Thorington 66, *10*: Thornbury (Glos) 66: Thorne (Yorks) *57*: Thorp: *44–5*, *52*, *61–2*, *89*: Thorpe (nr. Norwich) *132*; (Ness) 75; (Rocks) *51*: Thorpeness *113*, *132*: Thurton 8, *24*: Thwaite *74*, *142*; (Minerva Cottage) *142*: Tobago, West Indies *119*: Tonning *124*: Toft Monks *111*: Trimingham 45: Trinidad *84*: Trowse 1n., 53: Tunbridge Wells 109: Tunstall *43*

Uggeshall 114–5, 121, 131, *20*, *24*, *49*, *97–8*, *114*, *120*

Walberswick 1, 1n., 2–3, 5–6, 8, 8n., 15–6, 19, 29, 40, 43, 45, 48, 52, 54–6, 58–9, 61–2, 65, 66, 68, 70, 72–6, 79, 84–5, 92, 94, 96–7, 103, 108–18, 121, 123–5, 128–9, 132, 134, 136, 140, 145, *2, 8–10, 13, 25, 30–1, 33, 35–6, 41–4, 46, 54, 62–3, 65–6, 72, 75–7, 83, 86, 91–3, 99–100, 104–5, 108–9, 116, 118, 121–2, 132, 135, 140–2*; (Lime Kiln) 68; (Primitive Methodist Chapel) *142*; (Sluice) *8, 101–2*; (St. Helena Farm) *122*; (Windmill) 70: Wallsend 66: Walpole 13n., 21–2, 31, 142–3; (Meeting House) 22n: Walton on the Naze 74, *93*: Wangford 5, 30, 32, 51, 54, 58, 66, 73, 76, 78, 93, 95–6, 109, 114, 116, 119–26, 128n., 135, 137–8, 140, *8–14, 18, 24, 29–31, 33–4, 41, 44–5, 50, 53, 56, 62, 67, 75–6, 79–80, 86, 92–3, 98–100, 102, 104, 107, 109–10, 112, 114, 117–18, 121, 123–5, 135, 140–2*; (Hill) *141*; (Barnaby Green) *53*; (Windmill) 73: Warley Barracks (Essex) *43*: Warwick (St Nicholas) *121*: Wells (Norfolk) 81: Wenhaston 2, 36, 52, 57, 85, 114, 119, 122, 124–5, 127–8, *21, 29, 34, 42, 52, 54–6, 65, 67, 69, 79, 82–3, 86, 92, 100–1, 105, 109–10, 114, 117, 122, 124*; (Wesleyan Chapel) *92*: Westleton 77, 139, *13, 20, 42, 46, 49, 62, 67, 90, 92, 97*: Weston 21, *24*: West Wretham *52*: Westhall 55, *99*: West Indies *25, 63*: Westwood Lodge 37, *98*: Wherstead Park *109, 113*: Whitehaven *49*: White Notley 135n., *143*: Whitby 43, 127, *16, 35, 82–3, 88, 100, 117–18, 123*: Wickham Market 6, 60, 98; (Union House) *85, 104*: Wilford 74: Willingham *96*: Windsor *32*: Winterton Ridge *119*: Wisbech 140, *24*: Wivenhoe *53*: Woodbridge 115–16, 130, *11, 44, 77, 127, 148*; (River) *63*: Woolwich 6, 66, 78; (Prospect Place) *48*: Worcester *96*: Worlingham 126n: Worthing (York Terrace) 132: Wrentham 15, 23n., 24, 28, 65, 84, 94, 113, 115, 119, 121, 127, 131, 138, *8, 12, 17–19, 25, 30, 33, 37, 41, 46, 49–50, 53–56, 64, 68–9, 72, 77–81, 83–4, 87–90, 92, 96–8, 101, 105–9, 111–2, 114, 116–17, 120, 139, 141*; (Mills) *106*; (Park Farm) *88*: Wymondham 25n., *24*: Yarmouth 6, 21, 30–1, 42n., 43, 53–4, 57, 64, 66, 73–4, 78–9, 81, 91–3, 98, 100, 104, 106, 109–10, 112, 115, 117–20, 124–127n., 129–32, 134, 136, *6, 7, 12–3, 24, 26, 29–31, 33, 36, 43, 44, 46, 48, 51–3, 69, 71, 81, 83–4, 99, 103, 114, 132–3, 149*; (Fair) *119*; (Howard Street) *125*; (Southtown) 42, *124*: Yoxford 8n., 70–1, 81, 92, *30, 33, 46, 51, 76, 79–80, 117, 136*; (Cockfield Hall) 94, 134, *116*

II. INDEX RERUM

Poor Law Commissioners 85, *80*
Post and Post Office 32–3, 106, *42*, *105*
Public Houses 35–7, *79* (See also in *Index Locorum* "Inns")
Publications include Beccles Monthly Advertiser *89*; Bury Post *143*; East Suffolk Mercury and Lowestoft Weekly News *94*; Fishermen's Friendly Visitor *95*; Halesworth Times *80*, *99*; Ipswich Journal 128n., *15, 22, 27, 37n.*, *95, 108, 118, 120, 127, 141, 144–6, 148–9*; Lloyd's *Weekly Messenger 77*; Norfolk News *26–7*; Oxford Herald *21*; Suffolk Chronicle 148, *37, 94–6*; Suffolk Mercury *132*; Times *90*; Yarmouth Free Press *81*
Railways *91*; accident at Thorpe *132*; Blyth Valley *119*; East Suffolk Tramway *131*; East Suffolk (Halesworth to Southwold) 87; Eastern County 136; Eastern Counties and Haddiscoe, Beccles and Halesworth 77; Eastern Union (accident at Hadleigh) *148*; Great Eastern (accident on Oulton Marshes) *135*, to Ipswich 16; London to Yarmouth (times) *149*; Lowestoft Line 135; Southwold to Darsham/Halesworth *104*; Southwold to Darsham *133*; Norwich and Lowestoft *143*
Regatta (Southwold) *91, 11, 26, 37, 68, 76, 81, 142*; (Lowestoft) 74
Royal Occasions: death of Prince Consort *107*; Prince of Wales's birthday 116, *139*; Prince of Wales's marriage *110*; Queen's coronation *137*; Queen's marriage *138*
Sailors' Reading Room *111, 113, 125, 127, 131*
Saltworks 39, 133, *15, 25*
Salvage 39, 41, 48
Serjeant at Mace 110, *109*
Ships:

Abeena 98	Bottle Sloop 43	Curlew *86, 118*
Abeona 125–6	British Queen 45	Cynthia *112*
Accommodation 79	British Tar 109, 123–4,	
Active 79, 118, 122, 123,	127, 129, *30*	Damsel 54
85	Briton 44	David *129*
Agenonia 95	Buckingham 46	Den Junge Herrman *24*
Aid *35*	Burletta 49	Deo Gloria 101
Albion 105, 116, *132*	Bywell 134	Derwent 45
Alert 44		Diamond 45
Alfred *74, 116*	Cape Horn *3, 82*	Diana 133–*4*
Alice *92*	Carteret 37	Dispatch *75*
Albertina *75*	Caster 101	Dolphin 126, 135, *109*
Alma *132*	Cataraqui 130	Dorset 44
Alnwick *63*	Catharine 46	Dove 43
Amicitia 44, 125	Celeste Maria *124*	Dreadnought 134
Andrew *68, 105, 113, 116*	Ceres 1, 44, 125	Dunwich 53
Anna *101*	Charles 85, *52, 88, 123*	
Anne 45	Charley *88*	Earl of Liverpool *9*
Ann Emma *100–1*	Cheverell *88–90*	Ebenezer 58, 77, 127
Anna Maria *33*	Clansman 138	Effort 81
Ann and Mary *61, 62*	Clase 124	Eiderstedt *124*
Ant 45, 110	Cleofrid *7, 8, 14*	Eliza 45, 109, *65*
Arctic 77	Columbus 106	Elizabeth *115*
Ariel 45	Commerce 114, 119	Elizabeth-Ann 46, 114
	Conservative 110, *4*	Ellen 93, *92*
Barbara 45	Content *107*	Elsinore *122*
Barley 124	Coronella *124*	Elton 110–*1*
Billy *117–8, 123*	Cricketer *4, 17, 30, 97*	Emerald 126
Billy Boys *84*	Cumberland 44	Emma *3, 82, 88*

163

III. INDEX NOMINUM

101; Ellen *81*; J. *41*; J. J. 27–8, 146; J. Johnson *50, 71, 76, 81–3, 87–8, 106*; Mrs. M. *78, 89, 90, 96*
Goldsberry, Miss 113
Goldsmith 121, *139*; Mr. 77; Mrs. *65*; E. 28, 64, 93, *21, 25, 49, 55, 65*; Elizabeth *63, 79*; J. 66, 116, 147; W. 24, 36, *78*
Gooch 28, 51, 138; Lady *56*; Borrett *133*; Sir E. Sherlock *55–6, 86–8, 113, 117–19, 123*; E. *9, 29*; Sir Fras. *124*; Georgianna 146; H. 42, 72; Matilda 146; Rev. Rd. *43, 76*; Capt. Rt. 14n.; Rosse 32; T. Sherlock 146; Sir T. 23n., 24, 64, 91, 105, *6, 51*; T. S. 146; W. *86*; W. Frederick Sherlock 9 (N.B. Rt. = R. H. = H.)
Gooderham, Mr. *36*
Gooding 16n., 123; Mr. *69*; Mrs. *86*; Donald 19n.; Jonathan 9, 18, 42, 57, 76, 94, 99, 103, 108, 130–2, *13, 19, 27, 34, 37n., 42–3, 55, 57, 66, 68–70, 72, 81, 142*; Jonathan Rt. 15, 61, 94, *54–5, 59, 70, 78–9, 81–2, 86–7, 89, 92, 96–7, 102–3, 106–8, 114, 117*; W. 26
Goodrick, G. 119
Goodwin, Ambrose *32*; Jas. 144–5; Jasper 102, 115; Sam. 115
Gorrard, Si. *10*
Gowing, Fred. *6*
Grand, Rd. *118*
Grant, C. 43; Rev. F. B. 68
Gray *86*; Mr. 125; Arthur Baldrey *30*; E. 26, 101, 127; *8, 44, 79, 124*; G. *90*; Joshua *105*; Peter *121*; Sarah Emma *121*
Grayston, Ben. 119; Jas. *91*
Green 135; Mr. *91*; David 92, 111, 7, *78*; Elizabeth 98; G. *74*; Sam. 44; T. 98; W. *7, 9*
Greener, Jas. *45*
Grimmer, W. 75
Grimsey, J. Rust 138, *55*
Grimson 45
Grimwood, T. *148*
Groome, Mr. *97*
Gross, Mr. 92
Grossmith, Jesse *6*

Grout, Solomon 12, 35, 55, 60, 63, 144, 146
Grubbe, Eustace 19; J. Eustace 112, *127, 132*
Gwyn, Agnes *112*; W., R.N. *112*

Hacon, H. *123*
Hadingham 28; J. 23–5, 43–5, 63, 86, 149, *8, 13*; M. *45*
Hading, Mrs. *42*
Hadley, Brian 23n.
Haggard, Dr. *73*
Hague, Jas. 36
Hailstone, W. 47
Haken, H. 107, *33*; Rd. *87*; W. 115, *32, 75, 79*
Hall, Mr. 121; Jacob 84; J. 30, *74*; M. 25, 28, *87*; Sarah *70–1*; T. 114, *45*
Hallett, Mr. 120, *10, 19*
Hallows, Mrs. 100; Fras. *48*
Hambling, Sarah 67
Hamilton, Rev. C. J. *119*; G. 50
Hammond, Mr. *140*; Mrs. *33*; Jas 26, 123; O. 59
Hanner, Walter Jones *102, 111*
Harber, Mr. *8*
Harbour, C. *78*
Hardwicke, Lord *43*
Hardy, Admiral T. *95*
Harman, Mr. 81; Jas. 93
Harris, Mrs. Elizabeth 120
Harrison, 126, 139; Rev. T. 94, 140, *66*
Harrisson, Walter *135–6*; W. 36, *132*
Hart, W. Jos. *114*
Hartley, Fountain 102, 120, *103*
Hartridge 96
Harvey *99, 122*; Mr. 10, 135; Mrs. 136; C. *24, 56*
Haslegrave, Rev. J. 101
Hatch, Miss 99
Hatton, Yvonne 19
Hawes 124; Adam 134; Jas. 134; Jane *109*
Haward 136; Mr. 65; Jas. 21; Jane 63; S. R. 26, 115, 130, *34, 75*
Haxell 115
Hay, Mr. *50*; Col. E. *43*
Hays, W. 32

175

176

Mealing, Mr. 71; J. *80*
Meering, G. *106*
Meire, Mr. 106
Meldrum, G. G. *65*
Mercer, Rev. 71; Jas. *103*; Mrs. Lucy 71, *90–1*, *105*
Merewether *21*
Merewether & Stephens 12n.
Merrells, J. 141, *149*
Metcalfe, Frances 84
Michell, Mr. *50*
Middleton 61
Milbourne, G. 25; W. 33
Miller 51; Mr. 82, 102–3, 106, 111, *55*; Rd. Newring *51*; Rt. Newring *51*; Sarah A. 68, 115; T. Carne *111*; W. B. *90*
Mills 6, *141*; Miss *132*; E. 53, 120, 137; *10*, *120*; Esther *64*, *98*; J. 68; Jos. *112*; M. *112*; Rt. 10, 53, 57, 77, 131, *120*
Mitchell Page 28, *56*
Mizzlebrook, Sam 55
Mole, Mrs. *118*
Molinari, Anthony 116
Mollet, E. *142*
Money, W. *107*
Montague, J. 44, 101, 110, 116
Moody, Mr. *40*; J. 115, *45–6*
Moore, Mr. 118; E. *129*; J. 35; Rt. *135*; Susan 25; W. 22, 67, 133, *101*, *132*
Morby, Mr. 111; Adolphus 140; C. 140; Jane *36*
Morley *109*, *111*
More *149*; Jas. 144
Moss, Mrs. *114*; widow 135; Philip *89*; Sam. 40, *19*, *59*
Mott, J. 87
Moulton, Mr. B. *11*
Mow, Borre 41
Musgrave, Sir Christopher 91
Muttet *121*; T. *91*
Myers, David *45*; Rev. J. S. 126

Nash, Mr. 141; Mrs. *79*
Naunton *120*, *134*; Albert *115*; C. 28, 47, 66, 98, 110, 122–3, *31*, *43*, *71*, *109*, *115*; G. 70, 82, 105, *33*; Rhoda 47; Sarah *46*; T. 82, 104, *90*, *136*; W. 33, *116*

Neale, J. Preston *149*; W. H. *93*
Neech, Rt. 113, 116
Nelson *92*; G. 27, 49
Newberry, Mrs. *91*; G. *100*; W. *44*, *62*
Newcomb, Col. 19
Newman, Mr. *79*, *90*
Newson 23; David 36; Jas. 24; J. 49–50, 78; M. A. *46*; Rd. *12*
Nicholson, T. *16*
Nieman, D. 101
Nightingale, Lady 59; Lieutenant-General Sir Miles 59
Nolan, Patrick *88*
Noott, Rev. 140, *54*
Norman *79*; J. 98 (see Errata), 109, *49*; Rachel 72
Norris, Rev. H. H. *137*
North 68
Norton, Mrs. 85, 131, *29*; Clara 85; Daniel 75; Rev. Eardley 8n., *54*, *58–9*, *73*, *85*, 146; Eardley *101*; Jonathan *124*
Norwich, Bishop of 111, 116, 138n., *13*, *29*, *72*, *97*, *100*, *119*, *129*, *144–5*
Nossiter 46
Notcutt 133
Nottage, Rev. T. 5, 9n.
Nunn family 7; Mrs. 59, 115; G. *44*; Judith *131–2*; Sam 38, 145; T. (elder) 30–1; T. (younger) 30; T. 33, 144–5, *132*
Nutt, G. H. *96*; Jas. 96

Odells/Odell, Mr./s. 105, 111, *90*
O'Hare 118, 133
Oldring 99, *34*; Mr. *33*, *138*; Mrs. 115; Ben 101, 115, 123; Eleanor 27; H. 50, 60, 102, 119, *27*, *30*, *32–3*, *36*; H. jun. 50; Jas. 25, 99, 113, 115, 117, *16*; Jos. 50, 77; Mrs. Jos. 76; M. *33*; Mrs. M. 26, 139, *148*
Olive, Mr. 111
Onley 123
Ord, J. H. *93*; J. T. *93*
Orton, Miss 81; Mrs. 81
Osborne 116; Daniel Betts 36; G. *62*
Oswald, R. *96*
Ouchin 48
Owles, Miss 109

Sadd, Mr. *76*
Sage, Mr. *105*
Sallows, E. 78; J. 62
Salomon, J. T. *8*
Samkin, Ben 93; W. 46
Sandby, Rev. 84
Sandford, Emily *15*
Sapcoat, W. *142*
Saunders, Jos. jun. 100; W. 100
Savage 128
Savill, G. *32*
Sawyer 121, 123–4, *128*; C. 71, *7–9*; J. 46, 75, *29–30, 36, 100, 102, 120, 128, 130*; W. *29*
Sayer 135; H. 103, *63, 74–5*; J. 70; Mrs. J. 113, *79*; Michael *96*; Sam. *96*
Scarlett, Jas *105*; W. *62*
Scott, Jas. *89–90*; J. 59; J. Alfred 121, *53*
Seaborne, Malcolm 3n.
Seago, W. R. *59, 111*
Seaman, Mr. *16*; Miss 82, 104
Searle *10*
Sevesque, Mr. *54*
Sewell, Rev. 71; W. *76*
Shafto, Rev. 117
Sharman, W. 58, *52*
Sharpen, E. 59
Sharpin, W. R. 94
Shawe 77
Shelley, Mr. *33*
Shenton 127
Shepperd, T. jun. 56
Sheriffe family 8; Mrs. 117, 121, 125, *9, 141*; Miss Harriett *51, 56, 64, 70, 84, 86, 101, 122*; Rev. T. 115, *20, 106*
Sherman, J. 142; Rev. J. *137*
Sherwood, M. 97
Short, Miss 82, 104
Shrimpton, Mr./s. 103, 105, 107; Mrs. 56; Amelia Alexandrine *96*; Emily *56*; Jos. 49, 68, 119, 135, *84, 96*; Louisa *84*
Siggars, Rd. *56, 72*
Simm, Jas. 7
Simmons, Rev. Dr. *9*; Catharine *6*; Jas. 6; W. *69*; Lieut. *69*; Lieut. W. Cress *93, 95–6, 120*
Simms, Mrs. *120*

Simpson 49, *86, 114, 116*; Mrs. 136; David *110*; H. *35, 104*; Jas. 130, *108, 118*; J. 85; M. *9*; Pallant *52*
Sisley, Dr. Rd. 73
Skelton, Humphrey 22; J. 25, *24, 93, 101, 120*; W. 49
Sketchley, Rev. Dr. *96*
Skill, Fred 104, 109, 143
Skinner, midshipman 49; G. *68*; Rd. *82, 108*
Skipsey, B. *99*
Skoulding, Mr. *101*; Jos. 21; Sarah 77
Skylman 22
Smith 70, 121, *5n., 80, 101, 114, 118*; Mr. 70; Mrs. *80*; A. 39, *117*; C. 102–3, 106, 135; E. 33, 106, *8, 105*; Lieut. Fred. Wetherell *54*; H. 75, *8, 9, 44, 65*; Jane 75; Jas. 64, 66, 100, *54, 105*; Jeremiah 74; J. 100, 131, *8, 67–8, 109*; J. sen. 62; Lydia *134*; M. 128, *141*; Rd. *33*; Rt. *53, 79*; Susan *35*; Sidney 134; T. 56, *103*; T. Bailey *31, 46, 48*; W. 130, *10, 80, 91, 113, 134*
Snell 140, *42*; aunt 54; A. 1, 1n., 41; J. *50, 79*; Sarah 1n.; W. 1n.
Soans 135; J. 134, *16, 32, 67, 80, 97*
Sones, Elisha 137; G. 63; Hannah 137; J. 137, *18*
Souper, Mrs. *117*; Mrs. Elizabeth 42, 58; Eliza Emily *84*; G. Fred *84*
Southwell, Mr. 116, 138
Spalding, Mr. *18*; Mrs. *132*; Miss *132*; Ben. Morse *132*; M. *108*
Spall, Mr. 118; Esau *90*; J. S. *105*; Sarah 128; W. 128; W. Lines 128
Sparrowe, Mr. 74; Miss 113; J. E. 117, *17*
Spelman, W. *69*
Spence, Ben. *93*; E. 108, *53*; Jas. 81; Rebecca *119*; W. Pott *20, 125*
Spencer, Jacob 48; Rev. T. *43*
Spenser, Mr./s. 95
Sperling, Rev. Jas. 144
Spicer, Ben. 43, 76; Jane 76; J. *119*; Si. 61–2, 92, 102, 104, *26, 29, 35, 116*
Spoore, J. *67, 118*; Job. 74, *3*; Patience 68; Rt. 68
Spratt's 140
Sprunt 125
Spurgeon, C. *49–50, 52, 55, 67, 71, 75,*

77–8, *91–2, 94, 113, 116*
Spurling, Mr. 48
Squires 109
Stacey, J. 100
Stafford, Countess of 77; Lord 147
Stall, T. *103*
Stamford, Jas. Alfred 134–5, *12, 29*
Stammers, Betsy *98*; Daniel 27, 49; J. *49*; W. *91*
Standford, Adolphus 77; M. *75*, 116
Stanhaw, Mr. 141
Stanley, Dr. *29*; Edmund *86*
Stannard *23*; Mr. 139; Christmas *111, 125*; Francis 44, *32, 66*; G. *117*; Jos. *148*; Rt. 72, 84, 110; Sarah *76*
Stead, Patrick *2*
Stebbings, Mr. 118
Steele, Capt. J. *9*
Steggall, Mr. 96
Stephens, Francis Metcalfe 84; Rev. W. 84
Sterry, Betsy 140; Jas. 26, 70–1, 96, 126, *3*; Jas. jun. 96; J. 96; Rt. 49; Sarah 104
Steward, C. *59*; Rev. Frank 81
Stewart, C. E. *104*; Mrs. C. *125*
Stockdale *92*; W. *53, 78*,
Stodart *15*
Stone, W. 127
Stopher, T. 84
Storkey 121; Moses 107, 115, 117, *40*; Mrs. Moses 107
Stradbroke, earl of 64, 66, 73, 81, 124; countess 66, 146; Lord *18, 43, 74–5, 85, 91–2, 123–4*
Strange, Sam. 26, 33, 84, *20, 49, 109, 120*; T. R. 66
Stratbarn/Strathern *52, 66*
Street, Sam. *48*
Strickland, Major *86*; Agnes 93n., 101n., *86, 135, 137–8*; Elizabeth 93; Jane *87*; Rt. Alexander *86*
Strowger 119, *120–1*; Jas. 77; J. Dandy 122, *50, 65*; W. 131
Suckling 1n.
Sutherland, Duchess of 103; Henrietta Maria *54*; J. 12, 13, 15, 19, 25, 35, 51–2, 61, 69, 76–7, 84, 86, 112–14, 116–17, 144, 148, *7, 37, 48–9, 54, 59, 62–3*; Mrs. M. A. 69, *62*

Sutton 109, *75, 118*; H. M. *106*; T. Hurr 134; W. sen. 86, 125; W. jun. 132, *50, 78*; W. 70, 73, 84, 100, 107, 117, 119, 125, 136, 148, *6, 30, 46, 63, 93*
Swabey, W. *67*
Swain *96*; W. 120, 129, 140
Swatman, Rev. E. 59
Syer *115*; Mrs. 50, *120*; E. *43, 91*; Priscilla *117*; T. 25, 28, 93
Symonds, Ben 22; J. 22, 29; Capt. Ley 112
Symons, Dr. *14*; Rev. H. *9*
Syrage, Rev. Fras. *114*

Tacon *67*
Tallent, W. 23n., 24
Tann, Rt. *12*
Tapley, Mr. 111
Tates, Mr. 105
Taylor 130, *81*; Mr. *53*; E. 101, *11*; G. 64, *125*; Hannah *116*; Jas. 105, 130, *25, 121*; J. 59; Oddin 113; W. *85*
Teasdell, Mr. 110; W. *5n.*
Terry, Jas. *18*; Mrs. Margaret *125*
Tharmes, G. 36, 145, *122*
Thomas, Rev. 109
Thompson 38, 45, 101, 104, 110, *75*; family 7; Mrs. Betsy *87–8*; Mrs. C. 50; J. 23, 39–40, 47; Rt. 25; T. Ayscough *17*; T. W. 24, 33n., 51, 56, 77, 94, 101, 112, 117, 123, 137, 140, *25, 72, 76*; W. 38, 145; W. Ayscough *25, 37, 149*
Thredgate/Thredgale T. *92*; Mr. 134
Thrower, G. 59; Sam 66
Thorneycroft *118*
Thornton, Rev. Cecil Claude *124, 127–31*
Thurston *71*
Thurtle 59
Till, Mr. *75*
Tindling, Capt. 47–8
Tink 11; Jas. *44*; J. *55*; Philip *64, 67*; W. 95, 114–15, 129, 132, 134, 137–8, *30*
Tippell, Mr. 108, 112; T. 16, *83*; W. 40
Todd, G. *103*; W. *66*
Toll, Mrs. 113; Miss 59
Toogood, Mr. *75*
Tooke, Eliza 15; Jas. 10, *63, 70, 81*; J. *82*; S. *107*
Tory 5, 50

181

Treneman, Mr. 115
Trinham 125
Tripp, Rt. Robinson *89–90*
Truman, H. *50*
Tubby *79*
Tunney, Rev. R. W. 76
Turnbull, W. *70*
Turner 102; Mr. 102; Emily 51; J. *100*;
J. Alfred Scott *53*; Rt. G. 114; Rt.
Godfrey 51, 73, *34*; Sam *96*; T. 133,
56; W. 127, *6, 8–9, 14*
Turrell, T. 6
Tuthill 109; G. *11*; Margaret 91; Rt.
114; T. 22n., *57–8, 85*
Twaddell, E. 43; Lydia 112; Marshall
41, 78, 84, *17, 27, 30, 32–4, 37, 40,
62, 67–8, 124*; Rowland 98, 123, *49,
69*; S. A. 95, 99; W. 99, 126
Tye, Ebenezer *111*
Tymms, S. *123*
Tyrell, Mr. *37*

Uhtoff, Miss 7; Rev. H. 19, 67, 144, *7*
Underwood, Jas. *110*
Upcraft, Fras. 98; Jas. *54*; J. 98–9, 122,
126; Margaret 78; W. 98
Upton, W. *91*
Usher 46
Utting *114*

Vanneck family 19; Mrs. 146; Hon.
Thompson 67, 146
Verden, Francis *39, 39n.*
Verez, Jean M. L. *124*
Vertue, Algernon Philip *112*; Francis
Henry 19, *54, 56–7, 61, 75, 108, 112,
115–16, 119*; Henrietta Maria 19; Paul
77; Susan 116; T. 77
Vincent, G. *90, 105*
Vineyard, J. *81*
Vlieland, J. 98; M. 115

Wacgone, Francis *44*
Wade, Miss 59
Waggoner, Rd. *13*
Wake, Dr. Rt. 18, 95, 105, 108–9, 112,
136, *9, 15, 17, 58–9, 62, 82, 120, 140,
142*
Wakeman, Miss 71

Wale *74*
Wales family 145; Miss 84, *42, 55*; C.
75, 85, *56*; Calver 40; Collings 96,
116; Collings jun. 96; Mrs. Collings
116; Isaac 75; J. 39, 75; Lydia 66; Rt.
75; Susan 40, *114*; T. *62, 118*
Walker 59, 106; Lieutenant & Mrs. 81;
Jas. *5n.*; W. *26, 93–4*; W. M. *36*
Wall, Rev. Sam. Jas 143
Wallace, T. 49, 135, 140, 146, *11, 33,
37, 42, 54–5, 77, 149*
Walmer, Miss 59
Walpole, W. *119*
Walsham, Sir J. *80*
Walters, Lieutenant 131, *64*
Walton, Miss 109
Ward, Mr. *29, 128*; Capt. R. N. *95*;
Rev. H. *119*; Elizabeth 85; W. 81
Warn 98; Elizabeth 98; W. 98, *25*
Warne, E. 92–3; *32*; G. 93, *22*; Hezekiah
118; Isaac 93; Jas. 92; J. 92; Lucy *90*;
Rt. *52*; *25, 76*
Warnes, Isaac *125*; J. *96*; Rt. *106, 109*;
W. 90
Warner, Jas. 114
Warren family 7, 14n.; Daniel *122*; Jas
44
Warton, W. H. *108*
Wason 112
Watering *68*
Waters *98, 107*; A. *33*; H. 98, 109, 121,
133; Jas. 58, 132, *71*; J. 43, 133, *74*;
Sam. *108, 110*; T. 104; T. Hurr 132;
W. 23, 98, 101, *51, 70, 83*
Waterson, Mr. 131
Watson 45, *114, 119*; Capt. *115*; H. *103*;
Rt. *115*; Susannah *108*; T. *108*; W.
66, *108*
Wayling, J. *132*
Wayth 30, 42, *40*; Mr. 95; E. Archer
122, *86, 118*; Elizabeth 42; Francis
30, 40, 40n., 41n., 54, 115, 146, *7, 86,
116*; Fras. G. *86*; Isabella 71, 125;
Sam 41, 95, 108, *30, 53, 55, 69, 99*; S.
Cooper *84, 99*
Webb, Mr./s. 99; Mr. 9, 102–3, 106
Weering, Rev. Mr. 143
Welby, Jabez *114*
Welham *140*

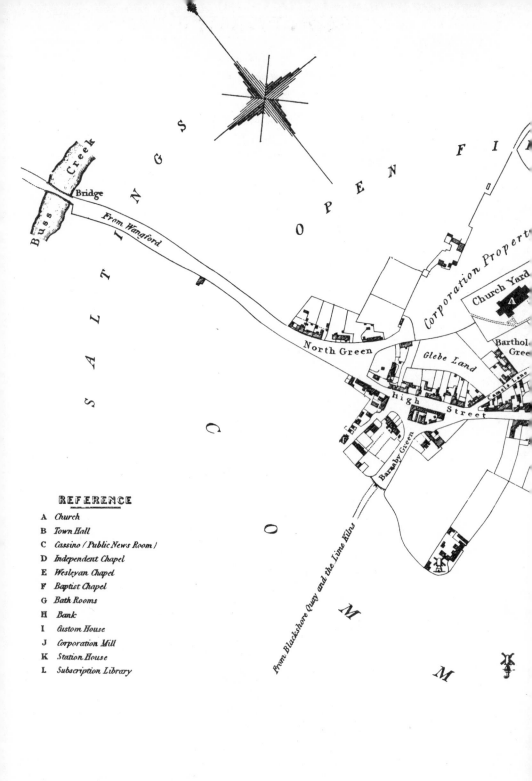

Creek

Bridge

Buss

From Wangford

S A L T I N G S

O P E N F I

Corporation Property

Church Yard

A

Barthol.
Gree

North Green

Glebe Land

Candle Lane

High Street

Barnaby Green

C

O

M

M

From Blackshore Quay and the Lime Kilns

REFERENCE

A Church
B Town Hall
C Cassino (Public News Room)
D Independent Chapel
E Wesleyan Chapel
F Baptist Chapel
G Bath Rooms
H Bank
I Custom House
J Corporation Mill
K Station House
L Subscription Library

C o r p o r a t i o n   M a r s h e s